criteria for the selection and use of visuals in instruction

a handbook

Educational Technology Publications
Englewood Cliffs, New Jersey 07632

George L. Gropper
Zita Glasgow

Printed in the United States of America.

Library of Congress Catalog Card Number: 70-158736.

International Standard Book Number: 0-87778-021-8.

First Printing: June, 1971.
Second Printing: December, 1972.

FOREWORD

This HANDBOOK is one part of a training program developed for personnel serving training or audio-visual functions. The program has been designed to train them in the preparation, selection, and use of visuals in instruction. It is intended for use by personnel who have had some prior training in the application of behavioral principles to the preparation of instructional materials.

The second part of the training program consists of a WORKBOOK designed to accompany the handbook. It provides the learner with practice opportunities in implementing the procedures described in the handbook.

The handbook is designed to assist the learner in solving practice problems. Accordingly, the learner should read each section of the handbook and, whenever directed to do so by instructions in the handbook, he should proceed to relevant practice exercises in the workbook. It is recommended that the learner not merely read the handbook; he should engage in the practice exercises specifically prepared to accompany it.

The HANDBOOK has also been designed to serve as a reference source and as a job aid to be consulted after completion of all workbook exercises. For this purpose, a table of contents and an index appear on the following pages.

ACKNOWLEDGMENTS

This volume was prepared by the American Institutes for Research, Pittsburgh, Pennsylvania for the Bureau of Naval Personnel under Contract No. N00022-68-C-0106. It was developed in the conduct of a project, under the direction of Dr. George L. Gropper, the principal aim of which was to develop guide lines for decisions about the use of film or instructional television in instruction.

The reproduction of this volume was heavily dependent on the skill of Miss Kathleen Gubala in preparing the manuscript.

CONTENTS

OBJECTIVES

INDEX

	PART I	PART II	PART III	PART IV	PART V
ACQUISITION					
definition of		19-20			
barriers to		32			
nature of		15-23			
rules for practice		25-37			
ACTION					
definition of visual action	22-27				
visual vs. non-visual action	9, 22-27				
criterion		2-6, 9-11			
mediating				15-17	
simulated			26-28, 43 62-63		
media requirements		49-51, 57			
ASSOCIATIONS					
result of failure in	38-41				
barriers to				15, 17	
assistance for				22, 25-29	
practice for		29			

	PART I	PART II	PART III	PART IV	PART V
CHAINS					
result of failure in	38-41				
barriers to				25	
assistance for				22, 25-29	
practice for		29			
CRITERION VISUALS					
definition of		6-7		21	
inputs		2-7, 10-11			
actions		2-6, 9-11			
outputs		2-6, 8, 10,11			
required practice with		7-13			
barriers to			8-14		
role in training		39-47			
media requirements		49-61			
DISCRIMINATIONS					
failure in	29-31, 34-35 40-41				
barriers to				13, 17	
assistance for				22-23, 26-29	

	PART I	PART II	PART III	PART IV	PART V
practice for		29			
FABRICATED VISUALS					
definition of	6-7				
fidelity of representation	54-57				
media requirements	52-57				
simulation and			24-25		
GENERALIZATIONS					
failure in	32-33, 36-37, 40-41				
barriers to				14, 17	
assistance for				22, 24, 26-29	
practice for		29-31			
relation to transfer		33, 40-42			
INPUTS					
definition of visual input	18-21				
criterion		2-7, 10-11			
mediating				13-14, 17	
simulated			24-25, 42, 60-61		
media requirements		49-56, 58-59			

	PART I	PART II	PART III	PART IV	PART V
LEARNING GOALS					
acquisition		19-25, 32-34, 37			
retention		19-25, 32, 34, 37			
transfer		19-25, 31-37, 40-47	35-40, 57-63		
LEVELS OF PERFORMANCE					
definition of				54-55, 62	
recognize			26-29, 33	69, 75-79	
edit			26-29, 33	69-72, 75-79	
produce			26-29, 33	70-71	
simulation and			26-33		
mediating practice and				69-79	
MEDIA					
definition of	44-45				
referents	47-55				
objects	47-48, 50-55, 57, 61				
abstractions	47, 49 51-52, 58-59, 61				
representation	40-59				
directness	58-61				

	PART I	PART II	PART III	PART IV	PART V
fidelity	50-61				
role of	44-45				
types of visuals	52-57				
fabricated	52-57				
realistic	52-55				
reproduced	52-57				
requirements		49-60			
inputs		49-56, 58-59			
actions		49-51, 57			
outputs		55-56, 60			
MEDIATING VISUALS					
definition of				9-12, 21-25	
inputs				13-14, 17	
actions				15-17	
assessing need for				13-17, 26-27	
discriminations				23, 35, 40-51	
generalizations				24, 35, 40-51	
chains				25, 35-51	

	PART I	PART II	PART III	PART IV	PART V
types of				31-81	
cues				35-51	
responses				53-81	
feedback				83-87	
types of learning and				28-29, 40-47	
motor				28-29, 40-44, 47	
verbal				28-29, 40-44, 46	
visual				28-29, 40-45	
OUTPUTS					
definition of visual output	10-17				
criterion		2-6, 8, 10-11			
mediating				83-87	
simulated			24-25		
media requirements		55-56, 60			
REALISTIC VISUALS					
definition of	6-7				
fidelity of representation	54-55				
media requirements	52-55				

	PART I	PART II	PART III	PART IV	PART V
simulation and			24-25		
REPRODUCED VISUALS					
definition of	6-7				
fidelity of representation	54-55				
media requirements	52-57				
simulation and			24-25		
RETENTION					
definition of		19-20			
barriers to		32			
practice for		15-23			
rules for practice		25-37			
SIMULATION					
transfer and			35-40, 57-63		
visual vs. verbal			20-23, 30-33, 44-45		
SIMULATED VISUALS					
definition of			5, 26-29	21	
inputs			24-25, 42, 60-61		
actions			26-28, 43, 62-63		

	PART I	PART II	PART III	PART IV	PART V
outputs			24-25		
assessing need for			7-16		
decision factors			55-75		
desirable characteristics			35-53		
levels of performance			26-29		
role of			9, 19		
types of visuals			24-25		
visual vs. verbal simulation			20-23, 30-33, 44-45		
TRANSFER					
definition of		19-20			
barriers to		31-33, 40-47			
practice for		15-23			
relationship to generalization		40-42			
simulation and			35-40, 57-63		
rules for practice		25-37			
TYPES OF VISUALS					
fabrications	6-7, 52-57		24-25		
reproductions	6-7, 52-57				

	PART I	PART II	PART III	PART IV	PART V
realistic visuals	6-7, 52-55		24-25		
VERBAL LEARNING	▓	▓	▓	▓	▓
concept learning				28-29, 40-44, 46	
directness of representation	47-49, 51-52, 58-59, 61				

√

PART I

Introduction to the Use of Visuals in Instruction

PART II

The Use of Criterion Visuals in Instruction

PART III

The Use of Simulated Criterion Visuals in Instruction

PART IV

The Use of Mediating Visuals in Instruction

PART V

Procedures to Follow in Selecting and Using Visuals
in Instruction

PART I

Introduction to the Use of Visuals in Instruction

OBJECTIVES

1.1 Distinguishing Between REALISTIC, REPRODUCED, and FABRICATED Visuals

1.2 Distinguishing Between VISUAL Inputs, Actions, and Outputs and NON-VISUAL Inputs, Actions, and Outputs

1.3 Identifying Training Situations in Which It Is Desirable for the Learner to Engage in Practice Involving VISUAL INPUTS, VISUAL ACTIONS, or VISUAL OUTPUTS

1.4 Identifying TYPES OF MEDIA Used in Instruction

1.1 OBJECTIVES OF THIS UNIT

At the end of this unit you will be able to distinguish between REALISTIC, REPRODUCED, and FABRICATED visuals.

DIAGRAM OF YOUR JOB

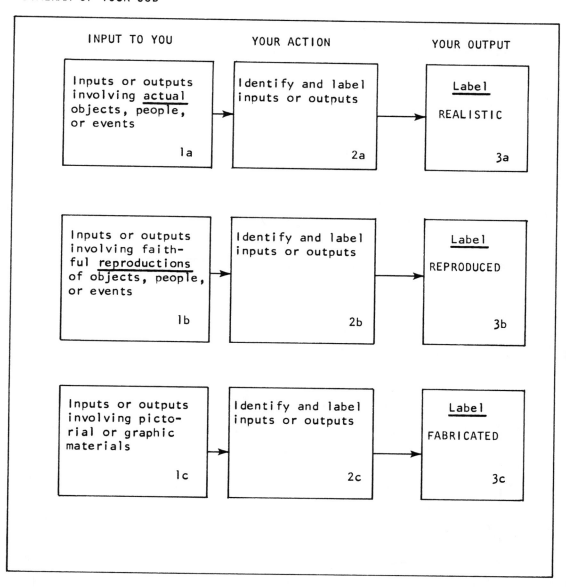

INPUT TO YOU	YOUR ACTION	YOUR OUTPUT
Inputs or outputs involving <u>actual</u> objects, people, or events **1a**	Identify and label inputs or outputs **2a**	<u>Label</u> REALISTIC **3a**
Inputs or outputs involving faithful <u>reproductions</u> of objects, people, or events **1b**	Identify and label inputs or outputs **2b**	<u>Label</u> REPRODUCED **3b**
Inputs or outputs involving pictorial or graphic materials **1c**	Identify and label inputs or outputs **2c**	<u>Label</u> FABRICATED **3c**

DISTINCTION BETWEEN REALISTIC, REPRODUCED, AND FABRICATED VISUALS

THREE TYPES OF VISUALS

	REALISTIC	REPRODUCED	FABRICATED
LABEL			
DEFINITION	actual objects, people, or events	hi-fidelity representation of objects, people, or events	low to moderate fidelity representation of objects, people, or events
			analogous representation of events or ideas
EXAMPLE	-actual customers or workers -actual equipment or tools -actual occurrences	-still photographs -film -TV tape -three-dimensional models	-pictorial materials (drawings, sketches) -graphic materials (charts, diagrams)

EXAMPLES OF REALISTIC, REPRODUCED, OR FABRICATED VISUALS

REALISTIC	REPRODUCED	FABRICATED
Screwdriver	Photograph of screwdriver	Drawing of screwdriver
Aircraft carrier maneuvering	Film of aircraft carrier maneuvering	Series of drawings of aircraft carrier maneuvering
		<u>Chart</u> showing increase in sales for 13 months
Retail customer smiling	Photograph of customer smiling	Sketch of customer smiling
Radar display	Film of radar display	Drawings of radar display
A building	A 3-dimensional model of the building (scaled-down)	Sketch of the building

NOW DO EXERCISE #1 ON PAGES <u>1.2</u> TO <u>1.5</u> IN THE WORKBOOK.

1.2 OBJECTIVES OF THIS UNIT

At the end of this unit you will be able to distinguish or discriminate between various types of visual inputs, actions, or outputs, on the one hand, and various types of non-visual inputs, actions, or outputs, on the other.

DIAGRAM OF YOUR JOB

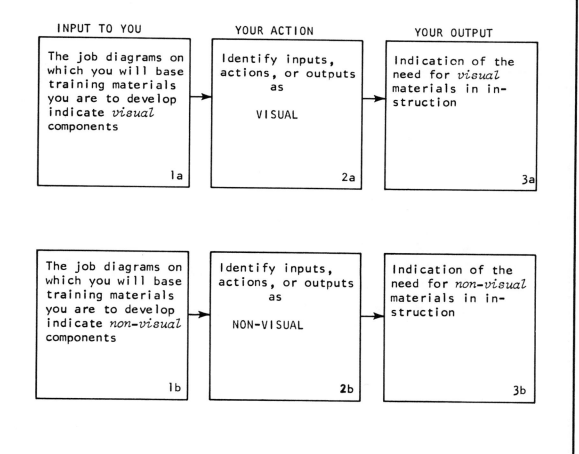

INPUT TO YOU

The job diagrams on which you will base training materials you are to develop indicate *visual* components

1a

YOUR ACTION

Identify inputs, actions, or outputs as

VISUAL

2a

YOUR OUTPUT

Indication of the need for *visual* materials in instruction

3a

The job diagrams on which you will base training materials you are to develop indicate *non-visual* components

1b

Identify inputs, actions, or outputs as

NON-VISUAL

2b

Indication of the need for *non-visual* materials in instruction

3b

DISTINCTION BETWEEN OUTPUTS
HAVING AND NOT HAVING RELEVANT VISUAL DISPLAY CHARACTERISTICS

TYPE OF OUTPUT

CLASSIFICATION

An output can provide
distinctively visual feedback
to the performer.

Based on the visual properties
of the output, the performer
either stops performing,
does something to correct
his performance,
or moves on to the next stage
of his performance.

Has relevant
VISUAL
display characteristics

An output can provide
feedback to the performer
that is not distinctively
visual in nature.

The performer
either stops performing,
does something to correct
his performance,
or moves on to the next stage
of his performance based on
feedback that is non-visual.
He does not need to attend
to the visual properties
of the output.

Does NOT have relevant
visual display characteristics

EXAMPLES OF THE DISTINCTION BETWEEN OUTPUTS

HAVING AND NOT HAVING RELEVANT VISUAL DISPLAY CHARACTERISTICS

OUTPUTS OF A DENTIST

Dentist inserts
a filling.

Output - filling

*The dentist makes discrimina-
tions about the adequacy of the
filling based on its visual
properties (e.g., smoothness,
covers whole area, etc.).*

CLASSIFICATION

Output
HAS
relevant visual
display characteristics

Dentist drills
a cavity (he can't see).

Output - drilled cavity

*The dentist makes discrimina-
tions about the adequacy of the
drilling based not on what it
looks like, but on resistance
to the drill.*

Output
DOES NOT HAVE
relevant visual
display characteristics

KEY SIGNIFICANCE OF THE DISTINCTION BETWEEN OUTPUTS HAVING
RELEVANT AND NON-RELEVANT VISUAL DISPLAY CHARACTERISTICS

TYPE OF OUTPUT	SKILLS THE PERFORMER NEEDS	CONTINUATION OF PERFORMANCE
1. has <u>relevant</u> visual display characteristics	performer <u>must</u> be <u>able to</u> discriminate between outputs based on their visual properties	stopping, correcting, or continuation of performance depends on <u>visual</u> discriminations
vs.	vs.	vs.
2. does <u>not</u> have <u>relevant</u> visual display characteristics	performer does <u>not</u> have to be <u>able to</u> discriminate between outputs based on their visual properties	stopping, correcting, or continuation of performance depends on <u>non-visual</u> discriminations

EXAMPLES OF THE DISTINCTION BETWEEN OUTPUTS
HAVING AND NOT HAVING RELEVANT VISUAL DISPLAY CHARACTERISTICS

EXAMPLES OF OUTPUTS

CLASSIFICATION

e.g., a man carving a piece of wood makes decisions about whether to stop, correct, or go on based on what the output looks like

e.g., a man reassembling a motor decides to stop, to redo, or to go on based on seeing the position of the parts that he has assembled

Has relevant
VISUAL
display characteristics

e.g., a man using the telephone for sales purposes raises the phone to his ear (the output), but whether he starts to talk does not depend on his seeing the phone in a certain position; feedback is kinesthetic

e.g., a computer operator may depress a "clear" button. The output is a clear dial; but the operator need not look at the dial (for visual information) before continuing. She does so without visual information

Does NOT have relevant
visual display characteristics

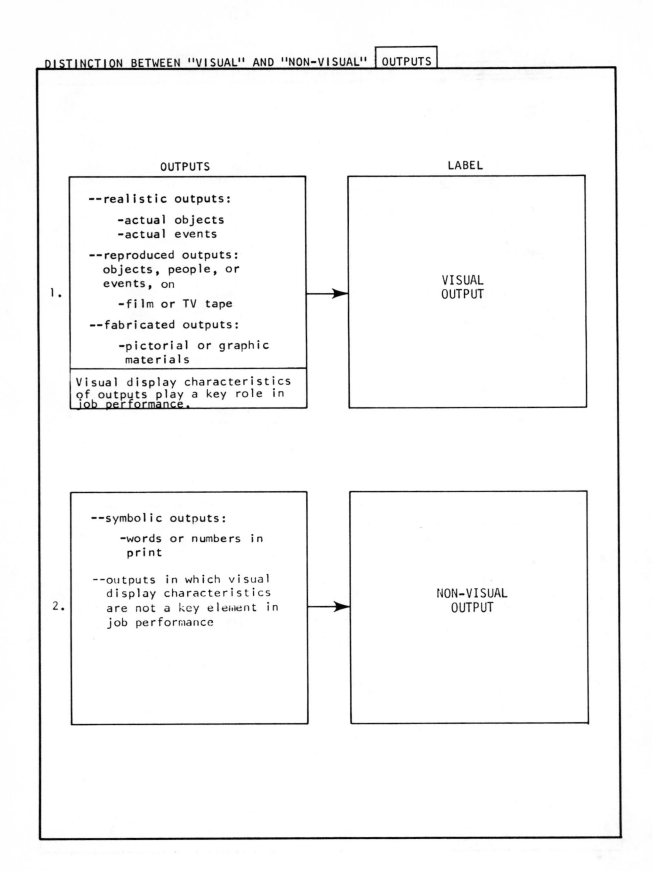

DISTINCTION BETWEEN "VISUAL" AND "NON-VISUAL" OUTPUTS

OUTPUTS   LABEL

1.
--realistic outputs:
    -actual objects
    -actual events

--reproduced outputs:
  objects, people, or
  events, on
    -film or TV tape

--fabricated outputs:
    -pictorial or graphic
     materials

Visual display characteristics
of outputs play a key role in
job performance.

→   VISUAL
         OUTPUT

2.
--symbolic outputs:
    -words or numbers in
     print

--outputs in which visual
  display characteristics
  are not a key element in
  job performance

→   NON-VISUAL
         OUTPUT

CONTRASTING EXAMPLES OF VISUAL AND NON-VISUAL OUTPUTS

	VISUAL OUTPUTS	vs.	NON-VISUAL OUTPUTS	vs.	COMBINATIONS OF VISUAL AND NON-VISUAL OUTPUTS
E.G. #1	A silent movie		A scenario for the movie		A movie with subtitles
	The output of a movie maker		The output of the writer of the movie		The output of a movie maker
E.G. #2	Black lines on a boundary map enclosing an area (for demolition)		"Starting at the southwest right of way, etc.": a legal boundary description		Boundary map with names of streets and other landmarks identified by a key
	The output of a city planner		The output of a lawyer		The output of a city planner or map maker
E.G. #3	Lamp glows on switchboard		Filled out message slip		Lamp glows on switchboard and voice of party called is heard
	The output of a PBX operator who plugs in a jack		The output of a PBX operator		The output of a PBX operator who plugs in a jack and connects the phone

1.15

EXAMPLES OF VISUAL OUTPUTS FOUND IN VARIED TYPES OF JOBS

JOB TYPES	REALISTIC VISUAL OUTPUTS	REPRODUCED VISUAL OUTPUTS	FABRICATED VISUAL OUTPUTS
Carpenter	A cabinet of a particular design		
Photographer		Picture of a cabinet	
Artist			Drawing of a cabinet
Economist			Graph
Gas Station Attendant	Clean wind- shield		
Draftsman			Blueprint
Nurse	Empty bedpan		Electrocardio- gram readout
Electrician	Lighted bulbs		
Salesman	Smiling customer		Sales graph

NOW DO EXERCISE #2 ON
PAGES 1.6 TO 1.11 IN
THE WORKBOOK.

1.17

DISTINCTION BETWEEN "VISUAL" AND "NON-VISUAL" INPUTS

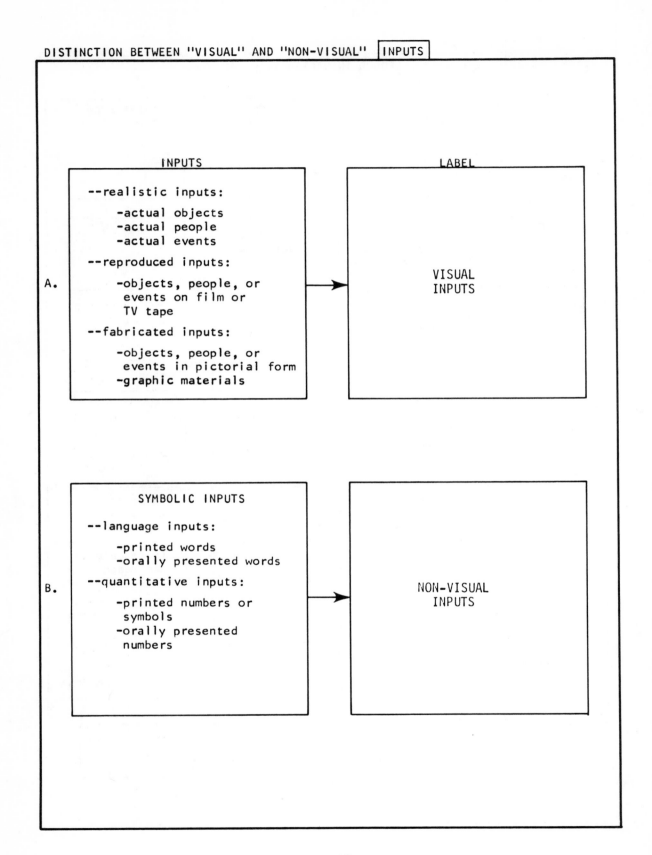

INPUTS

LABEL

A.
--realistic inputs:

-actual objects
-actual people
-actual events

--reproduced inputs:

-objects, people, or
events on film or
TV tape

--fabricated inputs:

-objects, people, or
events in pictorial form
-graphic materials

VISUAL
INPUTS

B.
SYMBOLIC INPUTS

--language inputs:

-printed words
-orally presented words

--quantitative inputs:

-printed numbers or
symbols
-orally presented
numbers

NON-VISUAL
INPUTS

	VISUAL INPUTS	vs.	NON-VISUAL INPUTS	vs.	COMBINATIONS OF VISUAL AND NON-VISUAL INPUTS

E.G. #1

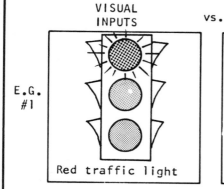

Red traffic light

Printed sign over a traffic lane

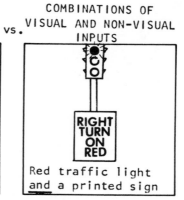

Red traffic light and a printed sign

E.G. #2

Pictorial illustration showing the orbit of an electron around the nucleus of an atom

"Electrons orbit around the nucleus of an atom."

A verbal description of the relationship of electrons to a nucleus of an atom

A pictorial (i.e., visual) and verbal (i.e., non-visual) illustration of the relationship of electrons to the nucleus of an atom

E.G. #3

A man who is to be rated, actually performing on the job

☐ works steadily

☐ makes few errors

☐ output high

A checklist describing a man's job performance serves as a basis for a rating

☐ works steadily
☐ makes few errors
☐ output high

Rating of performance is based on a visual input (man actually performing) and a verbal description of the performance

EXAMPLES OF VISUAL INPUTS FOUND IN VARIED TYPES OF JOBS

JOB TYPES	REALISTIC VISUAL INPUTS	REPRODUCED VISUAL INPUTS	FABRICATED VISUAL INPUTS
Manager	--an assembly line	--photograph of an assembly line	--sketch of a proposed assembly line
Mechanic	--engine parts to be assembled --tools to be used	--photograph of how part is to be oriented in engine	--diagram of part location
Salesman	--customer facial expression	--photographs of products	--graphs showing performance of product
Clerk	--products to be sold --bags for packing goods		
Physician	--color of patient's tongue --swelling of ankles	--X ray plate	--electro-cardiogram
Naval Officer	--enemy vessel to be identified	--photographs of enemy vessels	--silhouettes of enemy vessels
PBX Operator	--blinking light		
Foreman	--behavior of a work crew	--pictures of products showing acceptable tolerances	

NOW DO EXERCISE #3
ON PAGES 1.12 TO 1.13
IN THE WORKBOOK.

ACTION

LABEL

--identifies or recognizes
  visual display characteristics
  of inputs

--alters visual display
  characteristics of inputs
  (leading to a visual output)

--performs motor actions that
  produce an output that has
  visual properties the job
  holder (or someone else) has
  to attend to

     -draws, paints
     -creates objects

VISUAL
ACTIONS

1. identifies or recognizes
    symbolic (linguistic or
    quantitative) inputs

    alters symbolic inputs

    produces symbolic outputs

       -writes words, numbers

2. performs motor actions that
    produce an output involving
    no visual properties the
    job holder (or someone else)
    has to attend to

NON-VISUAL
ACTIONS

CONTRASTING EXAMPLES OF VISUAL AND NON-VISUAL ACTIONS

	VISUAL ACTION	NON-VISUAL ACTION	COMBINATION OF VISUAL AND NON-VISUAL ACTIONS
E.G. #1	Geographer *draws* a map and locates a city correctly.	Geographer *states* in print where a city is located.	Geographer *draws* a map, locates a city, and in addition *prints* the name of the city in the correct location.
E.G. #2	Chef stirs a sauce until the sauce clings to the spoon.	Chef writes out recipe and directions for preparing a sauce.	Chef heats pressure cooker until steam issues forth and nozzle indicator reaches correct reading.
E.G. #3	Naval officer picks out which ship in a group of ships is the aircraft carrier.	Naval officer describes verbally to a junior officer the characteristics of an aircraft carrier; Seaman sends morse code (no visual output)	Seaman sends semaphore message.

1.23

DISTINCTIONS AMONG THREE TYPES OF VISUAL ACTIONS

LABEL	IDENTIFICATION OF INPUTS	vs.	ALTERATION OF INPUTS	vs.	PRODUCTION OF OUTPUTS
DEFINITION	Identifying inputs based on their visual properties		Making a change in an input that results in an output having visual properties <u>relevant to job performance</u>		Working from raw materials creating an output having visual properties relevant to job performance
EXAMPLE	-Selecting inputs based on what they look like -Matching inputs based on what they look like -Recognizing conditions of inputs based on what they look like		-Making changes in inputs so that they achieve specified visual properties relevant to job performance		A visual output is created where none existed before

EXAMPLES OF | VISUAL ACTIONS | FOUND IN VARIED JOB TYPES

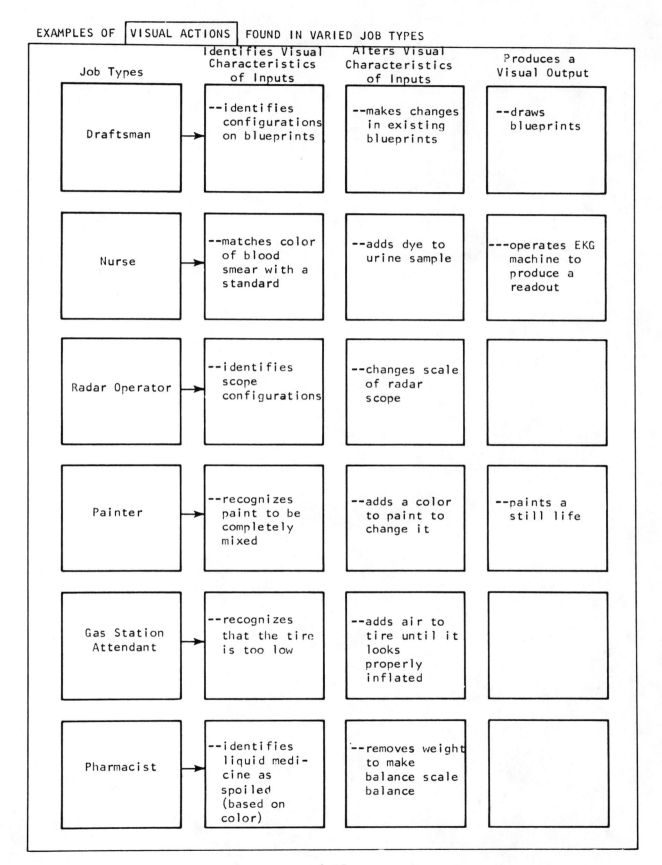

Job Types	Identifies Visual Characteristics of Inputs	Alters Visual Characteristics of Inputs	Produces a Visual Output
Draftsman	--identifies configurations on blueprints	--makes changes in existing blueprints	--draws blueprints
Nurse	--matches color of blood smear with a standard	--adds dye to urine sample	---operates EKG machine to produce a readout
Radar Operator	--identifies scope configurations	--changes scale of radar scope	
Painter	--recognizes paint to be completely mixed	--adds a color to paint to change it	--paints a still life
Gas Station Attendant	--recognizes that the tire is too low	--adds air to tire until it looks properly inflated	
Pharmacist	--identifies liquid medi- cine as spoiled (based on color)	--removes weight to make balance scale balance	

EXAMPLES OF MOTOR ACTIONS THAT LEAD TO OUTPUTS THAT
HAVE AND HAVE NOT RELEVANT VISUAL DISPLAY PROPERTIES

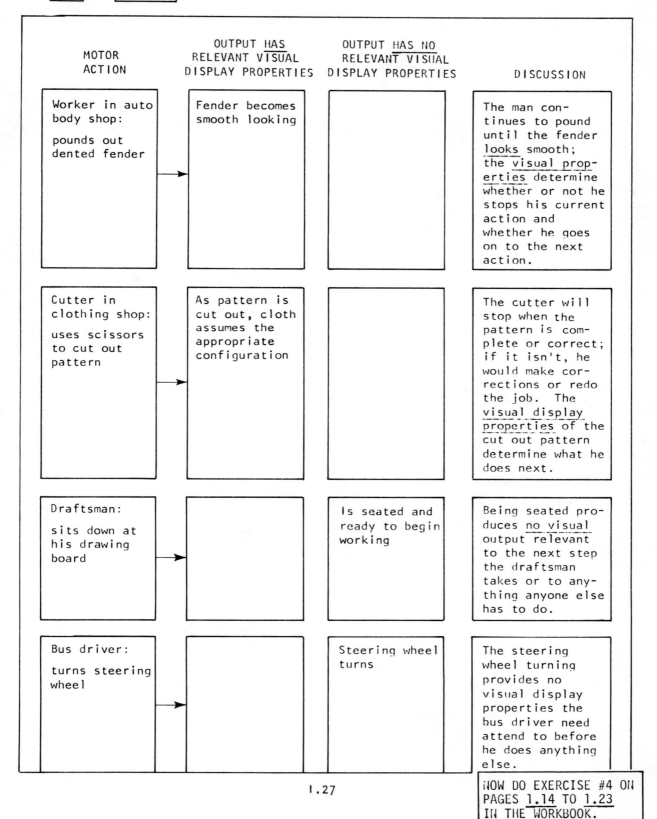

MOTOR ACTION	OUTPUT HAS RELEVANT VISUAL DISPLAY PROPERTIES	OUTPUT HAS NO RELEVANT VISUAL DISPLAY PROPERTIES	DISCUSSION
Worker in auto body shop: pounds out dented fender	Fender becomes smooth looking		The man continues to pound until the fender looks smooth; the visual properties determine whether or not he stops his current action and whether he goes on to the next action.
Cutter in clothing shop: uses scissors to cut out pattern	As pattern is cut out, cloth assumes the appropriate configuration		The cutter will stop when the pattern is complete or correct; if it isn't, he would make corrections or redo the job. The visual display properties of the cut out pattern determine what he does next.
Draftsman: sits down at his drawing board		Is seated and ready to begin working	Being seated produces no visual output relevant to the next step the draftsman takes or to anything anyone else has to do.
Bus driver: turns steering wheel		Steering wheel turns	The steering wheel turning provides no visual display properties the bus driver need attend to before he does anything else.

NOW DO EXERCISE #4 ON PAGES 1.14 TO 1.23 IN THE WORKBOOK.

1.3 OBJECTIVES OF THIS UNIT

At the end of this unit you will be able to identify training situations in which it is desirable for the learner to engage in active practice involving visual inputs, visual actions, or visual outputs.

DIAGRAM OF YOUR JOB

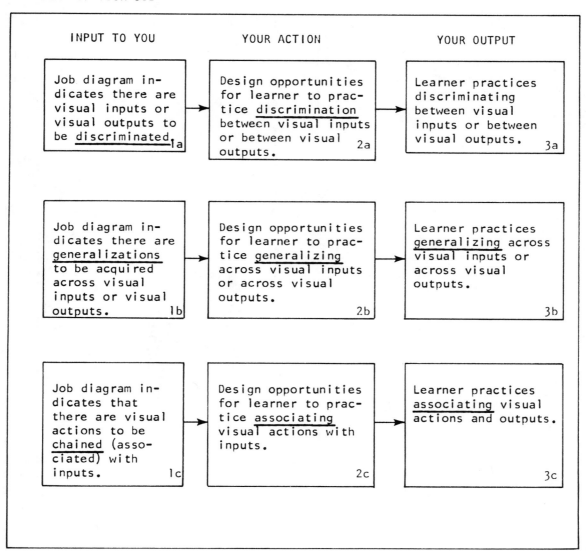

SITUATION

RESULT

A.

1. Job holder has produced an output and

CAN

<u>discriminate</u> between:

--completed and incompleted outputs
--correct and faulty outputs
--one type of output and another type.

Does <u>not</u> confuse correct and incorrect outputs.

1. Output becomes a <u>correct</u> INPUT for the next step in the chain; OR

2. Job holder <u>correctly</u> stops performing because his output in the step he has completed is <u>correct</u> or <u>complete</u>.

Job holder gets
CORRECT FEEDBACK

B.

1. Job holder has produced an output and

CANNOT

<u>discriminate</u> between:

--completed and incompleted outputs
--correct and faulty outputs
--one type of output and another type.

May confuse correct and incorrect outputs.

1. Output becomes an <u>incorrect</u> INPUT for the next step in the chain; OR

2. Job holder <u>incorrectly</u> stops performing despite the fact that his output in the step he has just completed is <u>incorrect</u> or <u>incomplete</u>. May also continue performing too long.

Job holder gets
INCORRECT FEEDBACK

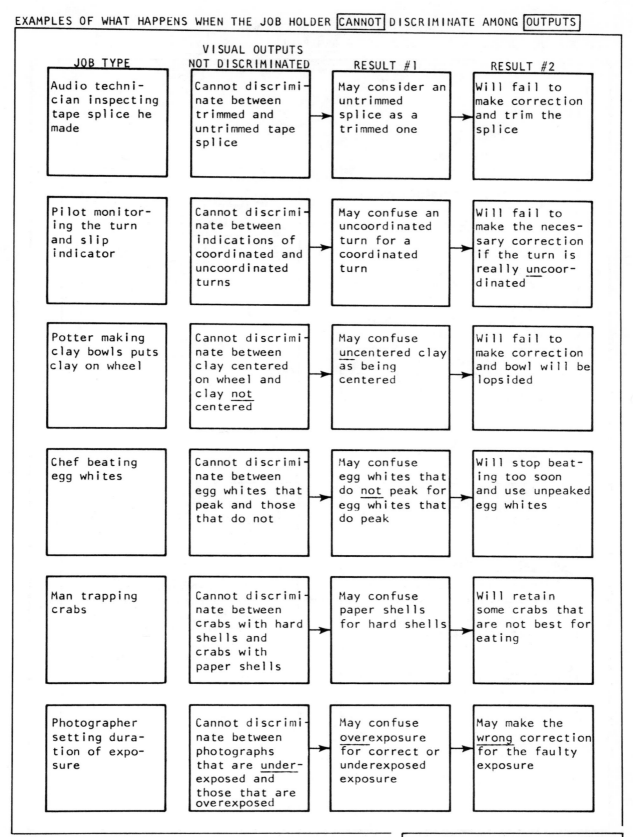

JOB TYPE	VISUAL OUTPUTS NOT DISCRIMINATED	RESULT #1	RESULT #2
Audio technician inspecting tape splice he made	Cannot discriminate between trimmed and untrimmed tape splice	May consider an untrimmed splice as a trimmed one	Will fail to make correction and trim the splice
Pilot monitoring the turn and slip indicator	Cannot discriminate between indications of coordinated and uncoordinated turns	May confuse an uncoordinated turn for a coordinated turn	Will fail to make the necessary correction if the turn is really uncoordinated
Potter making clay bowls puts clay on wheel	Cannot discriminate between clay centered on wheel and clay not centered	May confuse uncentered clay as being centered	Will fail to make correction and bowl will be lopsided
Chef beating egg whites	Cannot discriminate between egg whites that peak and those that do not	May confuse egg whites that do not peak for egg whites that do peak	Will stop beating too soon and use unpeaked egg whites
Man trapping crabs	Cannot discriminate between crabs with hard shells and crabs with paper shells	May confuse paper shells for hard shells	Will retain some crabs that are not best for eating
Photographer setting duration of exposure	Cannot discriminate between photographs that are underexposed and those that are overexposed	May confuse overexposure for correct or underexposed exposure	May make the wrong correction for the faulty exposure

NOW DO EXERCISE #5 ON PAGES 1.24 to 1.31 IN THE WORKBOOK.

CONDITION

RESULT

A.

Job holder has produced an output and

CAN

<u>gen</u>eralize across:

--variations in outputs that are still correct or complete

--variations in types of outputs that are fundamentally equivalent

Does <u>not</u> confuse <u>varied</u> instances of correct outputs as being incorrect (and converse).

(1) Output becomes a <u>correct</u> INPUT for the next step in the chain; OR

(2) Job holder <u>correctly</u> stops performing because his output in <u>this</u> step he has just completed is <u>correct</u> or <u>complete</u>

Job holder gets CORRECT FEEDBACK

B.

Job holder has produced an output and

CANNOT

<u>gen</u>eralize across:

--variations in outputs that are still correct or complete

--variations in types of outputs that are fundamentally equivalent

May confuse <u>varied</u> instances of correct outputs as being incorrect (and converse).

(1) Output becomes an <u>incorrect</u> INPUT for the next step in the chain; OR

(2) Job holder <u>incorrectly</u> stops performing despite the fact that his output in the step he has just completed is <u>incorrect</u> or <u>incomplete</u>; may also continue performing too long.

Job holder gets INCORRECT FEEDBACK

EXAMPLES OF WHAT HAPPENS WHEN THE JOB HOLDER [CANNOT] GENERALIZE ACROSS [OUTPUTS]

JOB TYPE	VISUAL OUTPUTS NOT PROPERLY GENERALIZED		CONFUSION	RESULT
Worker in photographic darkroom: taking photograph out of developer and putting it into stop bath when it is fully developed	One extreme of the tolerable range of being fully developed	Other extreme of the tolerable range of being fully developed	May confuse a fully developed photograph for one that was not	May leave photograph in the developer too long
Man grinding dies: paints dies and continues to grind until traces of pigment visible in grooves	Big trace acceptable	Medium trace or little trace also acceptable	May confuse an acceptable trace for an unacceptable trace	May continue too long if he cannot recognize any amount of trace is acceptable
Sandwich maker: slicing meat to put predetermined weight into sandwich	Six thin slices unacceptable	Eight thin slices unacceptable	May confuse eight thin slices for an acceptable amount	May stop slicing too soon, thinking he has enough meat
Electronic maintenance man doing soldering	Solder job #1 unacceptable	Solder job #2 unacceptable	May confuse an unacceptable solder job for an acceptable one	Cannot recognize that each job is within the unacceptable range and will stop too soon or fail to make correction

NOW DO EXERCISE #6 ON PAGES 1.32 TO 1.39 IN THE WORKBOOK.

1.33

CONDITION   RESULT

A.

Job holder has to respond to
a visual input and

CAN

discriminate between inputs
or classes of inputs, each of
which:

--requires different actions.

*Does not confuse one type of
input for another.*

Job holder can learn which
action goes with which input
and subsequently can take the
correct action for a given
input.

B.

Job holder has to respond to
a visual input and

CANNOT

discriminate between inputs
or classes of inputs, each of
which:

--requires different actions.

*May confuse one type of input
for another.*

Job holder cannot learn which
action goes with which input
and subsequently cannot take
the correct action for a
given input. Since he cannot
tell the difference among
inputs, he may confuse them
and therefore take a wrong
action.

EXAMPLES OF WHAT HAPPENS WHEN THE JOB HOLDER [CANNOT] DISCRIMINATE AMONG [INPUTS]

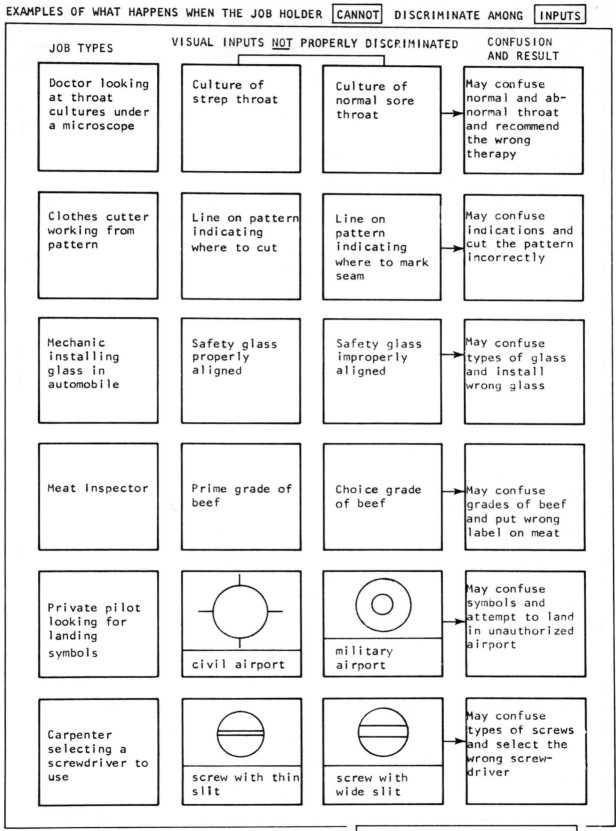

JOB TYPES	VISUAL INPUTS NOT PROPERLY DISCRIMINATED		CONFUSION AND RESULT
Doctor looking at throat cultures under a microscope	Culture of strep throat	Culture of normal sore throat	May confuse normal and abnormal throat and recommend the wrong therapy
Clothes cutter working from pattern	Line on pattern indicating where to cut	Line on pattern indicating where to mark seam	May confuse indications and cut the pattern incorrectly
Mechanic installing glass in automobile	Safety glass properly aligned	Safety glass improperly aligned	May confuse types of glass and install wrong glass
Meat Inspector	Prime grade of beef	Choice grade of beef	May confuse grades of beef and put wrong label on meat
Private pilot looking for landing symbols	civil airport	military airport	May confuse symbols and attempt to land in unauthorized airport
Carpenter selecting a screwdriver to use	screw with thin slit	screw with wide slit	May confuse types of screws and select the wrong screwdriver

1.35

NOW DO EXERCISE #7 ON PAGES 1.40 TO 1.47 IN THE WORKBOOK.

CONDITION | RESULT

A.

Job holder has to respond to a visual input and

CAN

<u>generalize</u> across inputs <u>all</u> of which:

--require the same action

Does <u>not</u> confuse <u>varied</u> instances of inputs that all belong to one class as belonging to another class.

Job holder can learn to take the <u>same</u> action for any of the <u>multiple</u> instances of an input and subsequently can take the correct action.

B.

Job holder has to respond to a visual input and

CANNOT

<u>generalize</u> across inputs <u>all</u> of which:

--require the same action

May confuse <u>varied</u> instances of inputs that <u>all</u> belong to one class as belonging to another class.

Job holder <u>cannot</u> learn to take the <u>same</u> action for any of the <u>multiple</u> instances of an input and subsequently <u>cannot</u> take the correct action.

Since he cannot see the similarity among inputs, he may incorrectly take a <u>different</u> action for one of them rather than taking the same action required for all instances of the input.

EXAMPLES OF WHAT HAPPENS WHEN THE JOB HOLDER CANNOT GENERALIZE ACROSS INPUTS

VISUAL INPUTS NOT PROPERLY GENERALIZED

JOB TYPE				RESULT
Pilot looking for any airport with facilities	Airport with facilities	Airport with facilities	Airport with facilities	May pass up an airport that actually has facilities / Treats it as if it is one without facilities
Farmer looking for a good day to plant	Fair weather clouds	Fair weather clouds	Fair weather clouds	May decide not to plant on what is really a good day / Treats it as if it were a bad day
Teacher trying to help children who exhibit emotional reactions to tension	Child laughs a lot / Indication of upset	Has tantrums / Indication of upset	Chews hair / Indication of upset	May ignore behavior that indicates emotional upset / Treats it as if it were not an indication of emotional upset
Electronic main-tenance man interpreting oscilloscope displays				May interpret one of the displays as being different when really they indicate the same condition

NOW DO EXERCISE #8 ON PAGES 1.48 TO 1.53 IN THE WORKBOOK.

1.37

CONDITION

RESULT

A.

Job holder has to take a
<u>visual action</u> in response to
a visual or non-visual input
and <u>has</u> learned to associate
the <u>action</u> with the input.

*Does <u>not</u> have any confusion as
to <u>which</u> action goes with which
input.*

Job holder <u>can</u> take the
correct vi<u>sual</u> action when
presented with a given input.

B.

Job holder has to take a
<u>visual action</u> in response to
a visual or non-visual input
and <u>has not</u> learned to
associate the action with
the input.

*May have a confusion as to
which action goes with which
input.*

Job holder <u>cannot</u> take the
correct visual action when
presented with a given input;
he may take an incorrect
action.

EXAMPLES OF WHAT HAPPENS WHEN THE JOB HOLDER DOES NOT
ASSOCIATE (OR CHAIN) VISUAL ACTIONS AND INPUTS

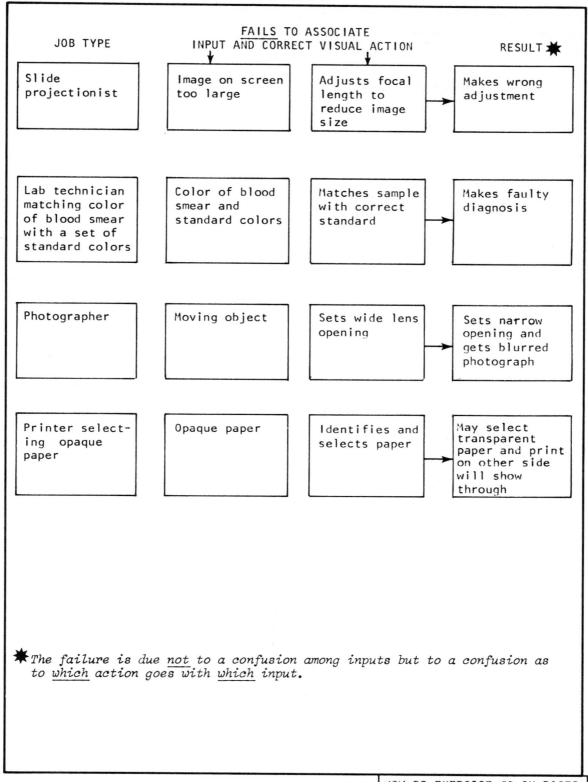

JOB TYPE	FAILS TO ASSOCIATE INPUT AND CORRECT VISUAL ACTION		RESULT ✱
Slide projectionist	Image on screen too large	Adjusts focal length to reduce image size	Makes wrong adjustment
Lab technician matching color of blood smear with a set of standard colors	Color of blood smear and standard colors	Matches sample with correct standard	Makes faulty diagnosis
Photographer	Moving object	Sets wide lens opening	Sets narrow opening and gets blurred photograph
Printer select-ing opaque paper	Opaque paper	Identifies and selects paper	May select transparent paper and print on other side will show through

✱ *The failure is due not to a confusion among inputs but to a confusion as to which action goes with which input.*

NOW DO EXERCISE #9 ON PAGES
1.54 TO 1.55 IN THE WORKBOOK

ULTIMATE CONSEQUENCE OF THE FAILURE TO ACQUIRE DISCRIMINATIONS AMONG INPUTS,
GENERALIZATIONS ACROSS INPUTS, OR ASSOCIATIONS BETWEEN INPUTS AND ACTIONS

The consequences of each of the three failures are the same. The job holder may TAKE THE WRONG ACTION. See the examples on the opposite page.

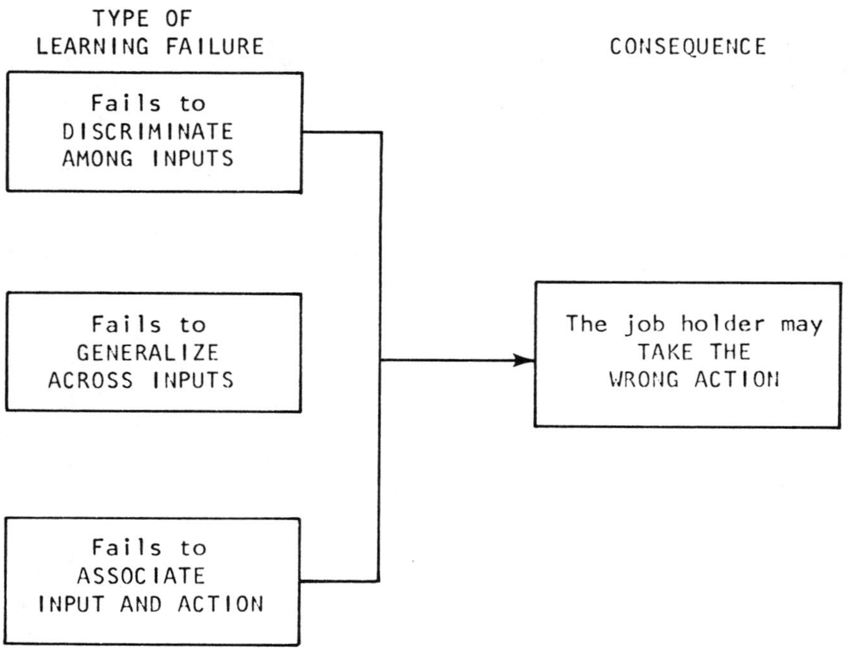

TYPE OF
LEARNING FAILURE   CONSEQUENCE

Fails to
DISCRIMINATE
AMONG INPUTS

Fails to
GENERALIZE   The job holder may
ACROSS INPUTS   TAKE THE
                                     WRONG ACTION

Fails to
ASSOCIATE
INPUT AND ACTION

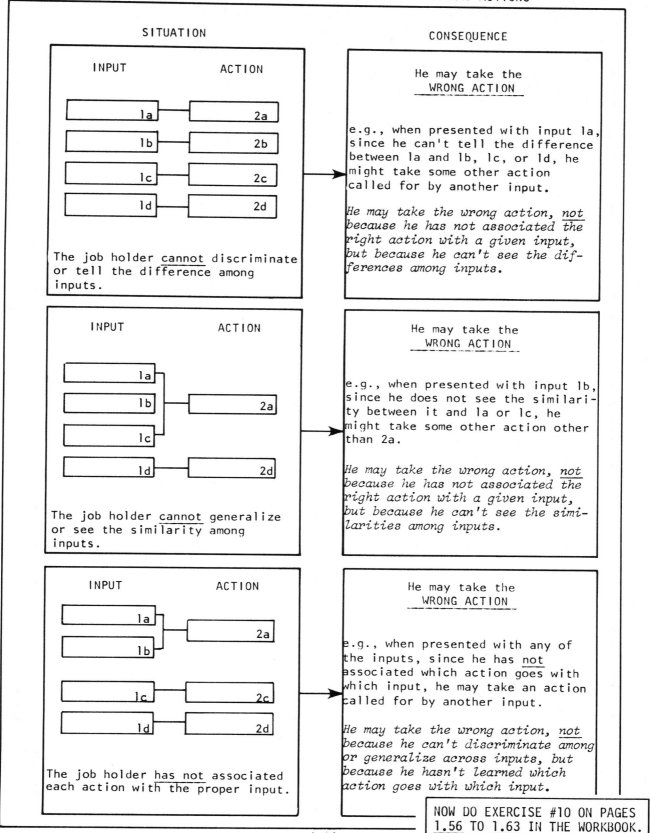

SITUATION

INPUT   ACTION

1a	2a
1b	2b
1c	2c
1d	2d

The job holder <u>cannot</u> discriminate or tell the difference among inputs.

CONSEQUENCE

He may take the
<u>WRONG ACTION</u>

e.g., when presented with input 1a, since he can't tell the difference between 1a and 1b, 1c, or 1d, he might take some other action called for by another input.

He may take the wrong action, <u>not</u> because he has not associated the right action with a given input, but because he can't see the differences among inputs.

INPUT   ACTION

1a	
1b	2a
1c	
1d	2d

The job holder <u>cannot</u> generalize or see the similarity among inputs.

He may take the
<u>WRONG ACTION</u>

e.g., when presented with input 1b, since he does not see the similarity between it and 1a or 1c, he might take some other action other than 2a.

He may take the wrong action, <u>not</u> because he has not associated the right action with a given input, but because he can't see the similarities among inputs.

INPUT   ACTION

1a	
1b	2a
1c	2c
1d	2d

The job holder has <u>not</u> associated each action with the proper input.

He may take the
<u>WRONG ACTION</u>

e.g., when presented with any of the inputs, since he has <u>not</u> associated which action goes with which input, he may take an action called for by another input.

He may take the wrong action, <u>not</u> because he can't discriminate among or generalize across inputs, but because he hasn't learned which action goes with which input.

NOW DO EXERCISE #10 ON PAGES <u>1.56</u> TO <u>1.63</u> IN THE WORKBOOK.

1.4   OBJECTIVES OF THIS UNIT

At the end of this unit, you will be able to identify the TYPES OF VISUAL MEDIA that are available for use in instruction.

DIAGRAM OF YOUR JOB

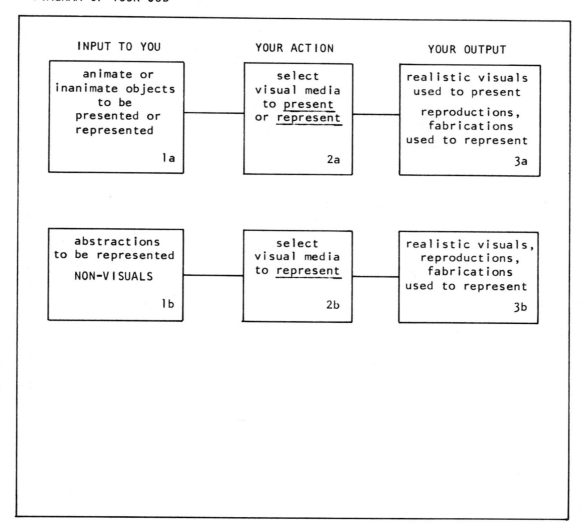

INPUT TO YOU | YOUR ACTION | YOUR OUTPUT

animate or inanimate objects to be presented or represented — 1a | select visual media to present or represent — 2a | realistic visuals used to present / reproductions, fabrications used to represent — 3a

abstractions to be represented NON-VISUALS — 1b | select visual media to represent — 2b | realistic visuals, reproductions, fabrications used to represent — 3b

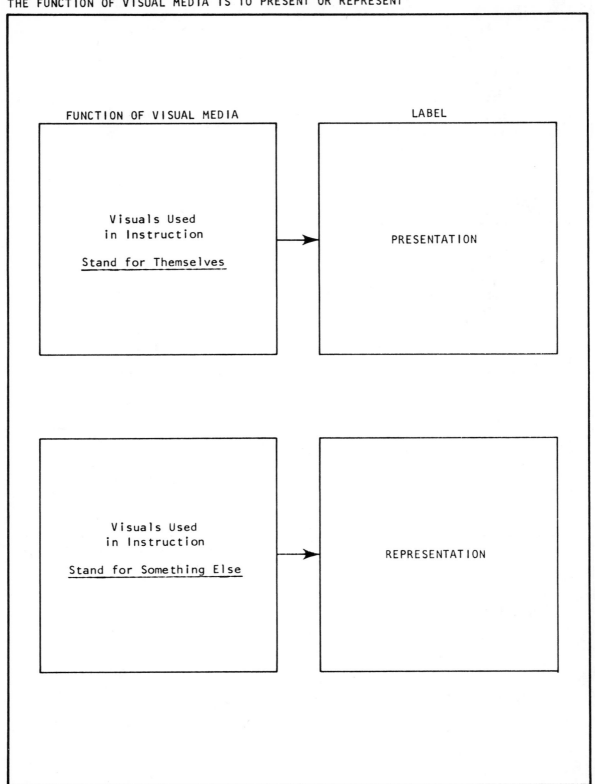

PRESENTATION

REPRESENTATION

The inside of
an automobile is used
in instruction

to stand for itself

A simulator
is used
in instruction

to stand for the automobile

An actual telephone switchboard
is used in instruction

to stand for itself

A photograph
of a telephone switchboard
is used in instruction

to stand for the switchboard

Naval guns firing at a target
are used in instruction

to stand for themselves

A motion picture film
of naval guns firing at a target
is used in instruction

to stand for the actual naval guns

NOW DO EXERCISE #11
ON PAGES 1.64 TO 1.67
IN THE WORKBOOK.

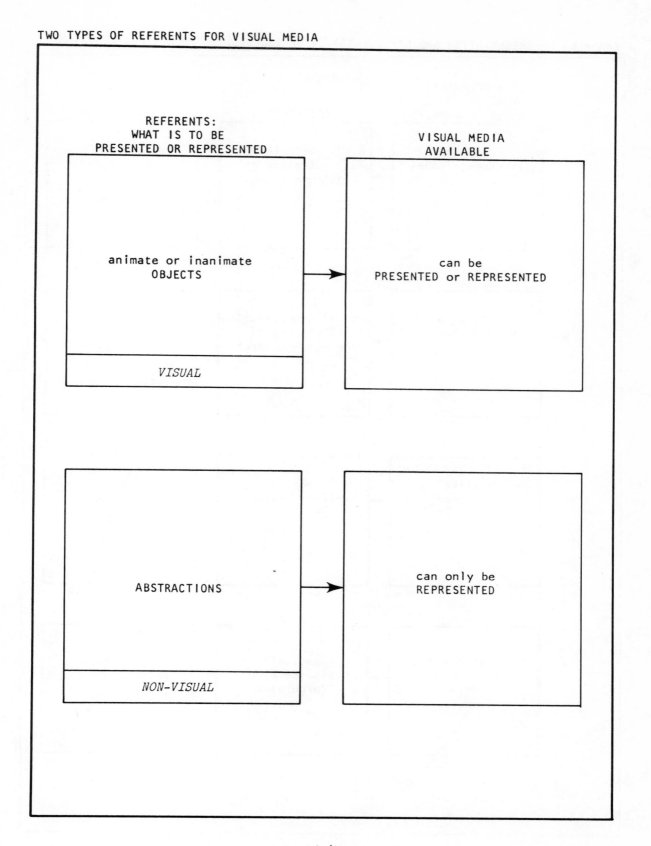

EXAMPLES OF PRESENTATION AND REPRESENTATION OF OBJECTS

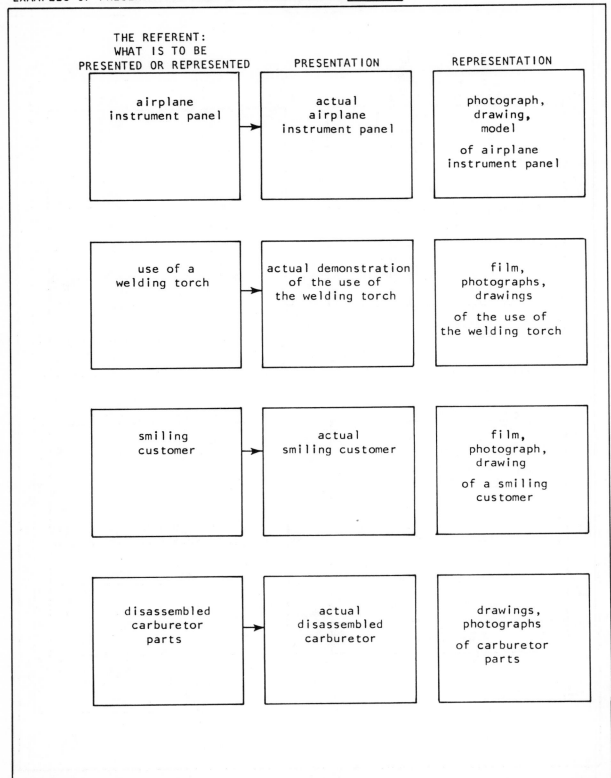

EXAMPLES OF REPRESENTATION OF ABSTRACTIONS

REFERENT: WHAT IS TO BE REPRESENTED	PRESENTATION	REPRESENTATION
concept of "peace"		dove
population statistics		bar chart
communication flow in an organization		diagram
concept of "leverage"		film of large object being raised with small force by using a lever

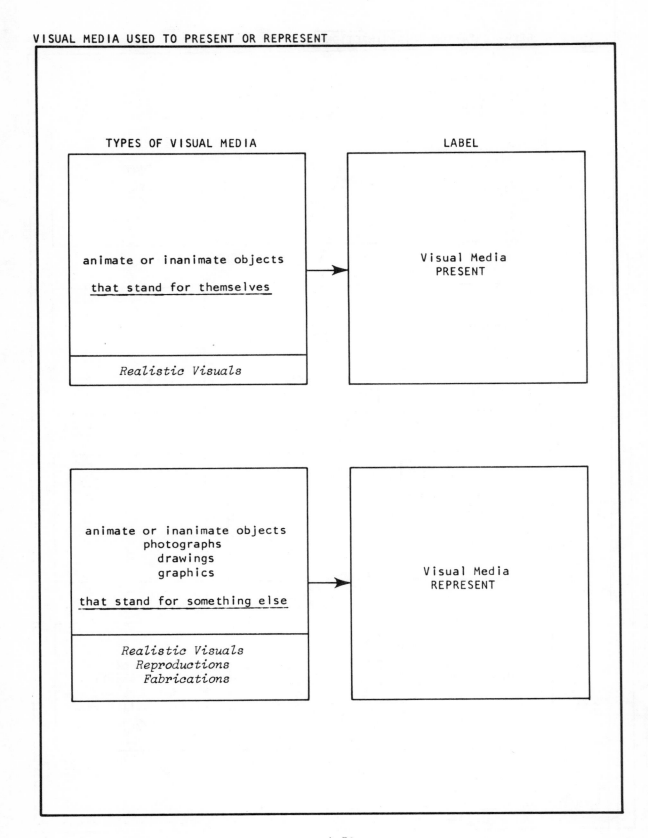

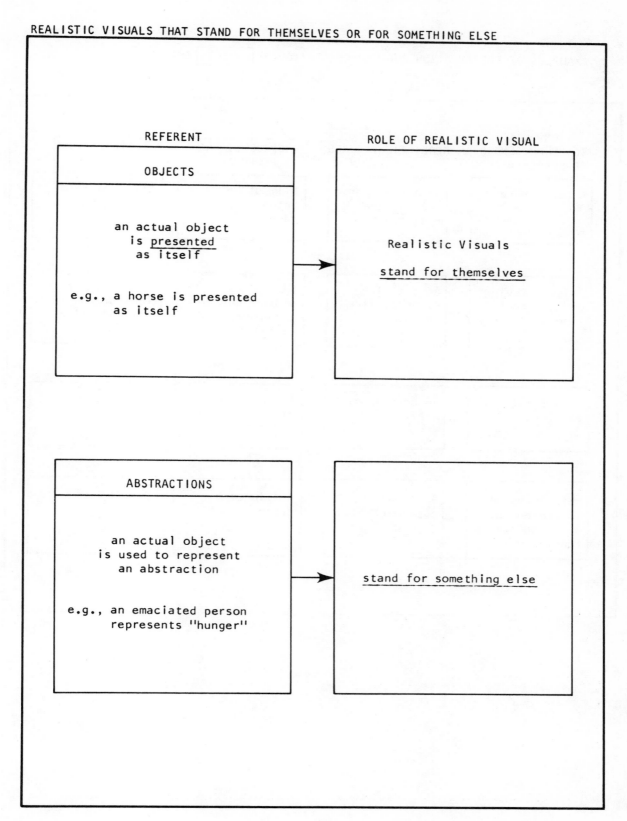

EXAMPLES OF PRESENTATION AND REPRESENTATION OF OBJECTS THROUGH MEDIA

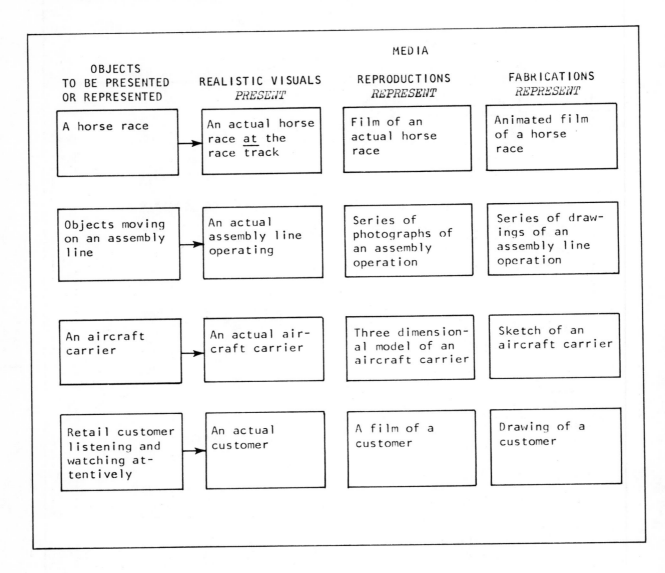

MEDIA

OBJECTS TO BE PRESENTED OR REPRESENTED	REALISTIC VISUALS *PRESENT*	REPRODUCTIONS *REPRESENT*	FABRICATIONS *REPRESENT*
A horse race	An actual horse race at the race track	Film of an actual horse race	Animated film of a horse race
Objects moving on an assembly line	An actual assembly line operating	Series of photographs of an assembly operation	Series of drawings of an assembly line operation
An aircraft carrier	An actual aircraft carrier	Three dimensional model of an aircraft carrier	Sketch of an aircraft carrier
Retail customer listening and watching attentively	An actual customer	A film of a customer	Drawing of a customer

EXAMPLES OF REPRESENTATION OF ABSTRACTIONS THROUGH MEDIA

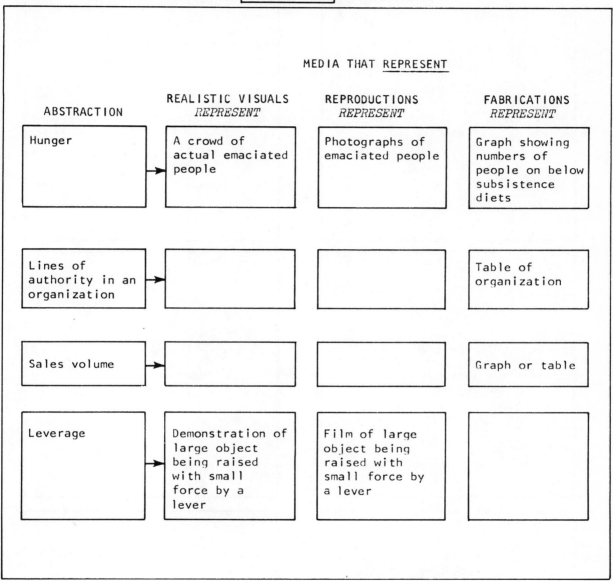

MEDIA THAT REPRESENT

ABSTRACTION	REALISTIC VISUALS *REPRESENT*	REPRODUCTIONS *REPRESENT*	FABRICATIONS *REPRESENT*
Hunger	A crowd of actual emaciated people	Photographs of emaciated people	Graph showing numbers of people on below subsistence diets
Lines of authority in an organization			Table of organization
Sales volume			Graph or table
Leverage	Demonstration of large object being raised with small force by a lever	Film of large object being raised with small force by a lever	

FIDELITY OF VISUAL MEDIA IN PRESENTING OR REPRESENTING OBJECTS

MEDIA

DEGREE OF
FIDELITY TO REFERENT

REALISTIC VISUALS

stand for themselves
(Present)

→ Very High

REPRODUCTIONS

stand for something else
(Represent)

→ Moderate to High

FABRICATIONS

stand for something else
(Represent)

→ Low to Moderate

1.54

EXAMPLES OF DEGREES OF FIDELITY IN PRESENTATION OR REPRESENTATION OF OBJECTS

OBJECT	VERY HIGH	HIGH	MODERATE	LOW
airplane cockpit panel	actual panel — *realistic visual presents*	mock-up of panel (simulation) — *reproduction represents*	close-up photograph — *reproduction represents*	sketch — *fabrication represents*
assembly of an engine	actual assembly of an engine — *realistic visual presents*	assembly of mock-up — *reproduction represents*	film of engine assembly — *reproduction represents*	animation of engine assembly — *fabrication represents*
irate customer	actual irate customer — *realistic visual presents*	role-play of irate customer — *reproduction represents*	photograph of irate customer — *reproduction represents*	drawing of irate customer — *fabrication represents*
suit of clothes fitted on person	suit of clothes fitted on person — *realistic visual presents*	suit of clothes fitted on dummy — *reproduction represents*	photograph of suit of clothes fitted on person — *reproduction represents*	sketch of suit of clothes fitted on person — *fabrication represents*

POSSIBLE VARIATIONS IN FIDELITY OF REPRESENTATION

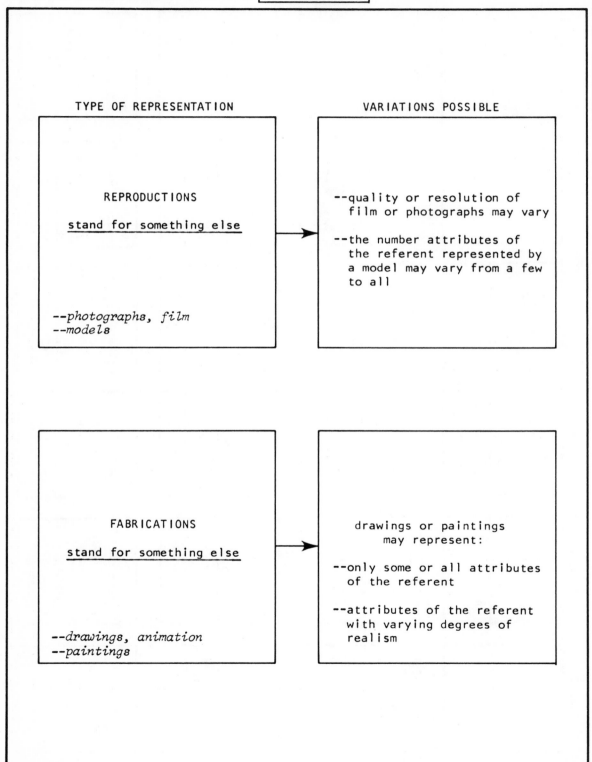

TYPE OF REPRESENTATION

VARIATIONS POSSIBLE

REPRODUCTIONS

stand for something else

--photographs, film
--models

--quality or resolution of
film or photographs may vary

--the number attributes of
the referent represented by
a model may vary from a few
to all

FABRICATIONS

stand for something else

--drawings, animation
--paintings

drawings or paintings
may represent:

--only some or all attributes
of the referent

--attributes of the referent
with varying degrees of
realism

EXAMPLES OF VARIATIONS IN FIDELITY OF REPRESENTATION OF OBJECTS

REFERENT REPRESENTED BY:	HIGH FIDELITY	MEDIUM FIDELITY	LOW FIDELITY
a man represented by REPRODUCTIONS	high detail photograph	medium detail photograph	low detail photograph
a man represented by FABRICATIONS	lifelike painting	stylized painting	stick figure
a battleship represented by FABRICATIONS	high detail model	medium detail model	low detail model

NOW DO EXERCISE #12 ON PAGES 1.68 TO 1.71 IN THE WORKBOOK.

1.57

REPRESENTATION OF ABSTRACTIONS VARIES IN DEGREES OF DIRECTNESS

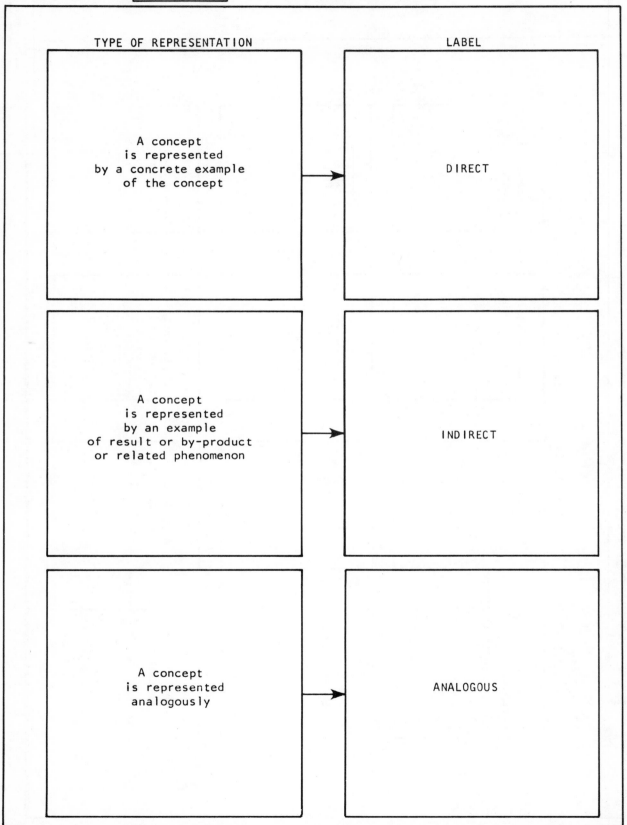

TYPE OF REPRESENTATION   LABEL

A concept
is represented
by a concrete example
of the concept

DIRECT

A concept
is represented
by an example
of result or by-product
or related phenomenon

INDIRECT

A concept
is represented
analogously

ANALOGOUS

EXAMPLES OF REPRESENTATION VARYING IN DIRECTNESS

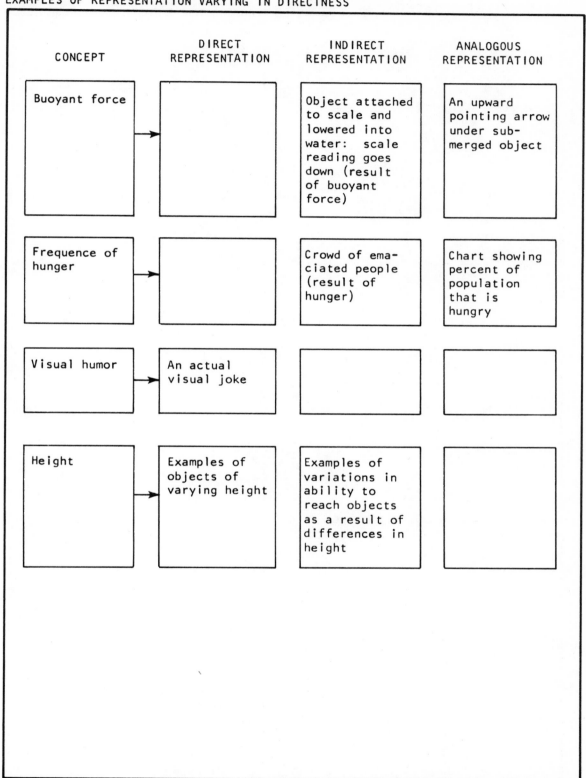

CONCEPT	DIRECT REPRESENTATION	INDIRECT REPRESENTATION	ANALOGOUS REPRESENTATION
Buoyant force		Object attached to scale and lowered into water: scale reading goes down (result of buoyant force)	An upward pointing arrow under sub-merged object
Frequence of hunger		Crowd of ema-ciated people (result of hunger)	Chart showing percent of population that is hungry
Visual humor	An actual visual joke		
Height	Examples of objects of varying height	Examples of variations in ability to reach objects as a result of differences in height	

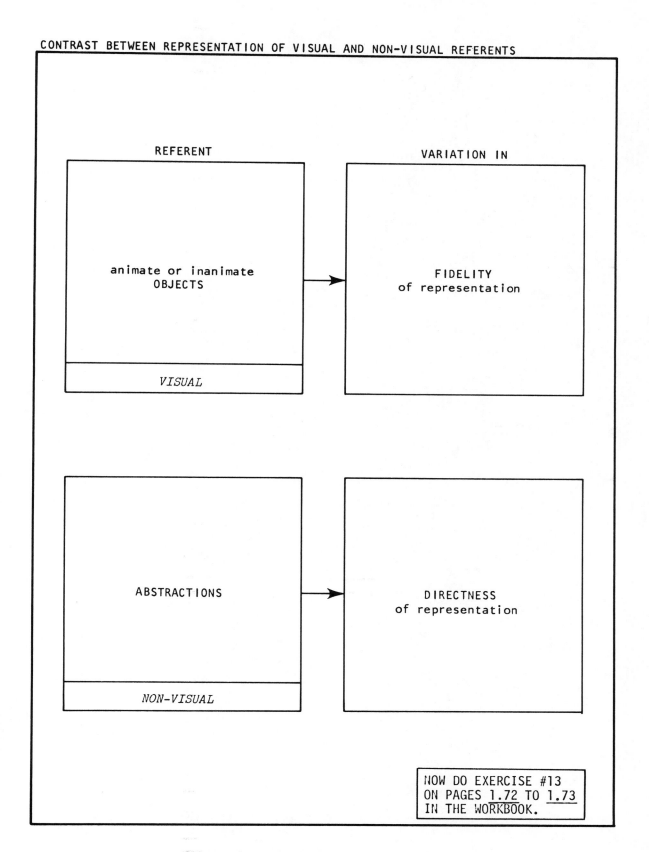

CONTRAST BETWEEN REPRESENTATION OF VISUAL AND NON-VISUAL REFERENTS

REFERENT

VARIATION IN

animate or inanimate
OBJECTS

VISUAL

FIDELITY
of representation

ABSTRACTIONS

NON-VISUAL

DIRECTNESS
of representation

NOW DO EXERCISE #13
ON PAGES 1.72 TO 1.73
IN THE WORKBOOK.

PART I

Introduction to the Use of Visuals in Instruction

PART II

 The Use of Criterion Visuals in Instruction

PART III

The Use of Simulated Criterion Visuals in Instruction

PART IV

The Use of Mediating Visuals in Instruction

PART V

Procedures to Follow in Selecting and Using Visuals
in Instruction

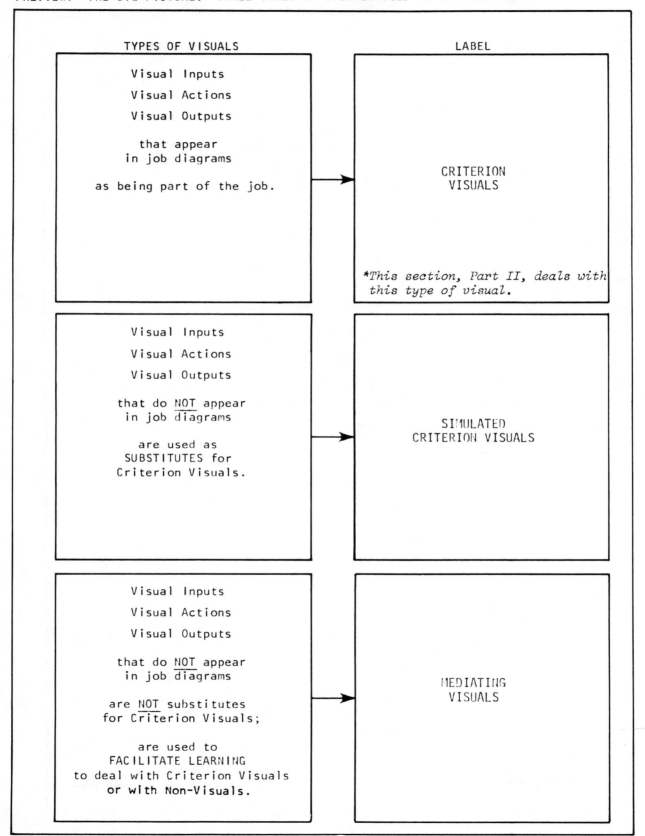

TYPES OF VISUALS

LABEL

Visual Inputs

Visual Actions

Visual Outputs

that appear
in job diagrams

as being part of the job.

CRITERION
VISUALS

*This section, Part II, deals with
this type of visual.*

Visual Inputs

Visual Actions

Visual Outputs

that do NOT appear
in job diagrams

are used as
SUBSTITUTES for
Criterion Visuals.

SIMULATED
CRITERION VISUALS

Visual Inputs

Visual Actions

Visual Outputs

that do NOT appear
in job diagrams

are NOT substitutes
for Criterion Visuals;

are used to
FACILITATE LEARNING
to deal with Criterion Visuals
or with Non-Visuals.

MEDIATING
VISUALS

PART II

The Use of Criterion Visuals in Instruction

OBJECTIVES

II.1 Identifying CRITERION VISUALS and Determining Their Use
in Instruction

II.2 Identifying INSTRUCTIONAL GOALS That Are Served When
ACTIVE PRACTICE IS INCORPORATED IN TRAINING

II.3 Identifying the KINDS OF PRACTICE Required to Achieve
INSTRUCTIONAL GOALS

II.4 Identifying the Consequences of Including or Not Including
Criterion Visuals IN TRAINING

II.5 Identifying MEDIA REQUIREMENTS for Use with CRITERION VISUALS

II.1 OBJECTIVES OF THIS UNIT

At the end of this unit you will be able to identify CRITERION VISUAL INPUTS, CRITERION VISUAL ACTIONS, AND CRITERION VISUAL OUTPUTS and to determine when to use them in instruction.

DIAGRAM OF YOUR JOB

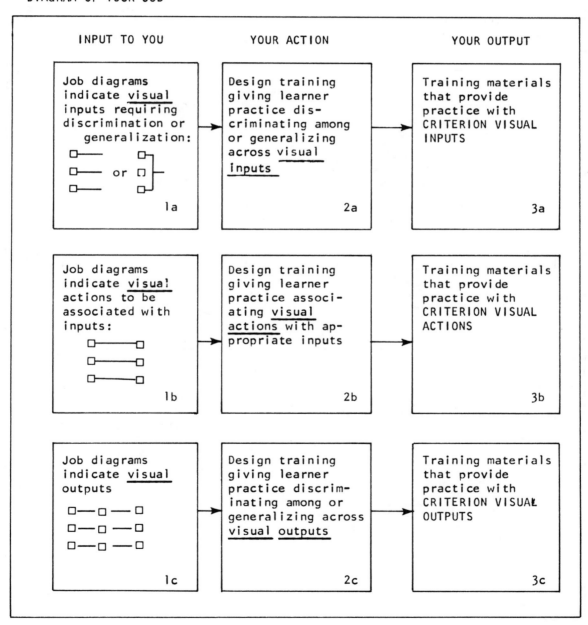

| INPUT TO YOU | YOUR ACTION | YOUR OUTPUT |

Job diagrams indicate visual inputs requiring discrimination or generalization:

1a

Design training giving learner practice discriminating among or generalizing across visual inputs

2a

Training materials that provide practice with CRITERION VISUAL INPUTS

3a

Job diagrams indicate visual actions to be associated with inputs:

1b

Design training giving learner practice associating visual actions with appropriate inputs

2b

Training materials that provide practice with CRITERION VISUAL ACTIONS

3b

Job diagrams indicate visual outputs

1c

Design training giving learner practice discriminating among or generalizing across visual outputs

2c

Training materials that provide practice with CRITERION VISUAL OUTPUTS

3c

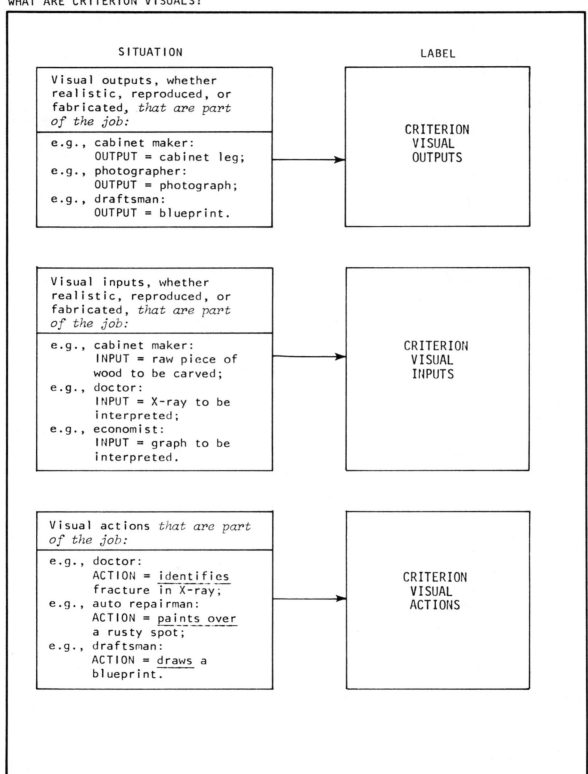

SITUATION   LABEL

Visual outputs, whether
realistic, reproduced, or
fabricated, *that are part
of the job:*

e.g., cabinet maker:
    OUTPUT = cabinet leg;
e.g., photographer:
    OUTPUT = photograph;   →   CRITERION
e.g., draftsman: VISUAL
    OUTPUT = blueprint.   OUTPUTS

Visual inputs, whether
realistic, reproduced, or
fabricated, *that are part
of the job:*

e.g., cabinet maker:
    INPUT = raw piece of
    wood to be carved;
e.g., doctor: →   CRITERION
    INPUT = X-ray to be   VISUAL
    interpreted;   INPUTS
e.g., economist:
    INPUT = graph to be
    interpreted.

Visual actions *that are part
of the job:*

e.g., doctor:
    ACTION = identifies
    fracture in X-ray;
e.g., auto repairman: →   CRITERION
    ACTION = paints over   VISUAL
    a rusty spot;   ACTIONS
e.g., draftsman:
    ACTION = draws a
    blueprint.

EXAMPLES OF REQUIRED PRACTICE WITH CRITERION VISUAL INPUTS

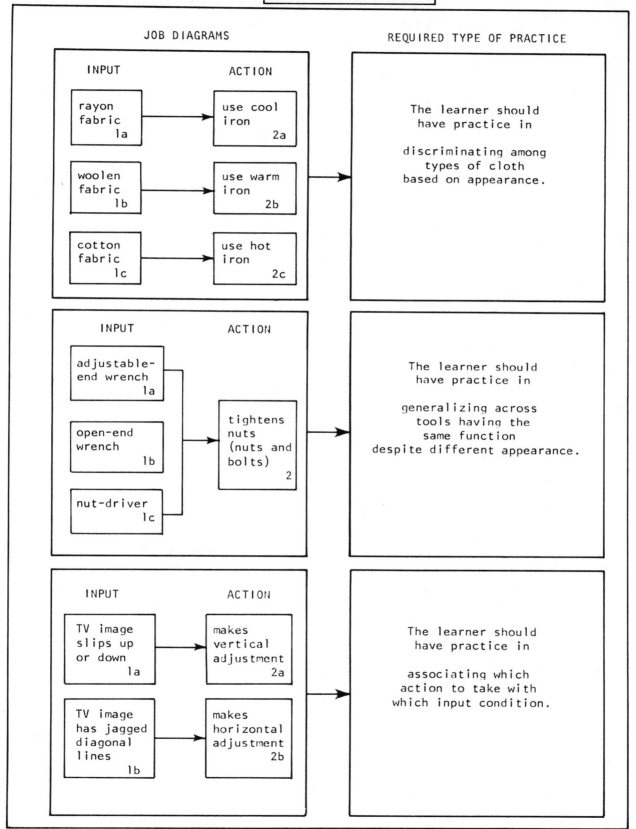

JOB DIAGRAMS

REQUIRED TYPE OF PRACTICE

INPUT   ACTION

rayon fabric 1a → use cool iron 2a

woolen fabric 1b → use warm iron 2b

cotton fabric 1c → use hot iron 2c

The learner should have practice in

discriminating among types of cloth based on appearance.

INPUT   ACTION

adjustable-end wrench 1a

open-end wrench 1b → tightens nuts (nuts and bolts) 2

nut-driver 1c

The learner should have practice in

generalizing across tools having the same function despite different appearance.

INPUT   ACTION

TV image slips up or down 1a → makes vertical adjustment 2a

TV image has jagged diagonal lines 1b → makes horizontal adjustment 2b

The learner should have practice in

associating which action to take with which input condition.

NOTE

(1) Job diagrams may not indicate outputs to be discriminated between or generalized across. It is always implied that the job holder has to be able to tell the difference between a correct and incorrect output.

(2) If the diagram indicates that the output becomes the input for the next step, then the diagram will identify the necessary discriminations or generalizations to be learned.

JOB DIAGRAMS

REQUIRED TYPE OF PRACTICE

WALL PAINTER

INPUT	ACTION	OUTPUT
wall	applies paint	wall with paint on it
wall covered	no further action	
wall not covered	applies a second coat	wall covered

The learner should have practice in

discriminating between walls that are adequately and inadequately covered with paint.

AUTOMOBILE DRIVER

INPUT	ACTION	OUTPUT
slowing or stopping vehicle ahead	applies brakes	car slows or stops

The learner should have practice in

discriminating between adequately and inadequately slowing-down cars and generalizing across varied instances of inadequately and across varied instances of adequately slowing-down cars.

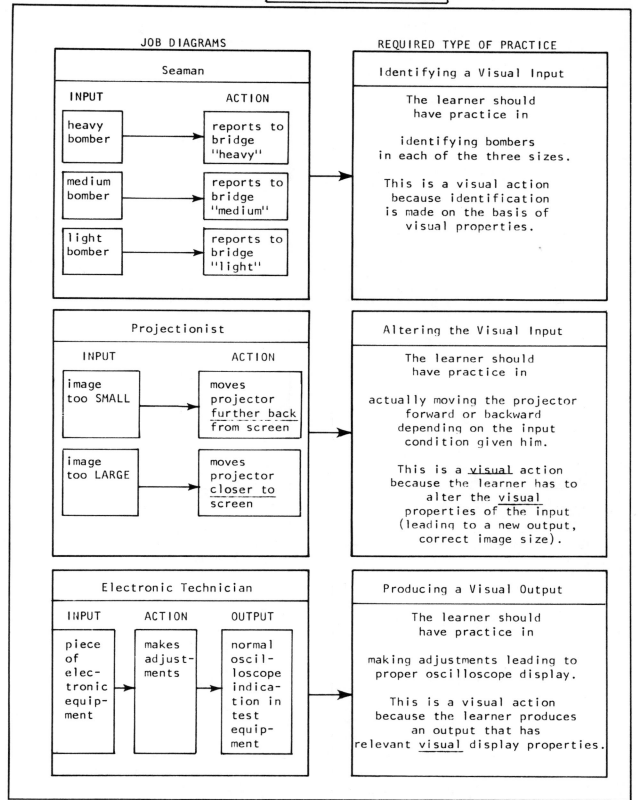

VISUAL PRACTICE	vs.	NON-VISUAL PRACTICE
INPUTS are VISUAL	vs.	**INPUTS** are NON-VISUAL
Discrimination or generalization practice should include VISUAL inputs.		*Discrimination or generalization practice should include NON-VISUAL inputs.*
ACTIONS are VISUAL	vs.	**ACTIONS** are NON-VISUAL
Association practice should include VISUAL actions.		*Association practice should include NON-VISUAL actions.*
OUTPUTS are VISUAL	vs.	**OUTPUTS** are NON-VISUAL
Discrimination or generalization practice should include VISUAL outputs.		*Discrimination or generalization practice should include NON-VISUAL outputs.*

EXAMPLES OF REQUIRED PRACTICE THAT IS VISUAL (VS. NON-VISUAL)*

INPUT	ACTION	OUTPUT	DISCRIMINATIONS OR GENERALIZATIONS FOR VISUAL INPUTS	ASSOCIATING VISUAL ACTIONS	DISCRIMINATIONS OR GENERALIZATIONS FOR VISUAL OUTPUTS
request to build stadium	draws sketch of stadium	sketch		X	X
color-coded resistors	reads off resistor values	resistance values	X		
undeveloped photograph	inserts in developer	developed photograph	X	X	X
TV symptom	adjusts set	good TV image	X	X	X
sound of gun	starts to race	running			

*X means VISUAL.

RULES ABOUT THE USE OF CRITERION VISUALS IN INSTRUCTION

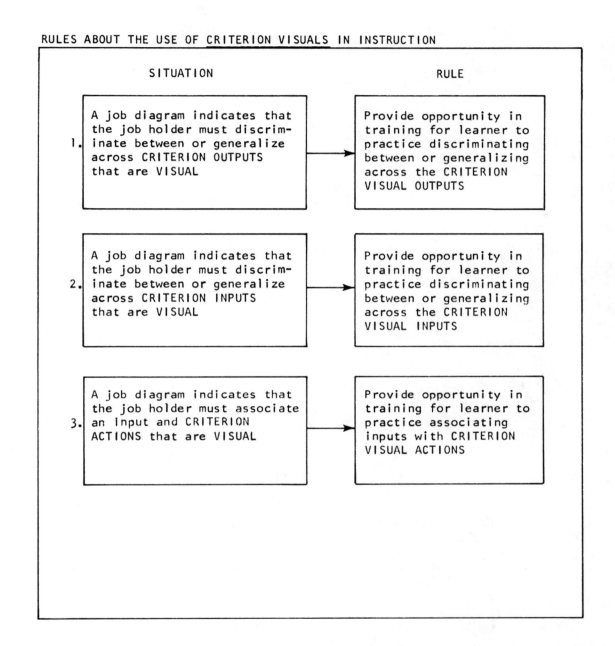

SITUATION

RULE

1. A job diagram indicates that the job holder must discriminate between or generalize across CRITERION OUTPUTS that are VISUAL

Provide opportunity in training for learner to practice discriminating between or generalizing across the CRITERION VISUAL OUTPUTS

2. A job diagram indicates that the job holder must discriminate between or generalize across CRITERION INPUTS that are VISUAL

Provide opportunity in training for learner to practice discriminating between or generalizing across the CRITERION VISUAL INPUTS

3. A job diagram indicates that the job holder must associate an input and CRITERION ACTIONS that are VISUAL

Provide opportunity in training for learner to practice associating inputs with CRITERION VISUAL ACTIONS

NOW DO EXERCISE #14 ON PAGES II.2 TO II.7 IN THE WORKBOOK.

II.2   OBJECTIVES OF THIS UNIT

At the end of this unit, you will be able to distinguish between three INSTRUCTIONAL GOALS that ACTIVE PRACTICE serves when it is incorporated in training.

DIAGRAM OF YOUR JOB

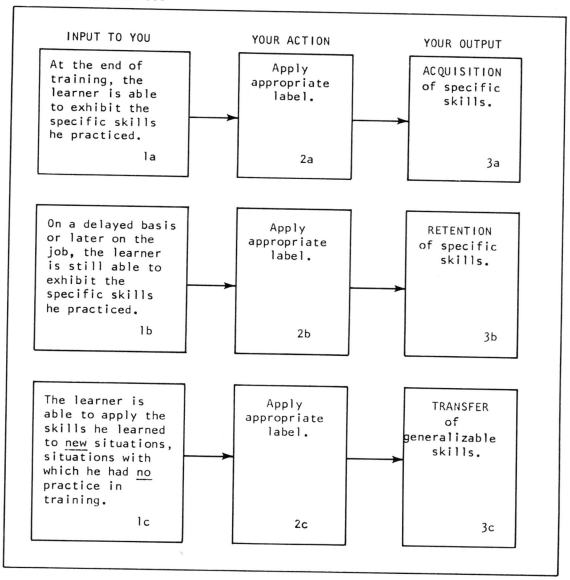

INPUT TO YOU

YOUR ACTION

YOUR OUTPUT

At the end of training, the learner is able to exhibit the specific skills he practiced.

1a

Apply appropriate label.

2a

ACQUISITION of specific skills.

3a

On a delayed basis or later on the job, the learner is still able to exhibit the specific skills he practiced.

1b

Apply appropriate label.

2b

RETENTION of specific skills.

3b

The learner is able to apply the skills he learned to new situations, situations with which he had no practice in training.

1c

Apply appropriate label.

2c

TRANSFER of generalizable skills.

3c

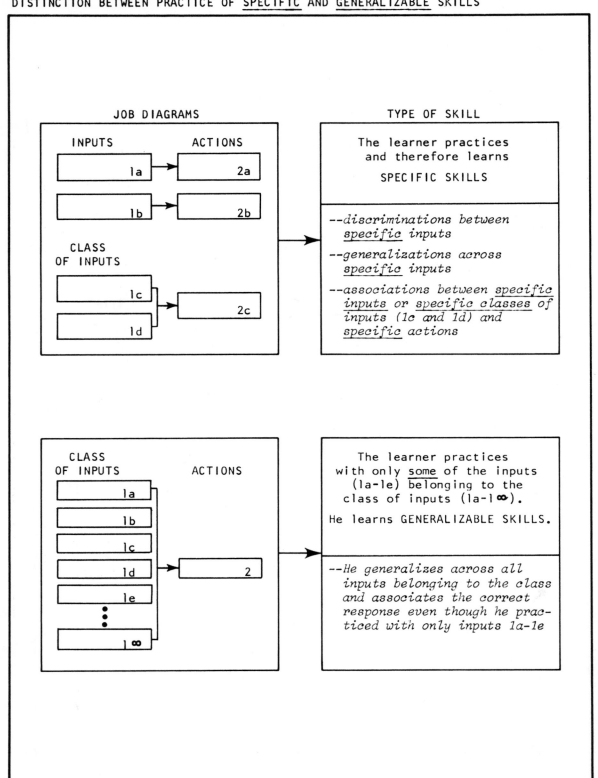

JOB DIAGRAMS

INPUTS   ACTIONS

[1a] → [2a]

[1b] → [2b]

CLASS
OF INPUTS

[1c]
        → [2c]
[1d]

practices

--discriminating between 1a, 1b, and the class that includes 1c and 1d

--generalizing across all instances in a class (1c and 1d)

--associating (1a and 2a), (1b and 2b), and (1c, 1d and 2c)

Practices all relevant specific skills

CLASS
OF INPUTS

[1a]
[1b]
[1c]
[1d] → [2]
[1e]
  •
  •
  •
[1∞]

practices

--generalizing across 1a-1e

--associating 1a, 1b, 1c, 1d, and 1e with 2

Does <u>not</u> practice with all relevant, specific skills (does not practice with 1f-1∞); based on the practice engaged in <u>generalizes</u> to other inputs (1f-1∞)

TYPES OF PRACTICE

LABEL

1. <u>All</u> the classes of inputs
   (and associated actions)
   <u>are</u> encountered in training.

2. <u>All</u> the individual inputs
   within <u>each</u> class of inputs
   (and associated actions)
   <u>are</u> encountered in training.

Practice of
ALL SPECIFIC SKILLS

1. <u>All</u> the classes of inputs
   (and associated actions)
   <u>are</u> encountered in training.

2. *Only <u>some</u> of the individual
   inputs within <u>each</u> class of
   inputs (and associated
   actions) <u>are</u> encountered
   in training.*

Practice of
GENERALIZABLE SKILLS

DEFINITION OF INSTRUCTIONAL GOALS

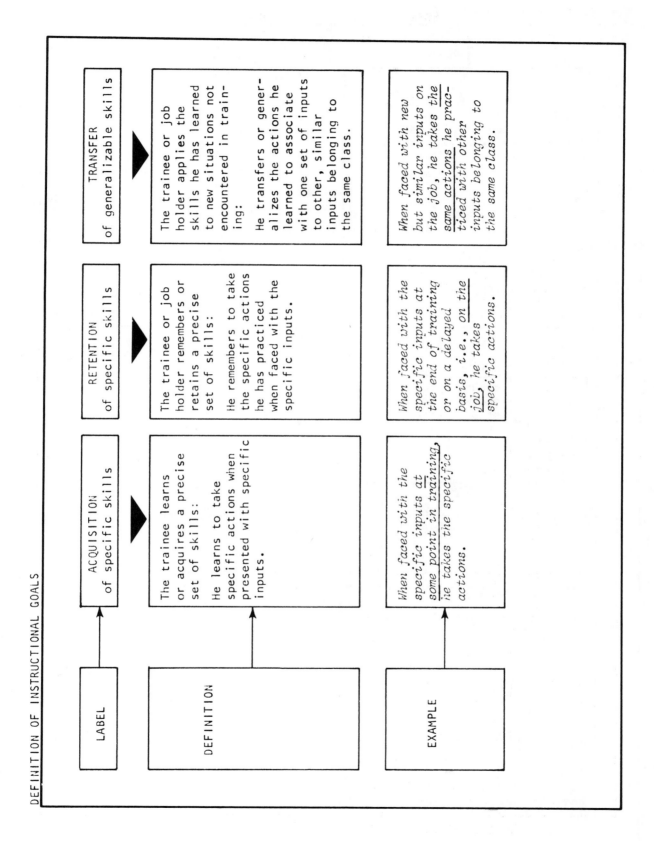

	ACQUISITION of specific skills	RETENTION of specific skills	TRANSFER of generalizable skills
LABEL	ACQUISITION of specific skills	RETENTION of specific skills	TRANSFER of generalizable skills
DEFINITION	The trainee learns or acquires a precise set of skills: He learns to take specific actions when presented with specific inputs.	The trainee or job holder remembers or retains a precise set of skills: He remembers to take the specific actions he has practiced when faced with the specific inputs.	The trainee or job holder applies the skills he has learned to new situations not encountered in training: He transfers or generalizes the actions he has learned to associate with one set of inputs to other, similar inputs belonging to the same class.
EXAMPLE	*When faced with the specific inputs at some point in training, he takes the specific actions.*	*When faced with the specific inputs at the end of training or on a delayed basis, i.e., on the job, he takes specific actions.*	*When faced with new but similar inputs on the job, he takes the same actions he practiced with other inputs belonging to the same class.*

11.19

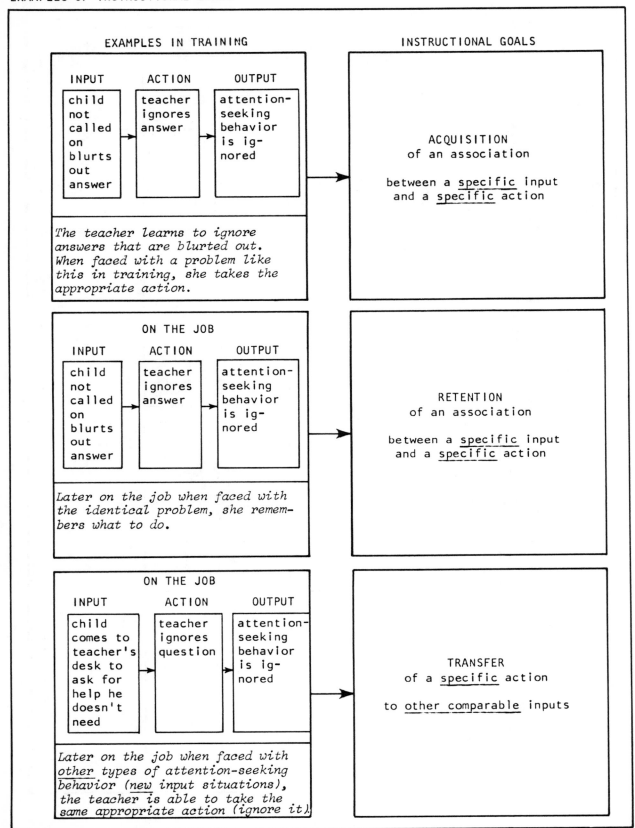

WHAT THE LEARNER MUST BE ABLE TO DO IN ORDER TO TRANSFER SKILLS TO NEW SITUATIONS

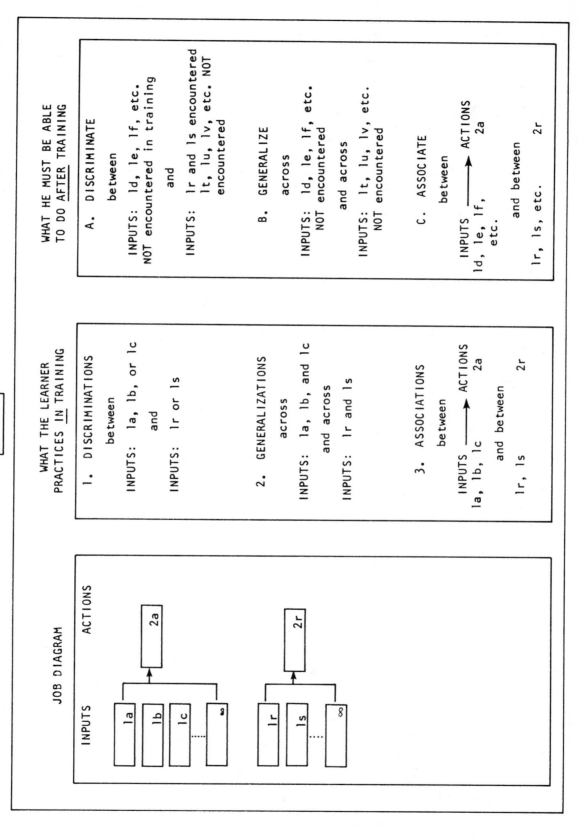

JOB DIAGRAM

INPUTS   ACTIONS

1a
1b   2a
1c
∞

1r
1s   2r
∞

WHAT THE LEARNER
PRACTICES IN TRAINING

1. DISCRIMINATIONS
    between

    INPUTS: 1a, 1b, or 1c
            and

    INPUTS: 1r or 1s

2. GENERALIZATIONS
    across

    INPUTS: 1a, 1b, and 1c
            and across

    INPUTS: 1r and 1s

3. ASSOCIATIONS
    between

    INPUTS ⟶ ACTIONS
    1a, 1b, 1c   2a
            and between

    1r, 1s   2r

WHAT HE MUST BE ABLE
TO DO AFTER TRAINING

A. DISCRIMINATE
    between

    INPUTS: 1d, 1e, 1f, etc.
    NOT encountered in training
            and

    INPUTS: 1r and 1s encountered
            1t, 1u, 1v, etc. NOT
            encountered

B. GENERALIZE
    across

    INPUTS: 1d, 1e, 1f, etc.
            NOT encountered
            and across

    INPUTS: 1t, 1u, 1v, etc.
            NOT encountered

C. ASSOCIATE
    between

    INPUTS ⟶ ACTIONS
    1d, 1e, 1f,   2a
    etc.
            and between

    1r, 1s, etc.   2r

ALL CRITERION SKILLS ARE INVOLVED IN THE ABILITY TO TRANSFER

DISCRIMINATIONS, GENERALIZATIONS, AND ASSOCIATIONS ARE ALL INVOLVED IN TRANSFER

TYPE OF INPUT	FAILURE TO DISCRIMINATE	FAILURE TO GENERALIZE	FAILURE TO ASSOCIATE	CONSEQUENCES
All classes of inputs and all individual inputs belonging to each class are encountered in training.	Between individual inputs or classes of inputs that were encountered in training.	Across all inputs belonging within a class that were encountered in training.	An action to any of the inputs encountered in training.	Failure in ACQUISITION or RETENTION of skills.
All classes of inputs are encountered in training. Only a sample of individual inputs belonging to a class are encountered in training.	Between any inputs belonging to one class that were NOT encountered in training and any input belonging to another class of inputs, whether encountered or not.	To any input NOT encountered in training.	An action with any input NOT encountered in training.	Failure in TRANSFER of skills.

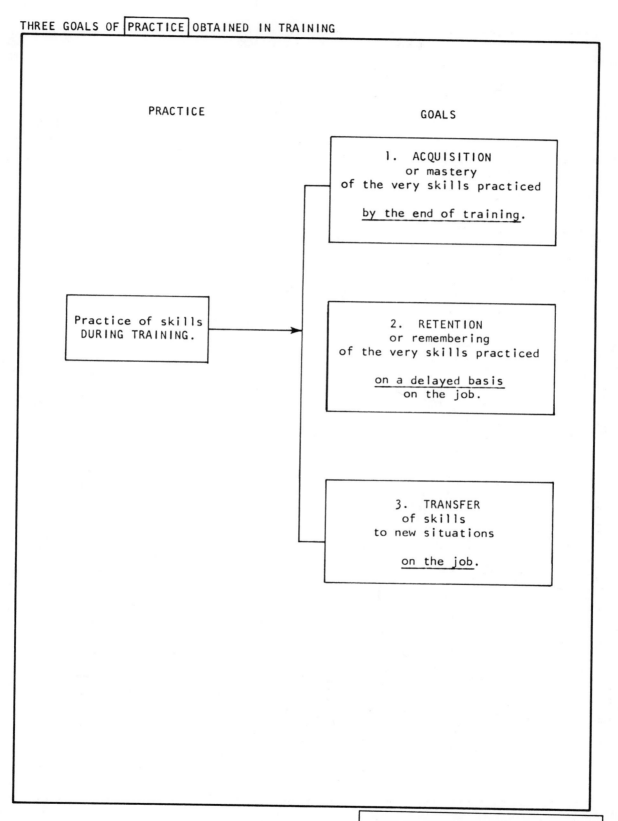

PRACTICE

GOALS

1. ACQUISITION
or mastery
of the very skills practiced

by the end of training.

Practice of skills
DURING TRAINING.

2. RETENTION
or remembering
of the very skills practiced

on a delayed basis
on the job.

3. TRANSFER
of skills
to new situations

on the job.

NOW DO EXERCISE #15 ON PAGES
II.8 TO II.11 IN THE WORKBOOK.

11.3   OBJECTIVES OF THIS UNIT

At the end of this unit, you will be able to identify the KINDS OF PRACTICE needed to achieve the INSTRUCTIONAL GOALS of acquisition, retention, and transfer.

DIAGRAM OF YOUR JOB

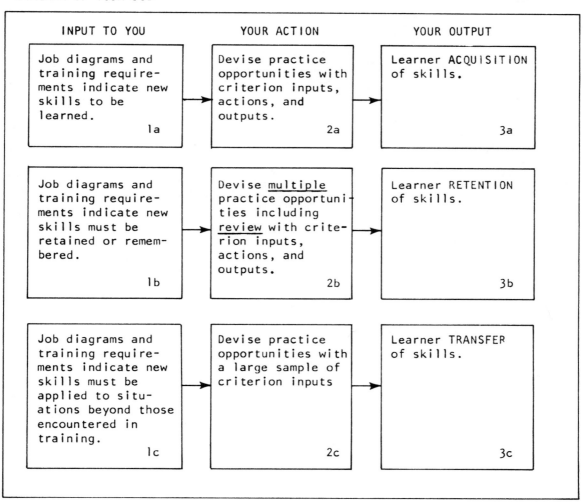

INPUT TO YOU	YOUR ACTION	YOUR OUTPUT
Job diagrams and training requirements indicate new skills to be learned. 1a	Devise practice opportunities with criterion inputs, actions, and outputs. 2a	Learner ACQUISITION of skills. 3a
Job diagrams and training requirements indicate new skills must be retained or remembered. 1b	Devise multiple practice opportunities including review with criterion inputs, actions, and outputs. 2b	Learner RETENTION of skills. 3b
Job diagrams and training requirements indicate new skills must be applied to situations beyond those encountered in training. 1c	Devise practice opportunities with a large sample of criterion inputs 2c	Learner TRANSFER of skills. 3c

SINGLE OPPORTUNITY

MULTIPLE OPPORTUNITIES

A program provides
only one practice item
in which the learner
practices discriminating between:

e.g., INPUTS 1a and 1r

e.g., INPUTS 1b and 1x

e.g., INPUTS 1r and 1x

DISCRIMINATIONS

vs.

A program provides
two or more practice items
in which the learner
practices discriminating between:

e.g., INPUTS 1a and 1r

e.g., INPUTS 1b and 1x

e.g., INPUTS 1r and 1x

DISCRIMINATIONS

A program provides
only one practice item
in which the learner
practices generalizing across:

e.g., INPUTS 1a and 1b

e.g., INPUTS 1r, 1s, and 1t

GENERALIZATIONS

vs.

A program provides
two or more practice items
in which the learner
practices generalizing across:

e.g., INPUTS 1a and 1b

e.g., INPUTS 1r, 1s, and 1t

GENERALIZATIONS

A program provides
only one practice item
in which the learner
practices associating between:

INPUTS and ACTIONS

e.g., 1a and 2a

e.g., 1s and 2r

e.g., 1x and 2x

ASSOCIATIONS or CHAINS

vs.

A program provides
two or more practice items
in which the learner
practices associating between:

INPUTS AND ACTIONS

e.g., 1a and 2a

e.g., 1s and 2r

e.g., 1x and 2x

ASSOCIATIONS or CHAINS

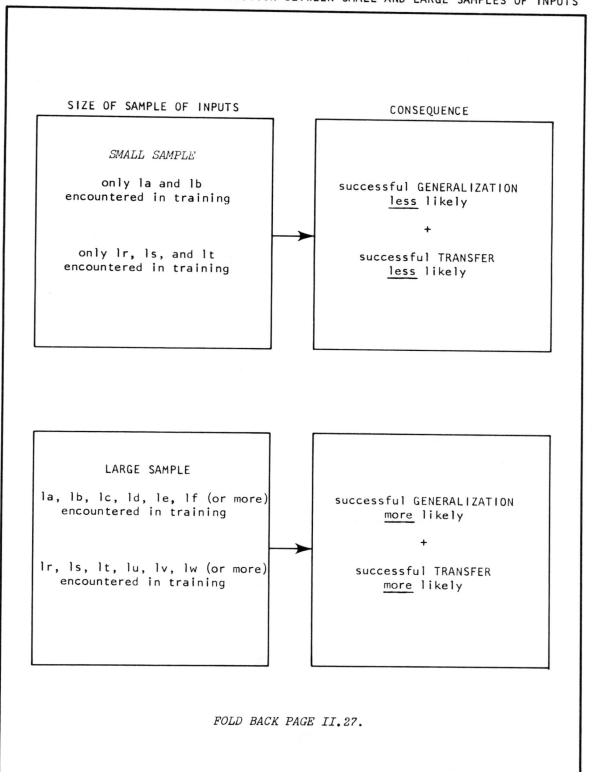

SIZE OF SAMPLE OF INPUTS

CONSEQUENCE

SMALL SAMPLE

only 1a and 1b
encountered in training

only 1r, 1s, and 1t
encountered in training

successful GENERALIZATION
<u>less</u> likely

+

successful TRANSFER
<u>less</u> likely

LARGE SAMPLE

1a, 1b, 1c, 1d, 1e, 1f (or more)
encountered in training

1r, 1s, 1t, 1u, 1v, 1w (or more)
encountered in training

successful GENERALIZATION
<u>more</u> likely

+

successful TRANSFER
<u>more</u> likely

FOLD BACK PAGE II.27.

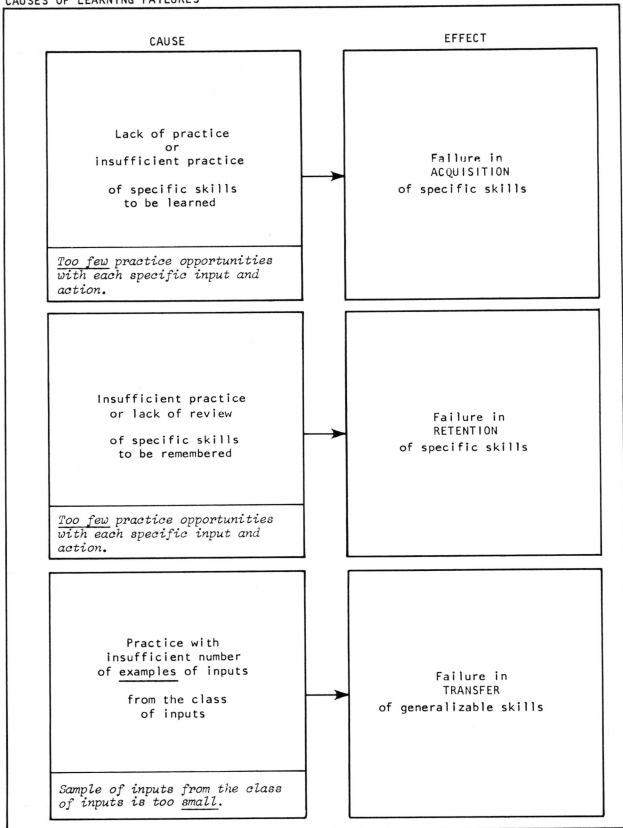

CAUSE

EFFECT

Lack of practice
or
insufficient practice

of specific skills
to be learned

Too few practice opportunities
*with each specific input and
action.*

Failure in
ACQUISITION
of specific skills

Insufficient practice
or lack of review

of specific skills
to be remembered

Too few practice opportunities
*with each specific input and
action.*

Failure in
RETENTION
of specific skills

Practice with
insufficient number
of examples of inputs

from the class
of inputs

*Sample of inputs from the class
of inputs is too small.*

Failure in
TRANSFER
of generalizable skills

THE SPECIAL PROBLEM OF "TRANSFER OF SKILLS"

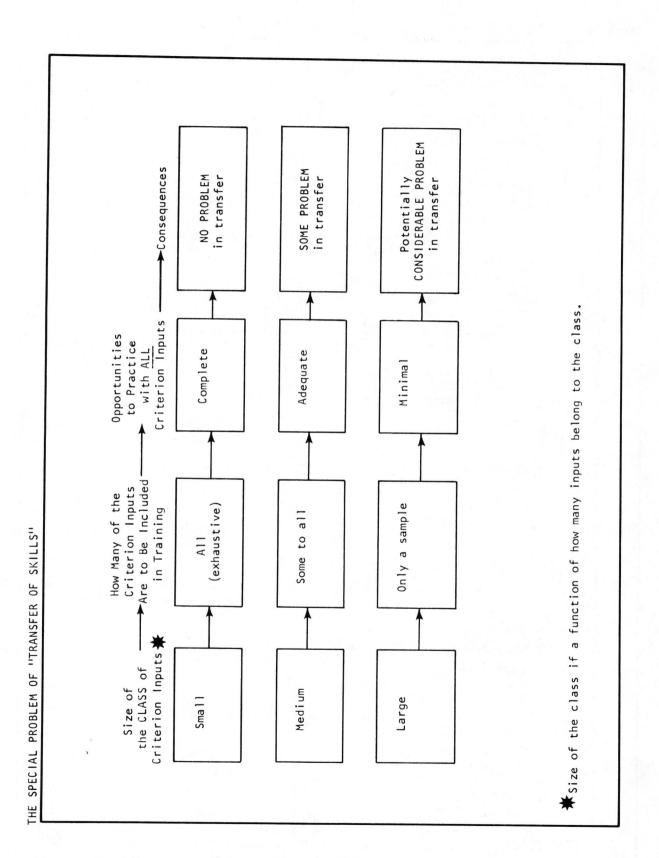

11.33

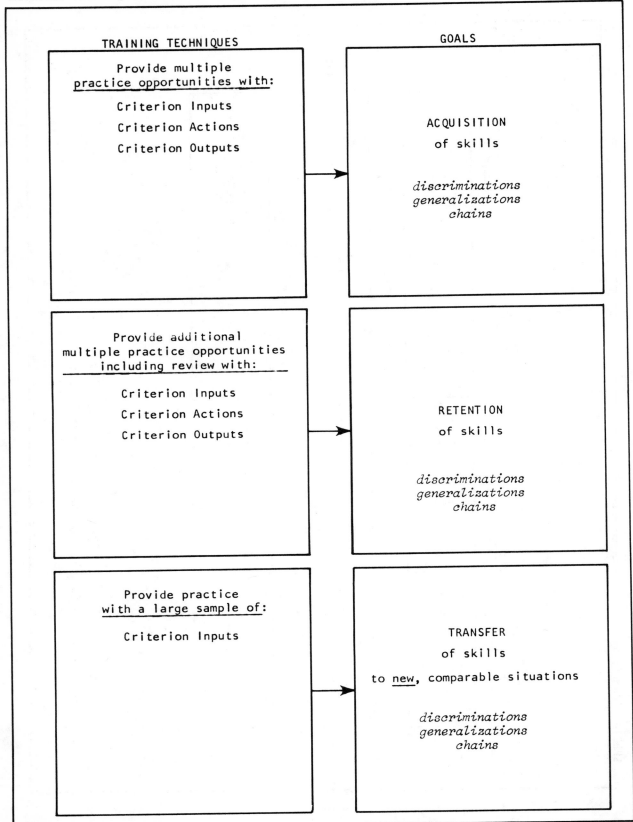

TRAINING TECHNIQUES

GOALS

**Provide multiple
practice opportunities with:**

Criterion Inputs

Criterion Actions

Criterion Outputs

ACQUISITION
of skills

*discriminations
generalizations
chains*

**Provide additional
multiple practice opportunities
including review with:**

Criterion Inputs

Criterion Actions

Criterion Outputs

RETENTION
of skills

*discriminations
generalizations
chains*

**Provide practice
with a large sample of:**

Criterion Inputs

TRANSFER

of skills

to <u>new</u>, comparable situations

*discriminations
generalizations
chains*

11.34

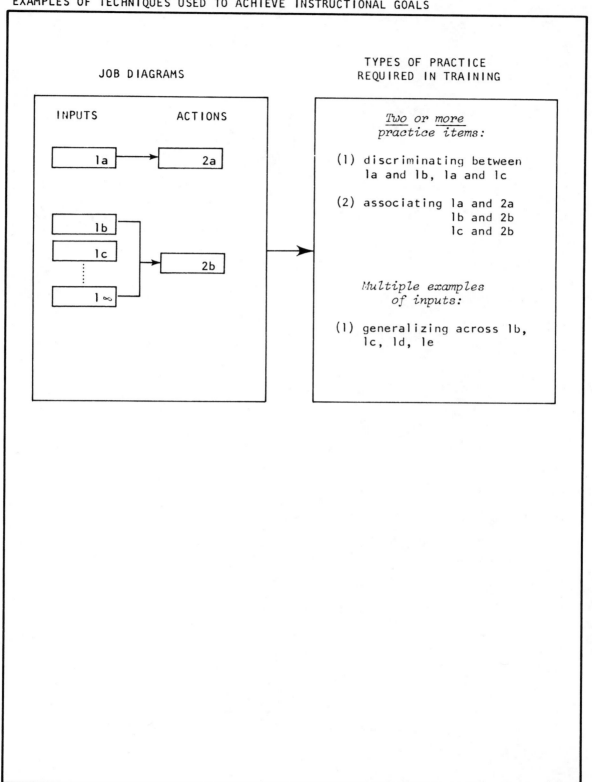

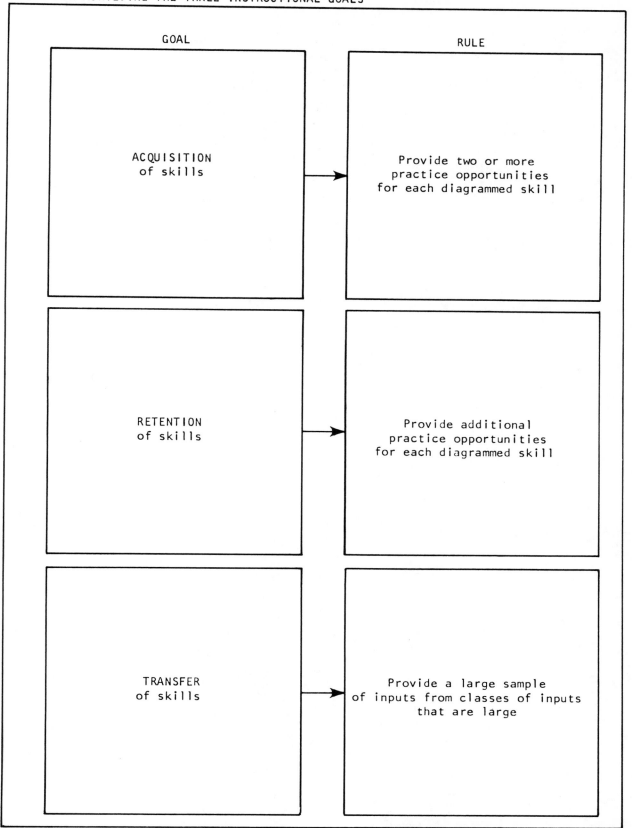

GOAL | RULE

ACQUISITION of skills → Provide two or more practice opportunities for each diagrammed skill

RETENTION of skills → Provide additional practice opportunities for each diagrammed skill

TRANSFER of skills → Provide a large sample of inputs from classes of inputs that are large

NOW DO EXERCISE #16 ON PAGES
II.12 TO II.17 IN THE WORKBOOK.

II.4   OBJECTIVES OF THIS UNIT

> At the end of this unit, you will be able to identify the consequences of including or <u>not</u> including CRITERION VISUALS in the type of practice provided in training.

DIAGRAM OF YOUR JOB

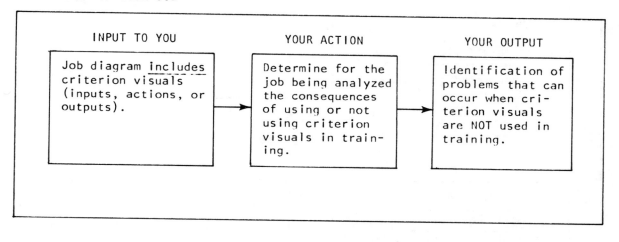

INPUT TO YOU

Job diagram <u>includes</u> criterion visuals (inputs, actions, or outputs).

YOUR ACTION

Determine for the job being analyzed the consequences of using or not using criterion visuals in training.

YOUR OUTPUT

Identification of problems that can occur when criterion visuals are NOT used in training.

TYPE OF PRACTICE
DURING TRAINING

CONSEQUENCE
ON THE JOB

1.

JOB DIAGRAM

INPUTS   ACTIONS

1. The class of inputs requiring generalization is large.
An insufficient sample of
inputs from the class is
encountered in training.

TRANSFER
WILL BE A PROBLEM

When inputs belonging to the
same class but not encountered
in training are encountered on
the job, the job holder may be
unable to take the appropriate
action.

2.

JOB DIAGRAM

| Visual Input | Visual Action | Visual Output |

Type of Practice
Used During Training:

Criterion Visuals Not Used

Substitute Inputs, Actions,
or Outputs Are Used

| Non-Visual Input | Non-Visual Action | Non-Visual Output |

TRANSFER
MAY BE A PROBLEM

When substitutes for criterion
inputs, actions, or outputs
specified in job diagrams are
used during training.

There may be a problem in
TRANSFERRING the skills learned
when CRITERION INPUTS are
encountered on the job.

EXAMPLES OF THE TWO TYPES OF TRANSFER PROBLEMS

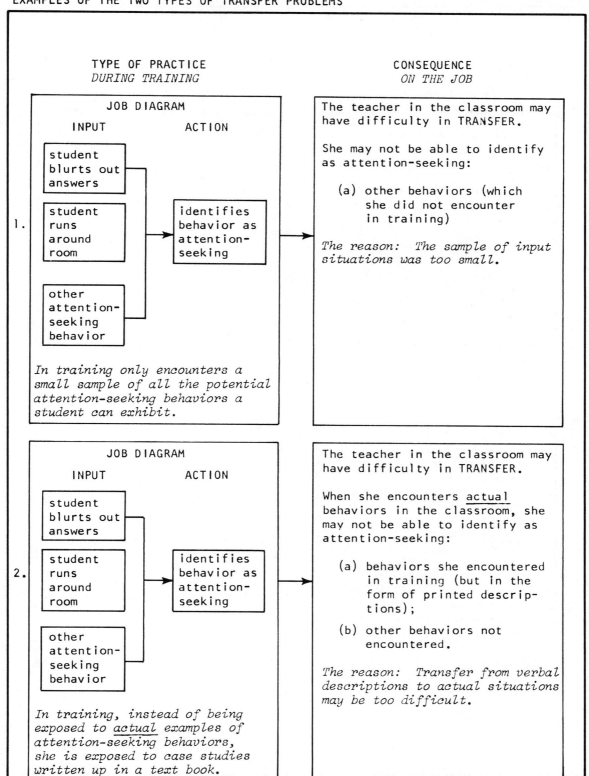

TYPE OF PRACTICE
DURING TRAINING

CONSEQUENCE
ON THE JOB

1.

JOB DIAGRAM

INPUT   ACTION

student blurts out answers

student runs around room

→ identifies behavior as attention-seeking

other attention-seeking behavior

In training only encounters a small sample of all the potential attention-seeking behaviors a student can exhibit.

The teacher in the classroom may have difficulty in TRANSFER.

She may not be able to identify as attention-seeking:

   (a) other behaviors (which she did not encounter in training)

The reason: The sample of input situations was too small.

2.

JOB DIAGRAM

INPUT   ACTION

student blurts out answers

student runs around room

→ identifies behavior as attention-seeking

other attention-seeking behavior

In training, instead of being exposed to <u>actual</u> examples of attention-seeking behaviors, she is exposed to case studies written up in a text book.

The teacher in the classroom may have difficulty in TRANSFER.

When she encounters <u>actual</u> behaviors in the classroom, she may not be able to identify as attention-seeking:

   (a) behaviors she encountered in training (but in the form of printed descriptions);

   (b) other behaviors not encountered.

The reason: Transfer from verbal descriptions to actual situations may be too difficult.

DEFINITION OF THE TWO TYPES OF TRANSFER PROBLEMS

TYPE OF PRACTICE DURING TRAINING

1. A class of inputs contains many inputs.
2. The learner must generalize across inputs.
3. The sample of inputs (from the class) used in <u>training</u> is small.
4. On the job when the learner encounters one of the inputs from the class which he did <u>not</u> encounter, he fails to generalize (i.e., treat it like the ones he did encounter in training).

TYPE OF TRANSFER PROBLEM

TYPE #1

A problem in
GENERALIZATION

---

1. Criterion inputs, actions, or outputs are <u>not</u> used in training.
2. Learner acquires discriminations, generalizations, or chains on the basis of <u>substitute</u> inputs, actions, or outputs (e.g., descriptions of inputs or actions instead of actual inputs or actions).
3. Faced with <u>criterion</u> inputs on the job, he may fail in discriminating, generalizing, or associating.

TYPE #2

A problem in
TRANSFERRING

skills acquired in a
substitute situation to the
actual job situation

TYPE OF PRACTICE
USED IN TRAINING

PERFORMANCE
ON THE JOB

Discriminations, generalizations, or chains

are practiced

with Criterion Visuals identified in job diagrams.

Performance requiring discriminations, generalizations, or chains

involving Criterion Visuals

is likely to be

EASIER

because skills practiced during training can more easily be transferred to actual job situations.

vs.

Discriminations, generalizations, or chains

are not practiced

with Criterion Visuals identified in job diagrams.

Performance requiring discriminations, generalizations, or chains

involving Criterion Visuals

is likely to be

HARDER

because skills practiced during training may be transferred to actual job situations only with difficulty.

JOB DIAGRAM

INPUT	ACTION	OUTPUT
disas-sembled rifle parts	assem-bles rifle	rifle assem-bled

TYPE OF PRACTICE
USED IN TRAINING

CRITERION VISUALS USED

Practice includes:

actual rifle parts
(inputs)

assembly of parts
(actions)

appropriate configura-
tion of assembled rifle
(output)

vs.

CRITERION VISUALS NOT USED

Practice includes:

photographs of parts
and verbal descriptions
of them (inputs)

photographs of assembly
operation and verbal
descriptions of them
(learner states what he
would do) (action)

photograph of correct
assembly configuration

CONSEQUENCES FOR
PERFORMANCE ON THE JOB

RELATIVELY EASY TRANSFER

Having practiced discrimination, generalization,
and chain with the criterion
visuals in training,

the learner has no diffi-
culty transferring the
skills to the job.

*POTENTIALLY DIFFICULT
TRANSFER*

Not having practiced dis-
criminations, generaliza-
tions, and chains with
the criterion visuals in
training,

the learner has difficulty
transferring the skills to
the job.

11.44

EXAMPLES OF WHAT HAPPENS WHEN PRACTICE DOES NOT INVOLVE CRITERION VISUALS APPEARING IN JOB DIAGRAMS

JOB TYPE	CRITERION VISUALS INVOLVED IN JOB PERFORMANCE	TYPE OF PRACTICE USED IN TRAINING	CONSEQUENCE ON THE JOB
EXAMPLE #1 Botanist identifies flowers or plants	Identifies flowers or plants on the basis of color, size, shape, etc.	Black and white photographs used or photographs not to scale	May not be able to identify actual specifications when identification must be made on basis of color or size
EXAMPLE #2 Cook making sauces	Stirring or adding water to sauces until they have the right consistency (the way they run off the spoon)	Practice involves identifying what the final sauce looks like from photographs	May not be able to distinguish between correct and incorrect consistency of actual sauces
EXAMPLE #3 Inspector of watch dials	Visual identification of defects in watch dials	Practice involves describing defects in words	May not be able to identify defects in actual watch dial

RULES ABOUT THE USE OF CRITERION VISUALS IN TRAINING

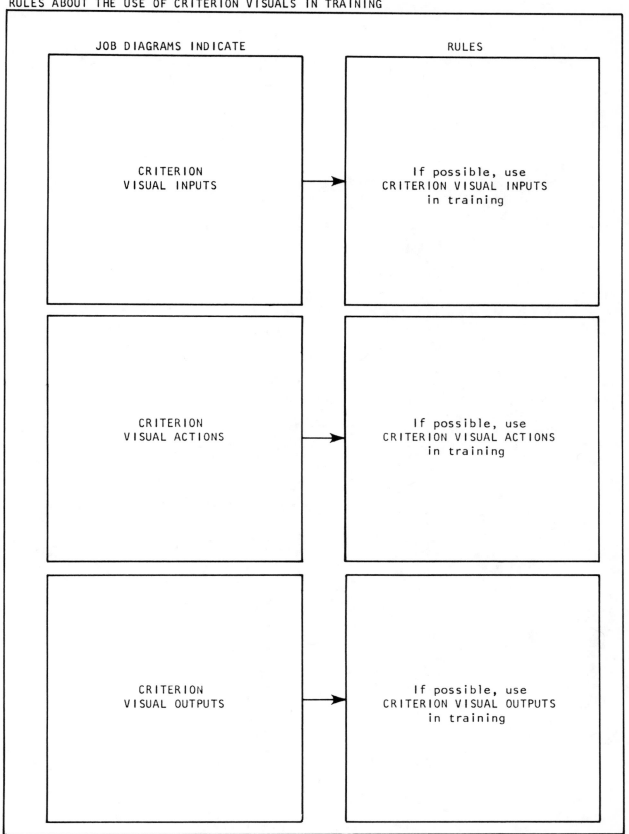

JOB DIAGRAMS INDICATE

RULES

CRITERION
VISUAL INPUTS

If possible, use
CRITERION VISUAL INPUTS
in training

CRITERION
VISUAL ACTIONS

If possible, use
CRITERION VISUAL ACTIONS
in training

CRITERION
VISUAL OUTPUTS

If possible, use
CRITERION VISUAL OUTPUTS
in training

NOW DO EXERCISE #17 ON PAGES
II.18 TO II.21 IN THE WORKBOOK.

II.5   OBJECTIVES OF THIS UNIT

At the end of this unit, you will be able to identify MEDIA REQUIREMENTS for training practice that involves CRITERION VISUALS: inputs, actions, or outputs.

DIAGRAM OF YOUR JOB

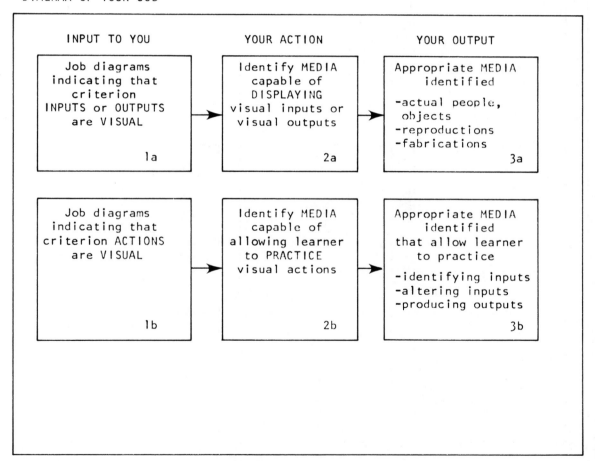

WHAT MEDIA MUST BE CAPABLE OF DOING IN TRAINING

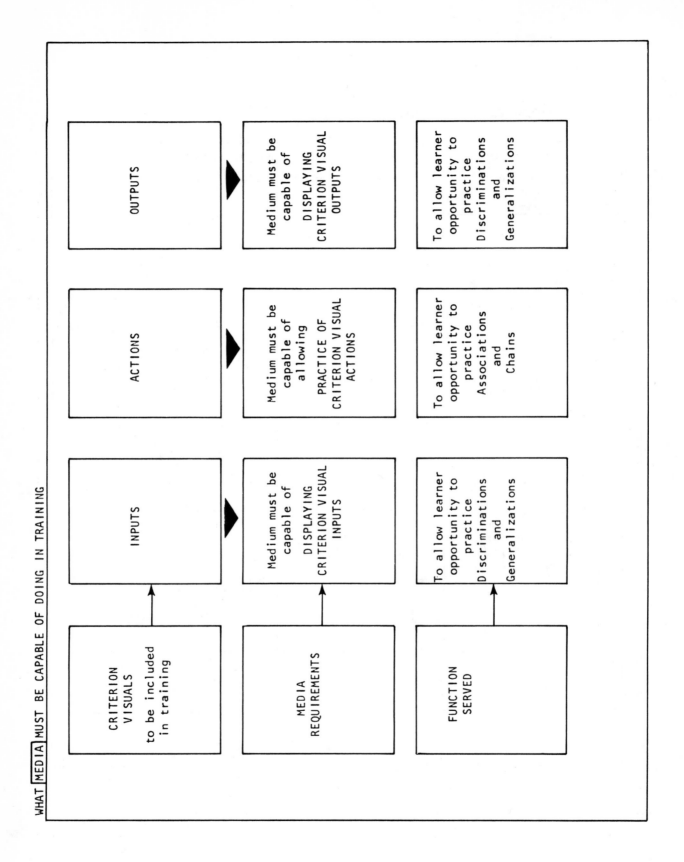

EXAMPLES OF REQUIRED MEDIA CAPABILITIES

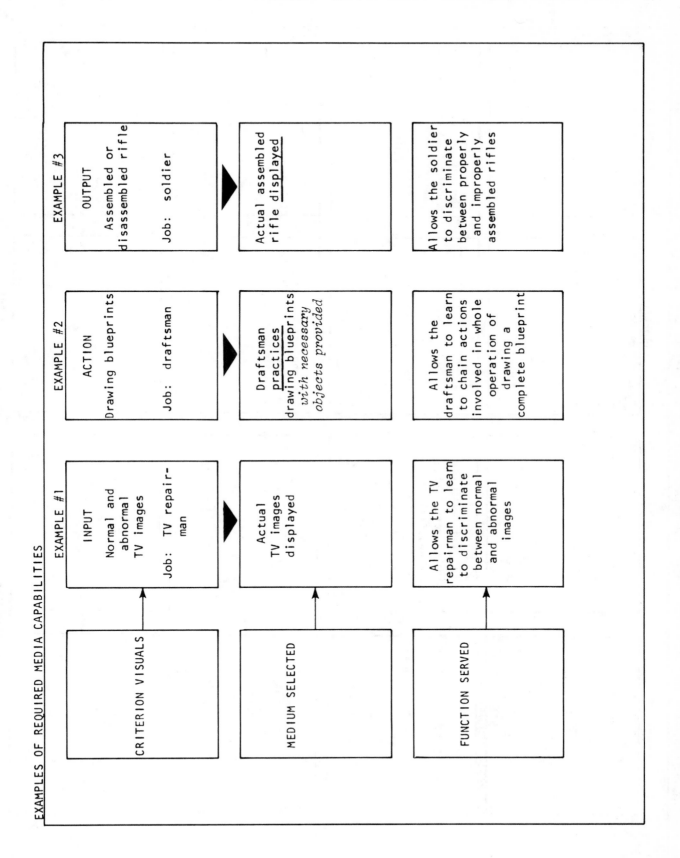

EXAMPLE #1

INPUT

Normal and abnormal TV images

Job: TV repair-man

EXAMPLE #2

ACTION

Drawing blueprints

Job: draftsman

EXAMPLE #3

OUTPUT

Assembled or disassembled rifle

Job: soldier

CRITERION VISUALS

Actual TV images displayed

Draftsman practices drawing blueprints *with necessary objects provided*

Actual assembled rifle displayed

MEDIUM SELECTED

Allows the TV repairman to learn to discriminate between normal and abnormal images

Allows the draftsman to learn to chain actions involved in whole operation of drawing a complete blueprint

Allows the soldier to discriminate between properly and improperly assembled rifles

FUNCTION SERVED

	EXAMPLE #1	EXAMPLE #2	EXAMPLE #3
JOBS	ELECTRICIAN	ANALYST OF AERIAL PHOTOGRAPHS	ARTIST
MEDIA REQUIREMENTS			
REALISTIC VISUALS actual objects, people, events	The electrician deals only with actual objects (switches, fixtures, etc.)	N.A.	The artist deals with models from which he paints; therefore, realistic visuals are part of his job
vs. REPRODUCTIONS film, photographs	N.A.	The analyst of photographs typically deals with photographs	N.A.
vs. FABRICATIONS drawings, paintings, tables, charts	N.A.	N.A.	The artist typically deals with drawings, paintings

N.A. = not applicable to this job and hence not a media requirement for this job

REALISTIC VISUALS actual objects actual people actual events	vs.	REPRODUCTIONS of objects, people, events	vs.	FABRICATIONS -of objects, people, events -analogously representing concepts and principles

| TYPES OF
CRITERION VISUAL
INPUTS OCCURRING
ON THE JOB | → | REALISTIC VISUALS | REPRODUCTIONS | FABRICATIONS |

(Diagram: three columns — REALISTIC VISUALS, REPRODUCTIONS, FABRICATIONS)

TYPES OF CRITERION VISUAL INPUTS OCCURRING ON THE JOB →
- actual objects / actual people / actual events
- of objects, people, events
- of objects, people, events / analogously representing concepts and principles

TYPES OF JOBS IN WHICH CRITERION VISUAL INPUTS ARE FOUND →
- all jobs
- photographers, film makers, TV producers
- artists, draftsmen / scientists, engineers, graphics specialists

MEDIA REQUIREMENTS FOR DISPLAYING CRITERION VISUAL INPUTS IN TRAINING →
- actual objects / actual people / actual events
- photographs / films / TV / slides
- drawings, paintings, sketches / tables, diagrams, charts

11.53

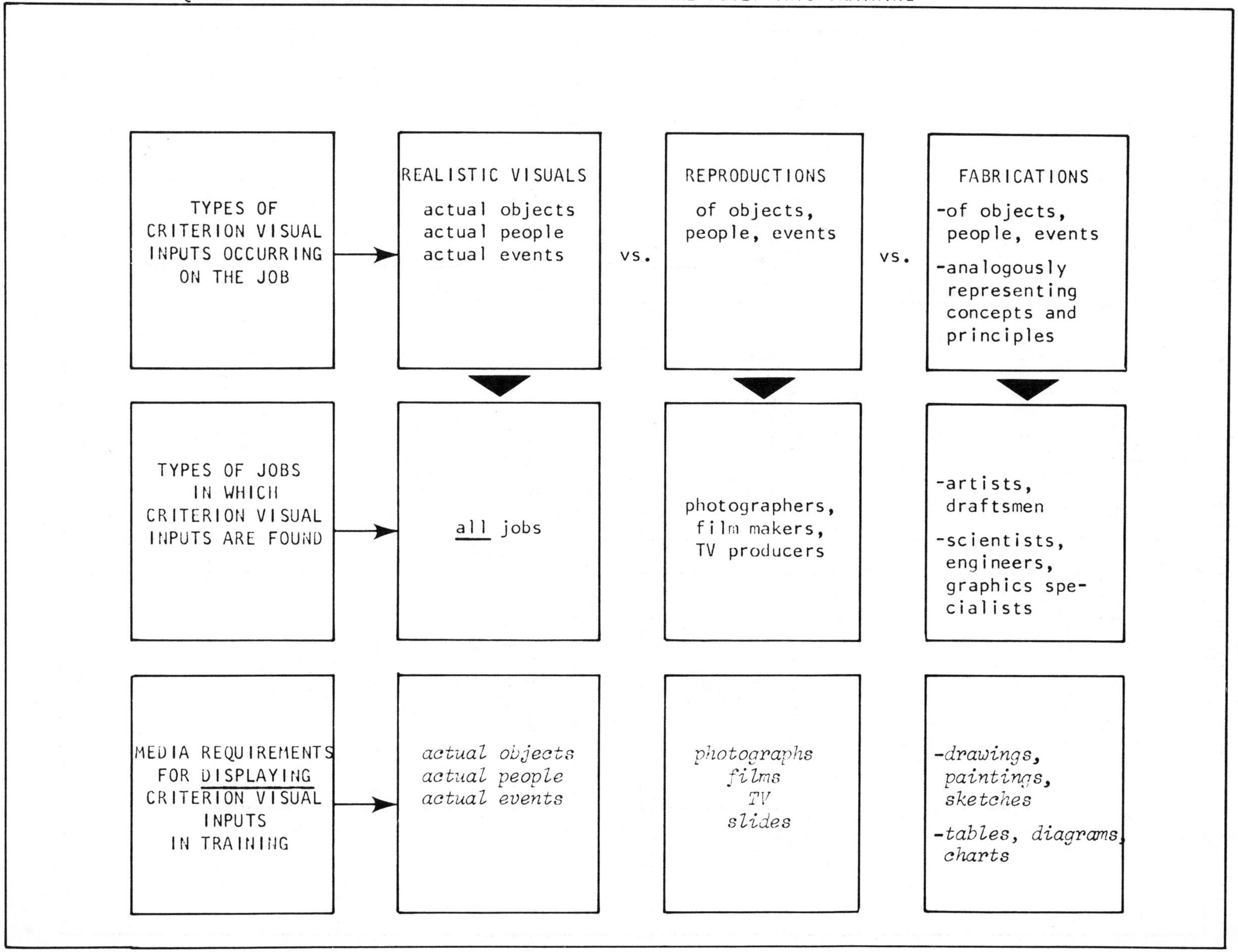

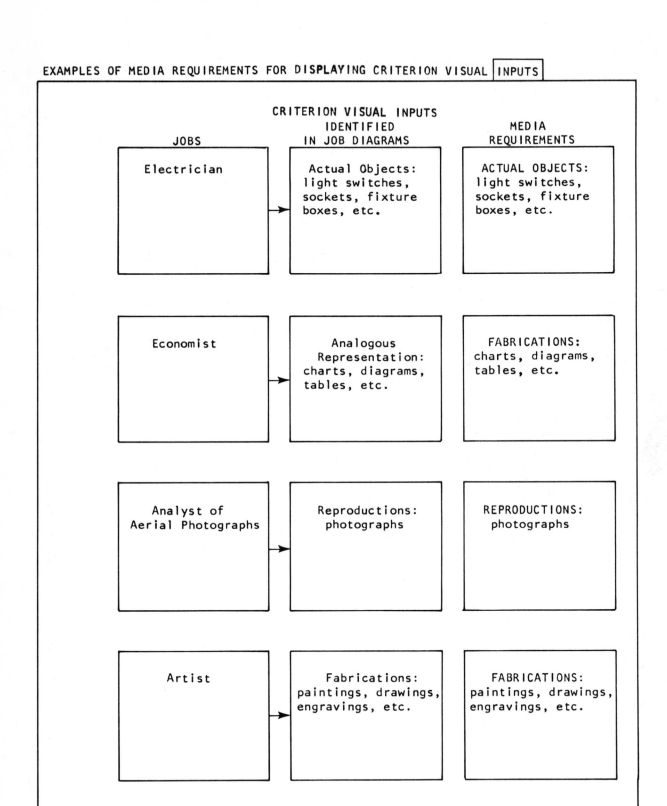

CRITERION VISUAL INPUTS
IDENTIFIED
IN JOB DIAGRAMS

JOBS

MEDIA
REQUIREMENTS

Electrician

Actual Objects:
light switches,
sockets, fixture
boxes, etc.

ACTUAL OBJECTS:
light switches,
sockets, fixture
boxes, etc.

Economist

Analogous
Representation:
charts, diagrams,
tables, etc.

FABRICATIONS:
charts, diagrams,
tables, etc.

Analyst of
Aerial Photographs

Reproductions:
photographs

REPRODUCTIONS:
photographs

Artist

Fabrications:
paintings, drawings,
engravings, etc.

FABRICATIONS:
paintings, drawings,
engravings, etc.

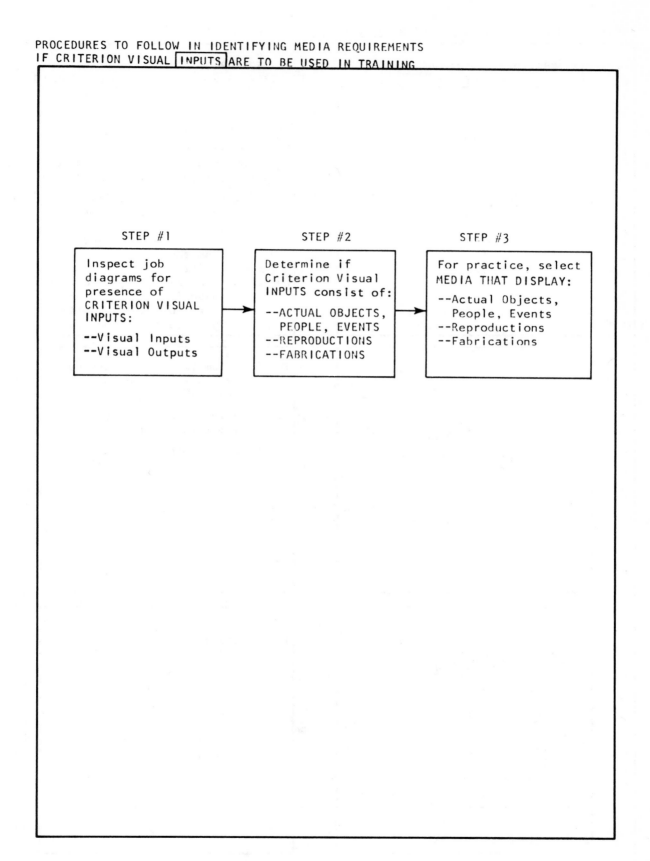

STEP #1

Inspect job
diagrams for
presence of
CRITERION VISUAL
INPUTS:

--Visual Inputs
--Visual Outputs

STEP #2

Determine if
Criterion Visual
INPUTS consist of:

--ACTUAL OBJECTS,
  PEOPLE, EVENTS
--REPRODUCTIONS
--FABRICATIONS

STEP #3

For practice, select
MEDIA THAT DISPLAY:

--Actual Objects,
  People, Events
--Reproductions
--Fabrications

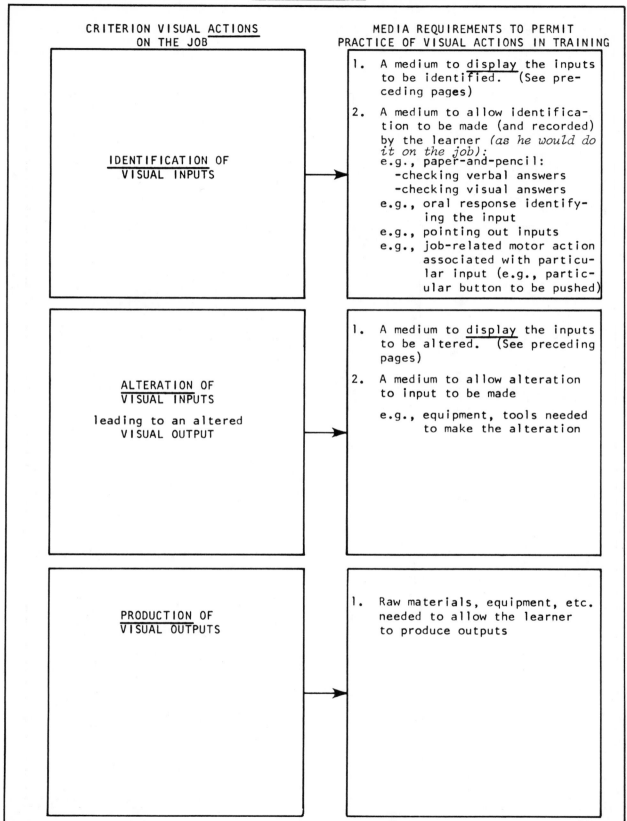

CRITERION VISUAL ACTIONS
ON THE JOB

MEDIA REQUIREMENTS TO PERMIT
PRACTICE OF VISUAL ACTIONS IN TRAINING

IDENTIFICATION OF
VISUAL INPUTS

1. A medium to display the inputs to be identified. (See preceding pages)

2. A medium to allow identification to be made (and recorded) by the learner *(as he would do it on the job)*:
   e.g., paper-and-pencil:
     -checking verbal answers
     -checking visual answers
   e.g., oral response identifying the input
   e.g., pointing out inputs
   e.g., job-related motor action associated with particular input (e.g., particular button to be pushed)

ALTERATION OF
VISUAL INPUTS

leading to an altered
VISUAL OUTPUT

1. A medium to display the inputs to be altered. (See preceding pages)

2. A medium to allow alteration to input to be made

   e.g., equipment, tools needed to make the alteration

PRODUCTION OF
VISUAL OUTPUTS

1. Raw materials, equipment, etc. needed to allow the learner to produce outputs

VISUAL ACTIONS	IDENTIFICATION OF INPUTS	vs.	ALTERATION OF INPUTS	vs.	PRODUCTION OF OUTPUTS
MEDIA DISPLAY REQUIREMENTS	Inputs to be identified should be displayed just as they appear on the job		Inputs to be manipulated or altered should be displayed just as they appear on the job		Inputs (raw materials) from which outputs are to be produced should be displayed just as they appear on the job
+					
MEDIA PRACTICE REQUIREMENTS	Media should allow learner to make identification just as he would on the job: -orally -in writing } *media* -through operation of equipment		Media should allow learner to make alterations in INPUTS just as he would on the job: -with equipment or tools provided (*media*)		Media should allow learner to produce outputs -from raw materials and equipment (*media*) provided him just as he would on the job

EXAMPLES OF MEDIA REQUIREMENTS FOR CRITERION PRACTICE: | IDENTIFICATION OF INPUTS |

EXAMPLE #1

EXAMPLE #2

EXAMPLE #3

IDENTIFICATION
OF INPUTS
TO BE PRACTICED

Dermatologist has to
identify skin symp-
toms reflecting dif-
ferent conditions

Radar operator has
to identify types of
objects and their
distance

Photographer has to
identify prints that
are overexposed,
underexposed, or
properly exposed

MEDIA DISPLAY
REQUIREMENTS

Dermatologist should
be presented with
actual patients
(inputs) who are
examples of the types
of skin conditions
to be identified

Radar operator
should be presented
with actual scope
configurations
(inputs)

Photographer should
be presented with
actual prints
(inputs): overex-
posed, underexposed,
and properly ex-
posed prints

+

MEDIA PRACTICE
REQUIREMENTS

Allow dermatologist
to do whatever he
does on the job after
identification is
made:

e.g., tell patient
what the condi-
tion is

e.g., write out
prescription

e.g., enter condition
in patient's
file

Allow radar operator
to do whatever he
does on the job after
the identification is
made:

e.g., enter in log

e.g., report to
superior

Allow photographer
to do whatever he
does on the job after
identification is
made:

e.g., put prints in
three piles

e.g., tear up poor
prints and throw
in wastebasket

e.g., label prints in
writing

11.58

EXAMPLES OF MEDIA REQUIREMENTS FOR CRITERION PRACTICE: ALTERATION OF INPUTS

	EXAMPLE #1	EXAMPLE #2	EXAMPLE #3
ALTERATION OF INPUTS TO BE PRACTICED →	Arc welder has to prepare surfaces (inputs) so that they are ready for welding	Captain has to change the direction of his ship or the distance of his ship (input) from other ships	Photographer has to develop prints from negatives (inputs)
MEDIA DISPLAY REQUIREMENTS →	Welder should be presented with actual unprepared surfaces that have to be prepared	Captain should be presented with actual situations (directions and distances) that require change	Photographer should be presented with actual negatives that have to be developed
+ **MEDIA PRACTICE REQUIREMENTS** →	Allow welder to prepare surface; provide him with necessary tools he would use on the job	Allow captain to make changes; i.e., provide him with the ship to steer	Allow photographer to develop prints; provide him with necessary equipment, materials, space to develop them

EXAMPLES OF MEDIA REQUIREMENTS FOR PRACTICE OF PRODUCTION OF OUTPUTS

	EXAMPLE #1	EXAMPLE #2	EXAMPLE #3
TYPES OF PRODUCTION TO BE PRACTICED	Artist painting pictures	Draftsman making drawings	Film director making movies
MEDIA DISPLAY REQUIREMENTS	human models, outdoor scenes, etc.	inputs are likely to be verbal (requests) *no visual media required*	actors, sets, outdoor scenes
MEDIA PRACTICE REQUIREMENTS +	canvas, paint brushes with which to practice	paper, pencils, rulers, etc. to permit practice	the equipment (cameras, meters, etc.) needed to practice taking motion pictures

PROCEDURES TO FOLLOW IN IDENTIFYING MEDIA REQUIREMENTS
IF CRITERION VISUAL ACTIONS ARE TO BE PRACTICED IN TRAINING

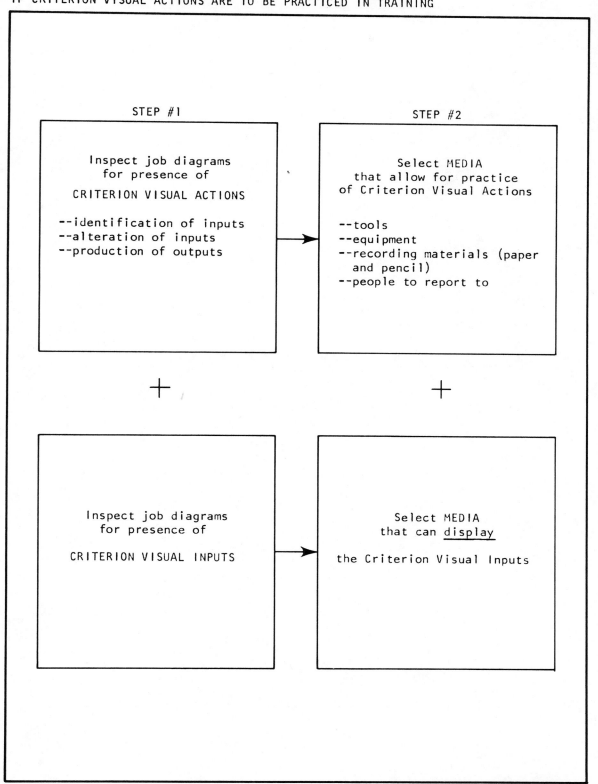

STEP #1

**Inspect job diagrams
for presence of
CRITERION VISUAL ACTIONS**

--identification of inputs
--alteration of inputs
--production of outputs

STEP #2

**Select MEDIA
that allow for practice
of Criterion Visual Actions**

--tools
--equipment
--recording materials (paper
  and pencil)
--people to report to

+

+

Inspect job diagrams
for presence of

CRITERION VISUAL INPUTS

Select MEDIA
that can <u>display</u>

the Criterion Visual Inputs

11.61

NOW DO EXERCISE #18 ON PAGES
II.22 TO II.27 IN THE WORKBOOK.

PART I

Introduction to the Use of Visuals in Instruction

PART II

The Use of Criterion Visuals in Instruction

PART III

 The Use of Simulated Criterion Visuals in Instruction

PART IV

The Use of Mediating Visuals in Instruction

PART V

Procedures to Follow in Selecting and Using Visuals
in Instruction

PART III

| The Use of <u>Simulated Criterion</u> Visuals in Instruction |

OBJECTIVES

III.1   Identifying CONDITIONS Under Which It Is Not Feasible or
        Possible to Use Criterion Visuals in Training

III.2   Identifying Various Ways to Substitute for or SIMULATE
        Criterion Visuals

III.3   Identifying DESIRABLE CHARACTERISTICS OF SIMULATION and
        Producing Examples of Simulation

III.4   Identifying PRIORITIES in Deciding Between CRITERION
        VISUAL PRACTICE and SIMULATED PRACTICE and Among Various
        Types of Simulated Practice

III.5   Identifying MEDIA REQUIREMENTS for <u>Simulated</u> Practice

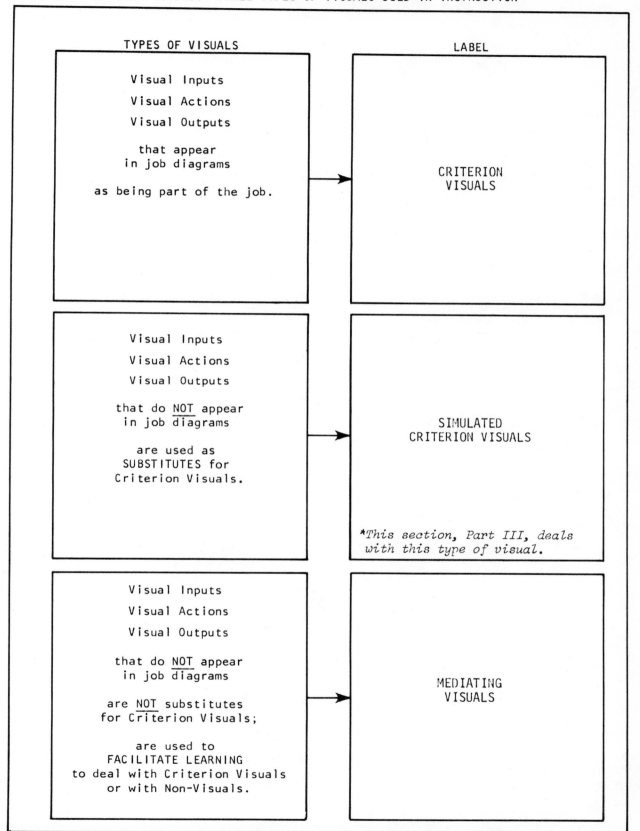

TYPES OF VISUALS

Visual Inputs

Visual Actions

Visual Outputs

that appear
in job diagrams

as being part of the job.

LABEL

CRITERION
VISUALS

Visual Inputs

Visual Actions

Visual Outputs

that do NOT appear
in job diagrams

are used as
SUBSTITUTES for
Criterion Visuals.

SIMULATED
CRITERION VISUALS

*This section, Part III, deals
with this type of visual.

Visual Inputs

Visual Actions

Visual Outputs

that do NOT appear
in job diagrams

are NOT substitutes
for Criterion Visuals;

are used to
FACILITATE LEARNING
to deal with Criterion Visuals
or with Non-Visuals.

MEDIATING
VISUALS

III.1   OBJECTIVES OF THIS UNIT

At the end of this unit, you will be able to identify CONDITIONS in which it is <u>not</u> possible or feasible to use criterion visuals in training.

DIAGRAM OF YOUR JOB

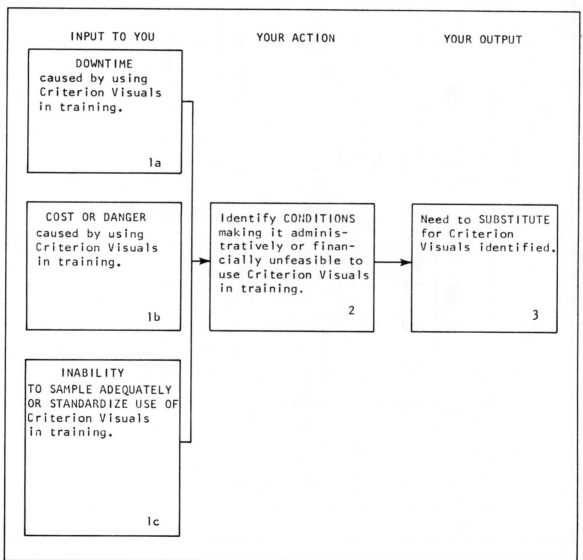

INPUT TO YOU   YOUR ACTION   YOUR OUTPUT

DOWNTIME
caused by using
Criterion Visuals
in training.

1a

COST OR DANGER
caused by using
Criterion Visuals
in training.

1b

Identify CONDITIONS
making it adminis-
tratively or finan-
cially unfeasible to
use Criterion Visuals
in training.

2

Need to SUBSTITUTE
for Criterion
Visuals identified.

3

INABILITY
TO SAMPLE ADEQUATELY
OR STANDARDIZE USE OF
Criterion Visuals
in training.

1c

DEFINITION OF THREE TYPES OF CONDITIONS REQUIRING SUBSTITUTES FOR CRITERION VISUALS

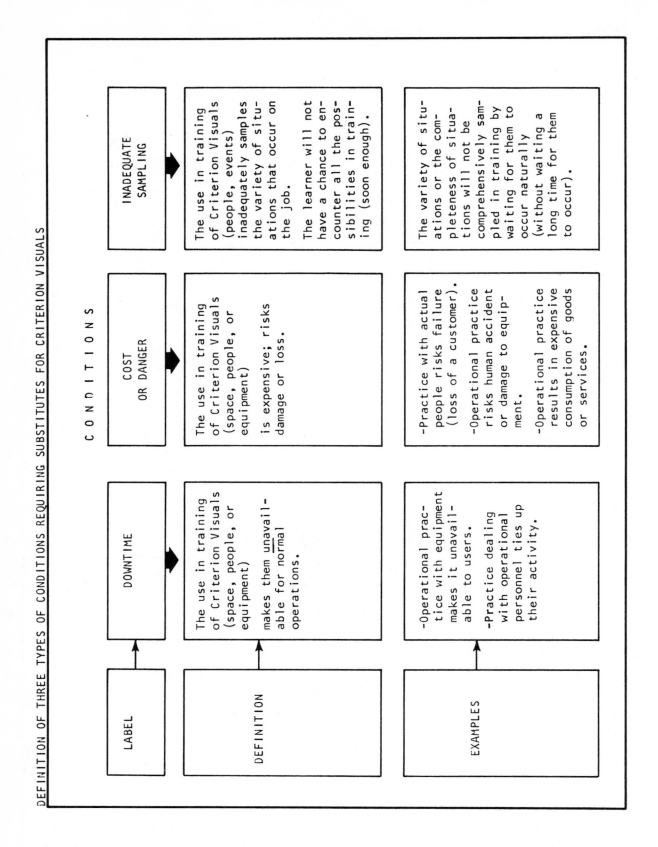

CONDITIONS

LABEL	DOWNTIME	COST OR DANGER	INADEQUATE SAMPLING
DEFINITION	The use in training of Criterion Visuals (space, people, or equipment) makes them unavailable for normal operations.	The use in training of Criterion Visuals (space, people, or equipment) is expensive; risks damage or loss.	The use in training of Criterion Visuals (people, events) inadequately samples the variety of situations that occur on the job. The learner will not have a chance to encounter all the possibilities in training (soon enough).
EXAMPLES	-Operational practice with equipment makes it unavailable to users. -Practice dealing with operational personnel ties up their activity.	-Practice with actual people risks failure (loss of a customer). -Operational practice risks human accident or damage to equipment. -Operational practice results in expensive consumption of goods or services.	The variety of situations or the completeness of situations will not be comprehensively sampled in training by waiting for them to occur naturally (without waiting a long time for them to occur).

HOW SIMULATED SUBSTITUTES OVERCOME PROBLEMS OCCASIONED BY USE OF CRITERION VISUALS

WHAT SUBSTITUTION ACCOMPLISHES

PROBLEM	SIMULATED SUBSTITUTION	OUTCOME
DOWNTIME	Mock-up of computer substitutes for real computer	Learner learns all the necessary operations without tying up an actual computer
COST OR DANGER	Automobile simulator substitutes for real automobile	Minimizes danger of accident
INADEQUATE SAMPLING	Airplane simulator substitutes for real airplane flying conditions	Can build into the training situation all varieties of flying conditions that would otherwise take a long time to occur in actual flying

EXAMPLES OF CONDITIONS |REQUIRING| AND |NOT REQUIRING|
SUBSTITUTES (OR SIMULATION) FOR CRITERION VISUALS IN TRAINING

	SUBSTITUTES LIKELY TO BE NECESSARY		USE OF CRITERION VISUALS FEASIBLE
	e.g., if a clerk learning to use a cash register in a busy supermarket were to practice in the actual supermarket setting, he would tie up the cash register	vs.	e.g., if a clerk learning to use a cash register in a small neighborhood store were to practice in the actual store setting, he would not tie up the cash register
	DOWNTIME A PROBLEM		*DOWNTIME NOT A PROBLEM*
	e.g., if a technician practiced taking actual X-rays of a patient, there would be danger to the patient (radiation); thus, there should be simulation either of the patient (input) or of the taking of the X-ray (action)	vs.	e.g., if a technician practiced taking actual X-rays of an airplane wing, there would not be any danger to the wing; the technician could practice with an actual plane (input) and actual X-rays (action)
	COST OR DANGER A PROBLEM		*COST OR DANGER NOT A PROBLEM*
	e.g., a Naval officer has to learn to identify all kinds of enemy vessels; he cannot wait until he encounters them all on the job; thus, he needs identification (action) practice with substitute inputs (e.g., photographs of all types of enemy vessels) because the real thing is not available during training readily and completely	vs.	e.g., a Naval officer has to learn to identify all the vessels of his own country; all types of vessels are probably available for him to view in person; he can practice identifying (action) with actual vessels (inputs) because they are available; (as a practical matter, he might still be given photographs to work with)
	SAMPLING OR STANDARDIZATION A PROBLEM		*SAMPLING OR STANDARDIZATION NOT A PROBLEM*

DEGREES OF SERIOUSNESS

PROBLEMS	SERIOUS	AVERAGE	NEGLIGIBLE
DOWNTIME	-Operations or equipment of very high importance to success or functioning of organization	-Operations or equipment of moderate importance to success or functioning of organization	-Operations or equipment of negligible importance to success or functioning of organization
COST OR DANGER	Very high cost or danger	Moderate to high cost or danger	Low cost or danger
INADEQUATE SAMPLING	-Number of situations to be sampled is large -All situations requiring practice occur infrequently and/or in incomplete detail	-Number of situations to be sampled is of medium size -All situations requiring practice occur with moderate frequency and/or in moderately complete detail	-Number of situations to be sampled is small -All situations requiring practice occur frequently and/or in complete detail

CONSEQUENCES OF USING CRITERION VISUALS IN TRAINING

DEGREES OF SERIOUSNESS

	SERIOUS	AVERAGE	NEGLIGIBLE
DOWNTIME EXAMPLE practice involves working with an actual automobile	If practice results in tying up production line in auto assembly plant *MOST IN NEED OF SIMULATION*	Slowing up auto going to next department for additional work in repair shop	Slowing up automobile going to next stage in autowash *LEAST IN NEED OF SIMULATION*
COST OR DANGER EXAMPLE practice involves working with actual computers or calculators	Damage to a large, electronic computer *MOST IN NEED OF SIMULATION*	Damage to an electronic desk calculator	Damage to an adding machine *LEAST IN NEED OF SIMULATION*
SAMPLING OR STANDARDIZATION EXAMPLE practice involves dealing with actual customers as the situations come up on the job	Long delay in encountering all the types of situations likely to occur; handling customers will suffer excessively *MOST IN NEED OF SIMULATION*		Short delay in encountering all the types of situations likely to occur; handling customers will suffer minimally *LEAST IN NEED OF SIMULATION*

EXAMPLES OF PROBABLE ESTIMATES OF THE SERIOUSNESS OF USING CRITERION VISUALS IN TRAINING

IF USED IN TRAINING

CRITERION VISUALS ON THE JOB	DOWNTIME	COST OR DANGER	SAMPLING OR STANDARDIZATION PROBLEM
EXAMPLE Missile Technician INPUT: missile trajectory ACTION: identifying acceptable/non-acceptable OUTPUT: correct identification	SERIOUS (launch pads and operations centers would be tied up)	SERIOUS (using an actual missile is expensive)	AVERAGE (the number of types of trajectory is not large)
EXAMPLE TV Repairman INPUT: TV symptoms ACTION: adjusts set OUTPUT: correct image	NEGLIGIBLE (using an actual TV set for training does not tie up customer sets)	NEGLIGIBLE (TV sets are not expensive and can easily be repaired)	SERIOUS (all the possible types of symptoms would not readily occur in ordinary operations)
EXAMPLE Draftsman INPUT: original blueprint ACTION: redraws blueprint OUTPUT: new blueprint	NEGLIGIBLE	NEGLIGIBLE	NEGLIGIBLE

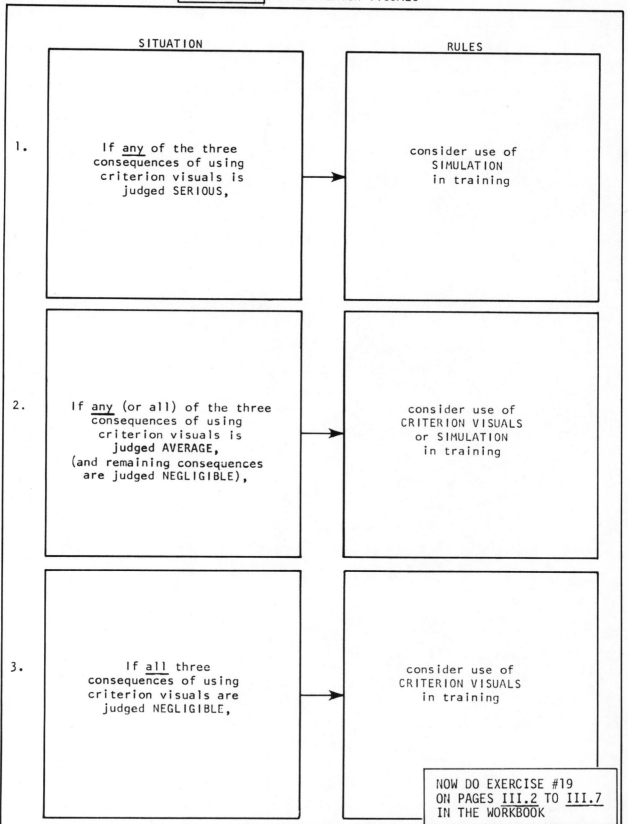

	SITUATION	RULES
1.	If **any** of the three consequences of using criterion visuals is judged SERIOUS,	consider use of SIMULATION in training
2.	If **any** (or all) of the three consequences of using criterion visuals is judged AVERAGE, (and remaining consequences are judged NEGLIGIBLE),	consider use of CRITERION VISUALS or SIMULATION in training
3.	If **all** three consequences of using criterion visuals are judged NEGLIGIBLE,	consider use of CRITERION VISUALS in training

NOW DO EXERCISE #19
ON PAGES III.2 TO III.7
IN THE WORKBOOK

III.2   OBJECTIVES OF THIS UNIT

> At the end of this unit, you will be able to identify various ways to SIMULATE or substitute for Criterion Visuals.

DIAGRAM OF YOUR JOB

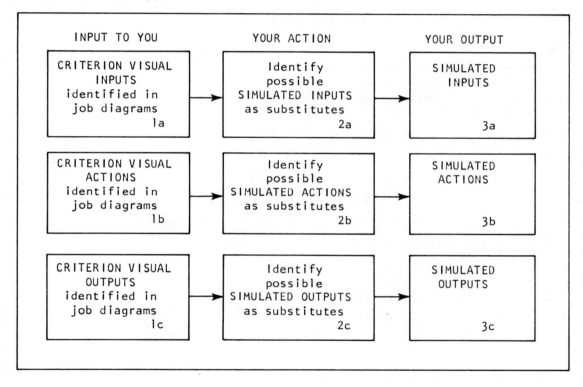

INPUT TO YOU | YOUR ACTION | YOUR OUTPUT

CRITERION VISUAL INPUTS identified in job diagrams 1a → Identify possible SIMULATED INPUTS as substitutes 2a → SIMULATED INPUTS 3a

CRITERION VISUAL ACTIONS identified in job diagrams 1b → Identify possible SIMULATED ACTIONS as substitutes 2b → SIMULATED ACTIONS 3b

CRITERION VISUAL OUTPUTS identified in job diagrams 1c → Identify possible SIMULATED OUTPUTS as substitutes 2c → SIMULATED OUTPUTS 3c

THE DIFFERENCE BETWEEN CRITERION AND SIMULATED PRACTICE

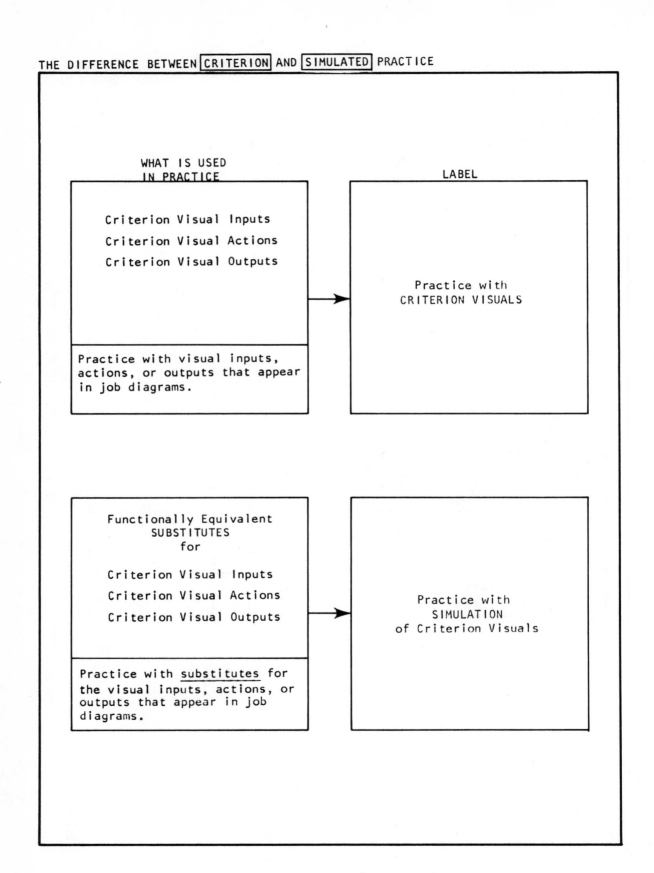

WHAT IS USED
IN PRACTICE

LABEL

Criterion Visual Inputs

Criterion Visual Actions

Criterion Visual Outputs

Practice with visual inputs,
actions, or outputs that appear
in job diagrams.

Practice with
CRITERION VISUALS

Functionally Equivalent
SUBSTITUTES
for

Criterion Visual Inputs

Criterion Visual Actions

Criterion Visual Outputs

Practice with substitutes for
the visual inputs, actions, or
outputs that appear in job
diagrams.

Practice with
SIMULATION
of Criterion Visuals

III.18

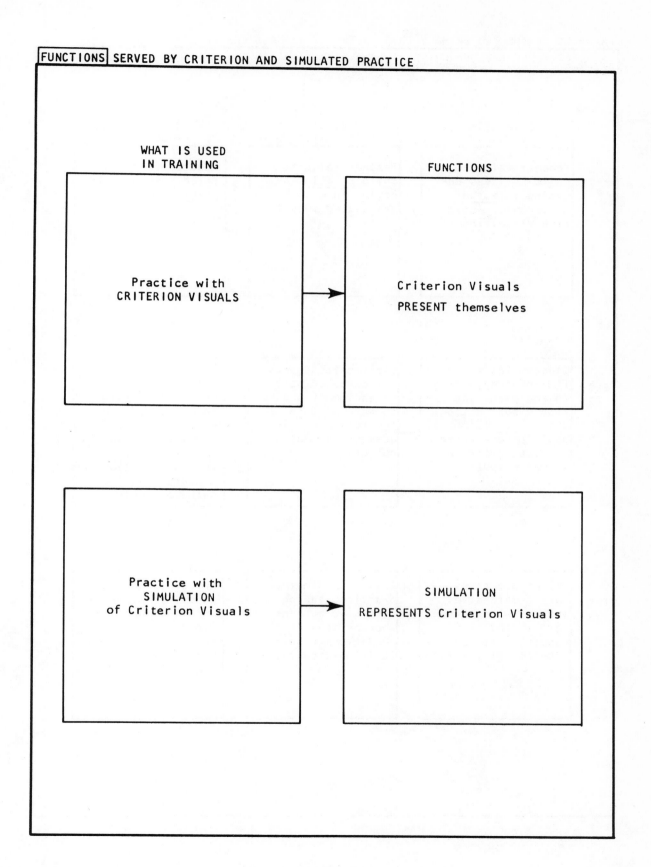

FUNCTIONS SERVED BY CRITERION AND SIMULATED PRACTICE

WHAT IS USED
IN TRAINING

FUNCTIONS

Practice with
CRITERION VISUALS

Criterion Visuals
PRESENT themselves

Practice with
SIMULATION
of Criterion Visuals

SIMULATION
REPRESENTS Criterion Visuals

	CRITERION VISUALS	VISUAL SIMULATION	NON-VISUAL SIMULATION
E.G. #1	Teacher talks to child she sees engaging in actual misbehavior (criterion visual input)	Teacher talks to child on film engaging in misbehavior (simulated input)	Teacher talks to child described in print as engaging in misbehavior (simulated input)
E.G. #2	Electronics specialist makes adjustment in equipment (criterion visual action) until actual, normal oscilloscope pattern results (criterion visual output)	Electronics specialist makes adjustment in equipment and is shown a picture of the result of his action (simulated output)	Electronics specialist indicates what he would do (simulated action) to adjust for problem in equipment and is told what the resulting oscilloscope pattern is (simulated output)
E.G. #3	Driver practices taking defensive actions when he sees actual conditions requiring it (criterion visual inputs)	Driver on simulator practices taking defensive actions when he sees film of conditions requiring it (simulated inputs)	Driver on paper-and-pencil problems indicates what he would do if he were to face given conditions (simulated inputs)

SELECTION OF
SIMULATION

NON-VISUALS:

WORDS

represent the
Criterion Visuals

REFERENT

CRITERION
VISUALS

or

Other
VISUALS

represent the
Criterion Visuals

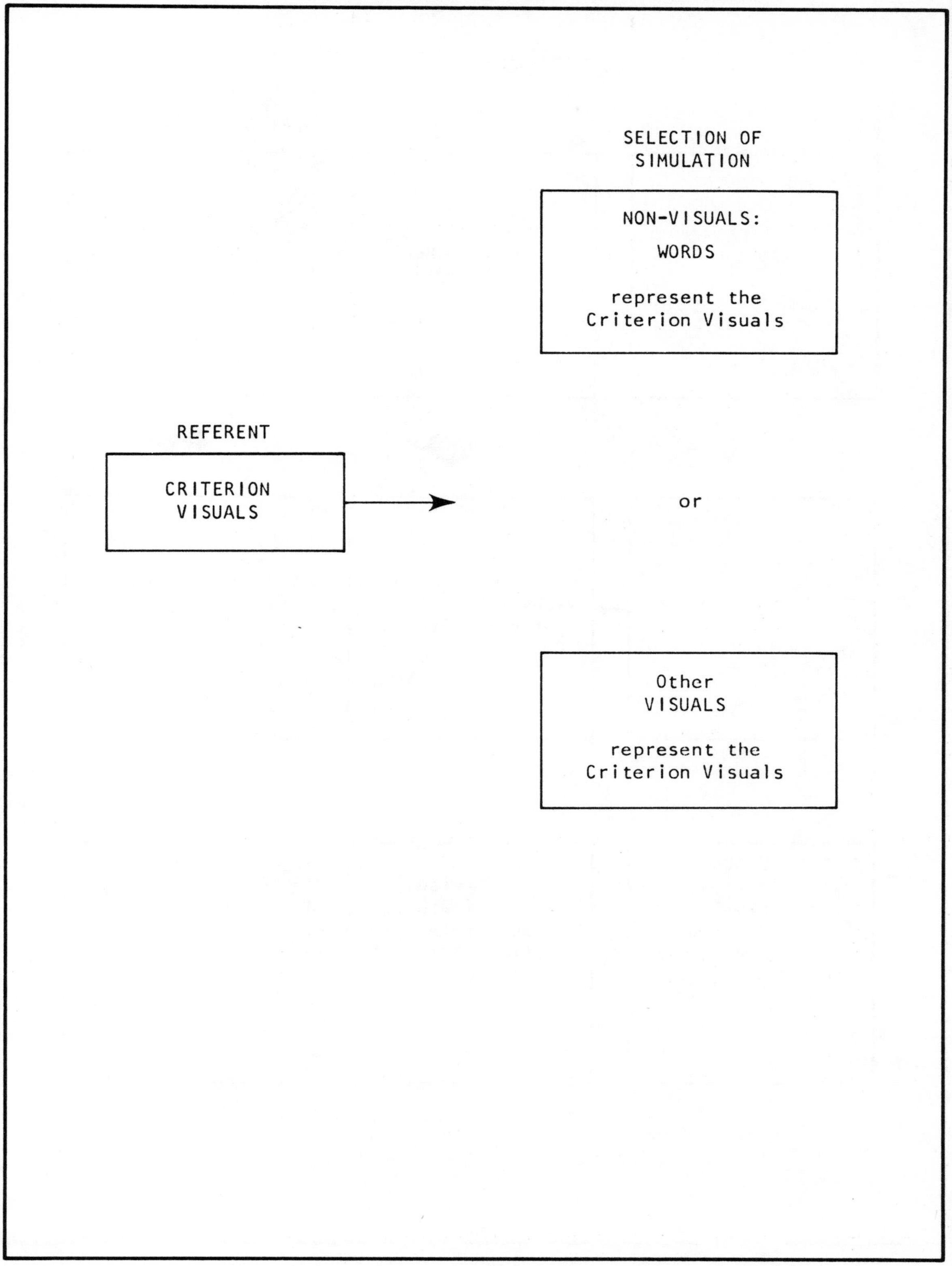

TWO PRIMARY WAYS CRITERION VISUALS CAN BE SIMULATED

TYPES OF SIMULATION

LABEL →	VISUAL SIMULATION	vs.	NON-VISUAL SIMULATION
DEFINITION →	Visual simulation substitutes for Criterion Visuals		Verbal simulation substitutes for Criterion Visuals
EXAMPLE →	Other visual inputs (outputs) substitute for Criterion Inputs (outputs)		Verbal description of Criterion Input situations substitute for Criterion Visual Inputs

EXAMPLES OF THE TWO PRIMARY WAYS CRITERION VISUALS CAN BE SIMULATED

EXAMPLE #1   EXAMPLE #2   EXAMPLE #3

Criterion Visuals to be simulated → Driver practices taking defensive actions when he sees actual conditions requiring it (criterion visual inputs)	Electronics specialist makes adjustment in equipment (criterion visual action) until actual, normal oscilloscope pattern results (criterion visual output)	Teacher talks to child she sees engaging in actual misbehavior (criterion visual input)
VISUAL SIMULATION → Driver on simulator practices taking defensive actions when he sees film of conditions requiring it (simulated inputs)	Electronics specialist makes adjustment in equipment and is shown a picture of the result of his action (simulated output)	Teacher talks to child on film engaging in misbehavior (simulated input)
NON-VISUAL SIMULATION → Driver on paper-and-pencil problems indicates what he would do if he were to face given conditions (simulated inputs)	Electronics specialist indicates what he would do (simulated action) to adjust for problem in equipment and is told what the resulting oscilloscope pattern is (simulated output)	Teacher talks to child described in print as engaging in misbehavior (simulated input)

vs.

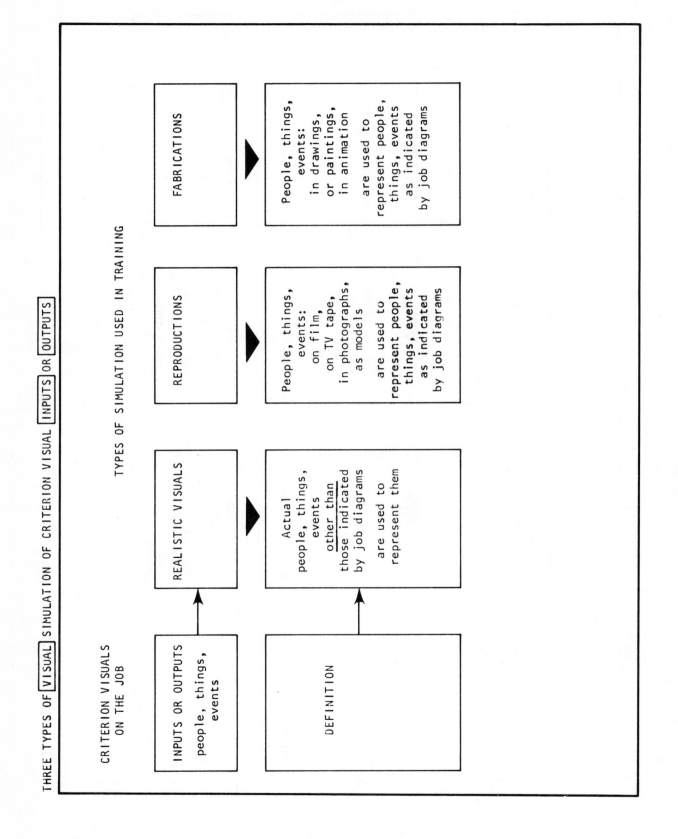

THREE TYPES OF VISUAL SIMULATION OF CRITERION VISUAL INPUTS OR OUTPUTS

CRITERION VISUALS
ON THE JOB

TYPES OF SIMULATION USED IN TRAINING

REALISTIC VISUALS

REPRODUCTIONS

FABRICATIONS

INPUTS OR OUTPUTS
people, things,
events

DEFINITION

Actual
people, things,
events
other than
those indicated
by job diagrams

are used to
represent them

People, things,
events:
on film,
on TV tape,
in photographs,
as models

are used to
represent people,
things, events
as indicated
by job diagrams

People, things,
events:
in drawings,
or paintings,
in animation

are used to
represent people,
things, events
as indicated
by job diagrams

EXAMPLES OF VISUAL SIMULATION OF INPUTS OR OUTPUTS

	EXAMPLE #1	EXAMPLE #2	EXAMPLE #3
Criterion Visuals (inputs or outputs) to be simulated	actual subordinates in an organization (supervisor has to deal with)	actual automobile (driver has to operate)	baby (to be diapered)
SIMULATION			
Simulation by REALISTIC VISUALS	actors playing subordinates	driver-training automobile (e.g., dual steering wheel)	chimpanzee
Simulation by REPRODUCTIONS	film of subordinates	auto simulator	doll
Simulation by FABRICATED VISUALS	animation of subordinates	sketches of dash, or drawing of gear shift positions	drawing of baby

III.25

THREE LEVELS OF PERFORMANCE AS CANDIDATES FOR SIMULATION OF VISUAL ACTIONS

L E V E L S   O F   P E R F O R M A N C E

	RECOGNIZE	vs.	EDIT	vs.	PRODUCE
LABEL					
DEFINITION	The learner is merely expected to recognize -whether an input, action, or output is correct or incorrect -which of two or more inputs, actions, or outputs is the correct one		The learner is merely expected to edit or change -an incorrect input, action, or output		The learner is expected to perform as he would on the job -identify inputs -alter inputs -produce outputs
DEGREE OF SIMILARITY WITH CRITERION SITUATION	LEAST		MIDDLE		MOST
PERFORMANCE EFFECTIVENESS IN PROMOTING TRANSFER	LEAST		MIDDLE		MOST

TYPE OF SIMULATION

CRITERION VISUAL ACTIONS	RECOGNIZE	vs.	EDIT	vs.	PRODUCE
IDENTIFY INPUTS: taking an action on the basis of an appropriate identification of inputs	-merely selecting one of two or more inputs -merely selecting one of two or more actions for the input that is presented		-merely editing an incorrectly labeled input -merely editing an incorrect action taken on the basis of an appropriate identification of inputs		-taking an action other than the criterion action on the basis of an appropriate identification of an input
ALTER INPUTS: making a change in an input leading to an output	-merely selecting one altered input from two or more possibilities		-merely editing an incorrectly altered input		-making an alteration in inputs (other than and as a substitute for criterion alteration)
PRODUCE INPUTS: producing an output (from raw materials)	-merely selecting an output from two or more possibilities		-merely editing an incorrectly produced output		-producing an output (other than and as a substitute for criterion production)

EXAMPLES OF VISUAL SIMULATION OF ACTIONS

	EXAMPLE #1	EXAMPLE #2	EXAMPLE #3
Criterion Visual Actions	On the job, the TV repairman is expected to make actual adjustments leading to the alteration of the poor TV image (input)	On the job, the draftsman is expected to draw (produce) actual blueprints	On the job, the electronics maintenance man is expected to identify oscilloscope patterns and to take an appropriate course of action
SIMULATION Simulated by RECOGNITION	In training, the learner merely selects which of two or more actions he would take	In training, the draftsman merely selects which of two or more blueprints satisfies requirements	In training, the maintenance man merely selects one of two or more patterns as the occasion for a stated course of action
Simulated by EDITING	In training, the learner merely edits an incorrect alteration (presented to him)	In training, the draftsman merely edits incorrect blueprints until they satisfy requirements	In training, the maintenance man is expected to change an incorrect course of action (presented to him), the course of action depending on the identification of the oscilloscope pattern
Simulated by PRODUCTION	In training, the learner may draw a picture of a correctly altered image (rather than make knob changes leading to an altered image)		In training, the maintenance man is expected to produce a specific pattern

LEVELS OF PERFORMANCE REQUIRED IN TRAINING	RECOGNIZE	vs.	EDIT	vs.	PRODUCE
DEGREE OF SIMILARITY WITH LEVEL OF PERFORMANCE REQUIRED IN CRITERION SITUATION	Least		Middle		Most
DEGREE OF DIFFICULTY COMPARABLE TO THAT FOUND IN CRITERION SITUATION	Least		Middle		Most
APPROPRIATENESS FOR SIMULATION	Least		Middle		Most

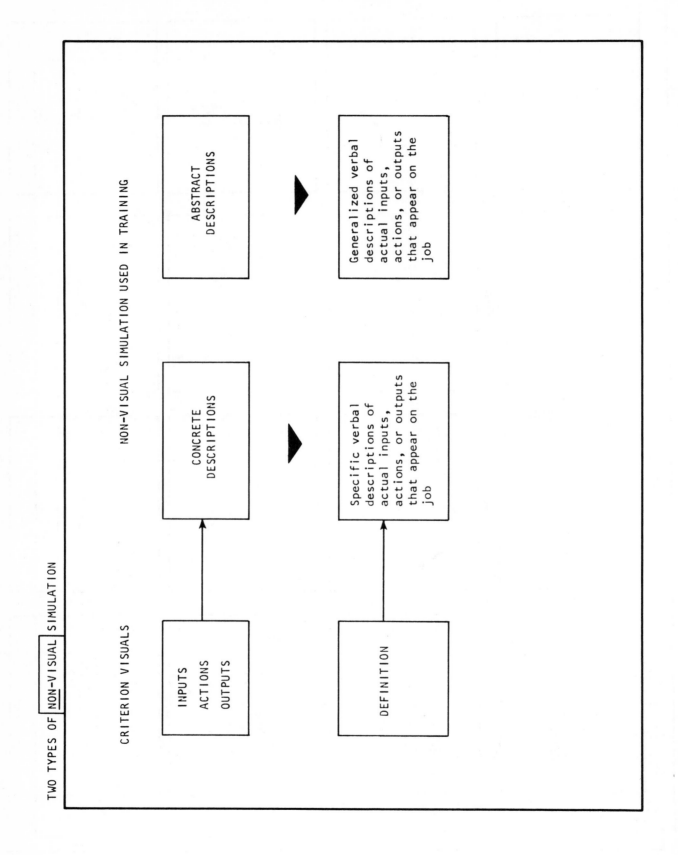

TWO TYPES OF NON-VISUAL SIMULATION

NON-VISUAL SIMULATION USED IN TRAINING

CRITERION VISUALS

ABSTRACT
DESCRIPTIONS

Generalized verbal
descriptions of
actual inputs,
actions, or outputs
that appear on the
job

CONCRETE
DESCRIPTIONS

Specific verbal
descriptions of
actual inputs,
actions, or outputs
that appear on the
job

INPUTS
ACTIONS
OUTPUTS

DEFINITION

	EXAMPLE #1	EXAMPLE #2	EXAMPLE #3
	A teacher has to practice identifying problem behavior (visual inputs) that takes place in her classroom	A TV repairman has to trouble-shoot and repair malfunction leading to normal TV image	A naval officer has to learn to identify types of friendly or enemy vessels
Criterion Visuals to be simulated	▶	▶	▶

SIMULATION

To be simulated by CONCRETE DESCRIPTION	Case study: "Johnny fails to look at board while teacher is writing on it; stares off into space"	Paper-and-pencil problem: "If the TV image continually rolls up, what would you do?"	Paper-and-pencil description: specific number of stacks described verbally

To be simulated by ABSTRACT DESCRIPTION	Case study: "Student fails to attend to classroom events and exhibits withdrawal"	Paper-and-pencil problem: "If a vertical symptom occurred, what adjustments would you consider?"	Paper-and-pencil description: size and configuration are key distinctions

III.31

SUMMARY OF POSSIBLE TYPES OF SIMULATION OF CRITERION VISUALS

V I S U A L   S I M U L A T I O N

CRITERION VISUALS

| INPUTS OUTPUTS | → | REALISTIC VISUALS | vs. | REPRODUCTIONS | vs. | FABRICATIONS |

| ACTIONS | → | RECOGNIZE | vs. | EDIT | vs. | PRODUCE |

N O N - V I S U A L   S I M U L A T I O N

CRITERION VISUALS

| INPUTS ACTIONS OUTPUTS | → | CONCRETE DESCRIPTIONS | vs. | ABSTRACT DESCRIPTIONS |

NOW DO EXERCISE #20 ON PAGES III.8 TO III.11 IN THE WORKBOOK.

III.3   OBJECTIVES OF THIS UNIT

At the end of this unit, you will be able to identify DESIRABLE CHARACTERISTICS OF SIMULATION and to PRODUCE EXAMPLES of effective simulation.

DIAGRAM OF YOUR JOB

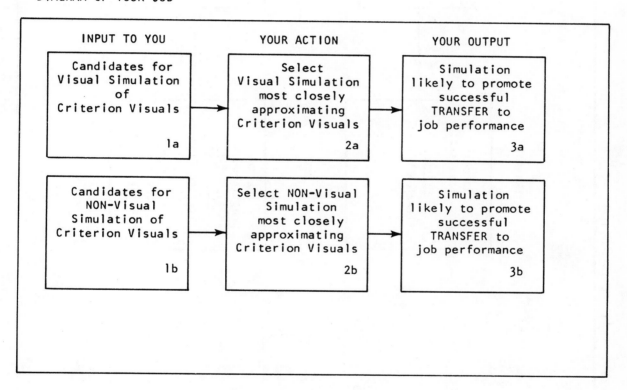

INPUT TO YOU	YOUR ACTION	YOUR OUTPUT
Candidates for Visual Simulation of Criterion Visuals 1a	Select Visual Simulation most closely approximating Criterion Visuals 2a	Simulation likely to promote successful TRANSFER to job performance 3a
Candidates for NON-Visual Simulation of Criterion Visuals 1b	Select NON-Visual Simulation most closely approximating Criterion Visuals 2b	Simulation likely to promote successful TRANSFER to job performance 3b

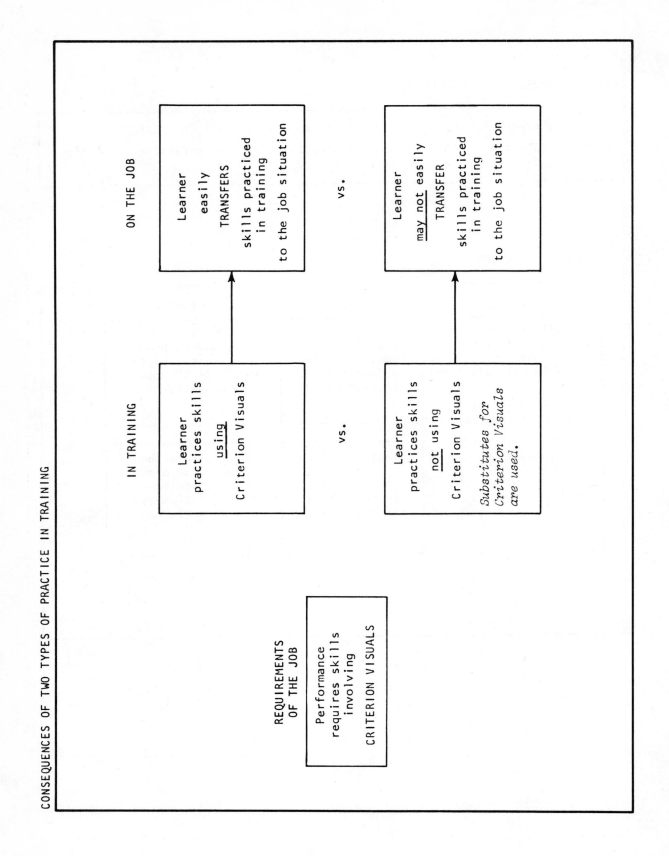

CONSEQUENCES OF TWO TYPES OF PRACTICE IN TRAINING

ON THE JOB

IN TRAINING

Learner easily TRANSFERS skills practiced in training to the job situation

Learner may not easily TRANSFER skills practiced in training to the job situation

vs.

Learner practices skills using Criterion Visuals

Learner practices skills not using Criterion Visuals

Substitutes for Criterion Visuals are used.

vs.

REQUIREMENTS OF THE JOB

Performance requires skills involving CRITERION VISUALS

EXAMPLES OF THE CONSEQUENCES OF TWO TYPES OF PRACTICE IN TRAINING

	EXAMPLE #1	EXAMPLE #2	EXAMPLE #3
Performance on the job involving criterion visuals	Air controller must identify flight patterns from radar screen (visual inputs)	Arc welder must produce surfaces of appropriate smoothness	Maintenance mechanic must spatially locate breakdown in equipment
Consequences of using criterion visuals in training	Having practiced with actual radar patterns, has no difficulty transferring skills in identifying pattern when on the job	Having practiced producing actual welded surfaces, has no difficulty transferring skills to the job setting	Having practiced actually locating breakdowns, has no difficulty transferring skills to the job setting
vs. Consequences of using substitutes for criterion visuals in training	Having practiced with pictures of or verbal descriptions of radar patterns, may have difficulty transferring skills to the job setting	Having practiced only recognizing the differences between appropriately and inappropriately smooth surfaces, may have difficulty transferring skills to the job setting	Having practiced locating breakdowns from diagrams, may have difficulty transferring skills to the job setting

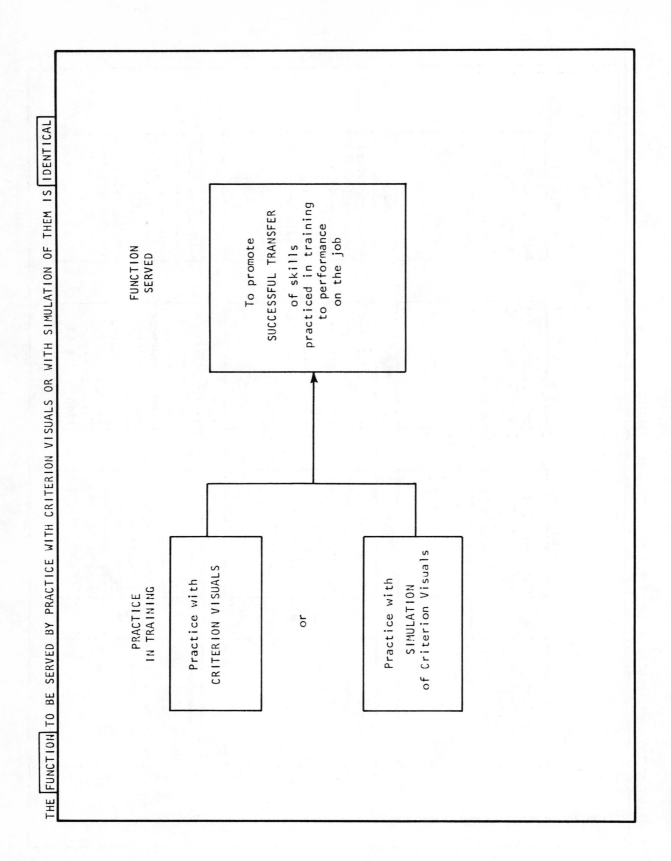

THE [FUNCTION] TO BE SERVED BY PRACTICE WITH CRITERION VISUALS OR WITH SIMULATION OF THEM IS [IDENTICAL]

FUNCTION
SERVED

To promote
SUCCESSFUL TRANSFER
of skills
practiced in training
to performance
on the job

PRACTICE
IN TRAINING

Practice with
CRITERION VISUALS

or

Practice with
SIMULATION
of Criterion Visuals

111.38

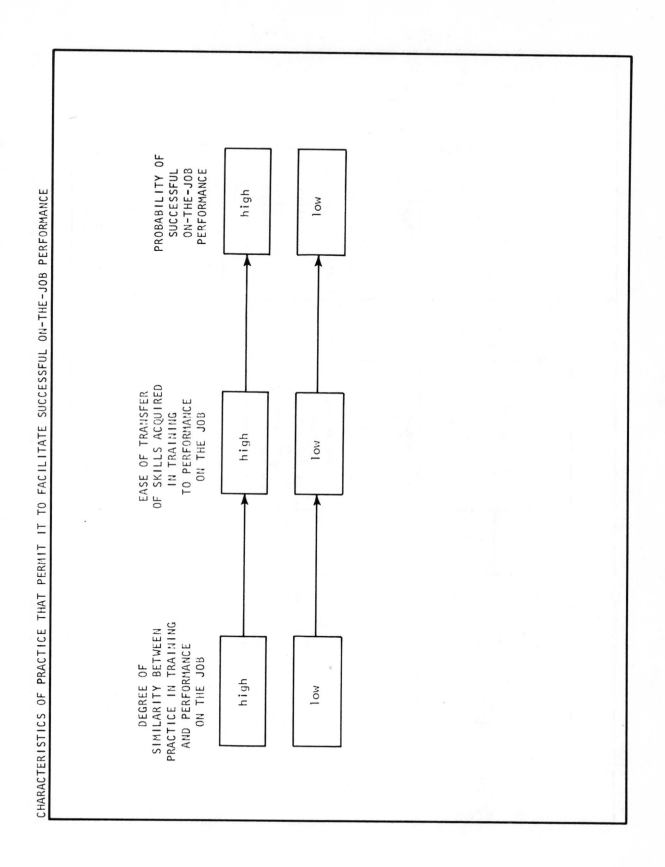

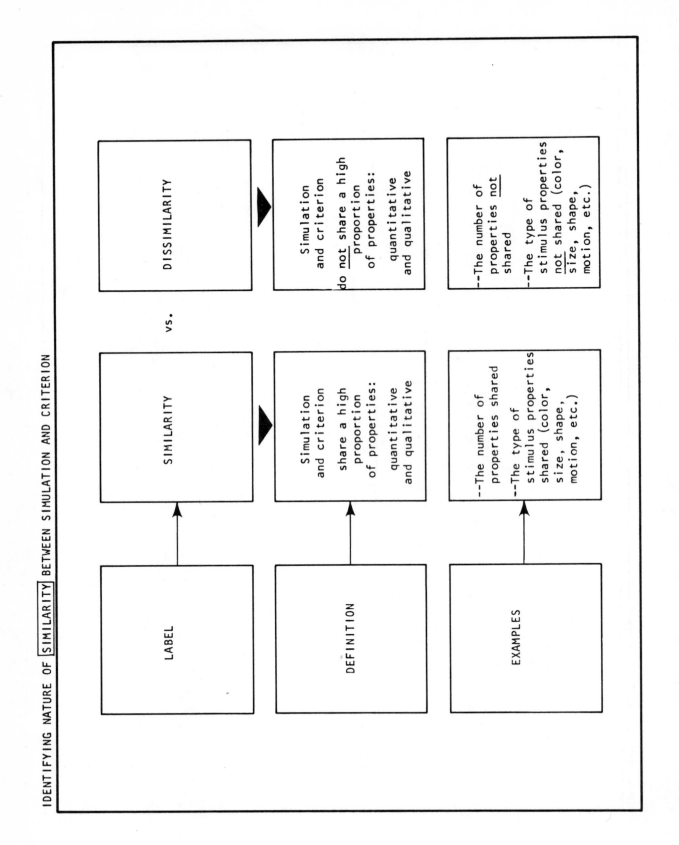

IDENTIFYING NATURE OF [SIMILARITY] BETWEEN SIMULATION AND CRITERION

LABEL

SIMILARITY

vs.

DISSIMILARITY

DEFINITION

Simulation and criterion share a high proportion of properties: quantitative and qualitative

Simulation and criterion do not share a high proportion of properties: quantitative and qualitative

EXAMPLES

--The number of properties shared
--The type of stimulus properties shared (color, size, shape, motion, etc.)

--The number of properties not shared
--The type of stimulus properties not shared (color, size, shape, motion, etc.)

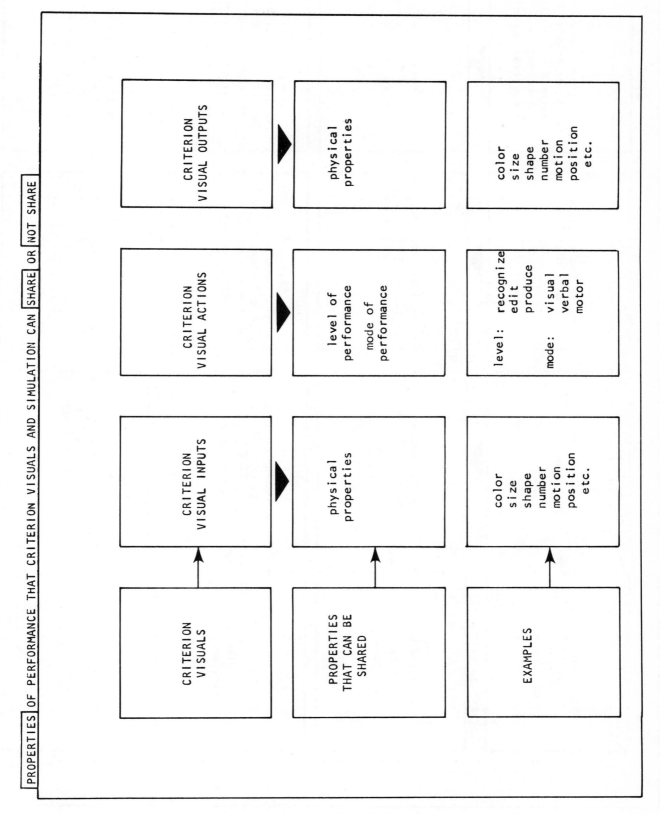

EXAMPLES OF DIFFERING DEGREES OF SIMILARITY SHARED BY SIMULATED AND CRITERION VISUAL INPUTS

	EXAMPLE #1	EXAMPLE #2	EXAMPLE #3
CRITERION VISUAL INPUTS to be simulated	airplane instrument panel	tracking the trajectory of a missile	behavior and facial expression of workers bringing problems to industrial nurse
DEGREE OF SIMILARITY			
Simulated with HIGH similarity	Simulated by a mock-up of panel with all dials, knobs, lights represented	Simulated by film of missile trajectory	Simulated by actors role playing
vs.			
Simulated with MEDIUM similarity	Simulated by a mock-up of panel with many of the dials, knobs, lights represented	Simulated by still photographs of different phases of the trajectory (motion absent)	Simulated by case studies providing concrete description of behavior and facial expression (visual properties absent)
vs.			
Simulated with LOW similarity	Simulated by a mock-up of panel with only a small number of the dials, knobs, lights represented	Simulated by verbal description of phases of missile trajectory (actual visual properties absent)	Simulated by case studies providing abstract description of behavior and facial expression (specifics absent)

EXAMPLES OF DIFFERING DEGREES OF SIMILARITY SHARED BY SIMULATED AND CRITERION VISUAL ACTIONS

	EXAMPLE #1	EXAMPLE #2	EXAMPLE #3
CRITERION VISUAL ACTIONS to be simulated	preparing blueprints	welding plates	wrapping bandages
DEGREE OF SIMILARITY			
Simulated with HIGH similarity	preparing rough sketches	making movement with mock-up torch	verbal description of what to do
Simulated with MEDIUM similarity	editing blueprints	verbally describing the details of movements	editing or verbal description of what to do
Simulated with LOW similarity	recognizing good or bad examples of blueprints	verbally describing principles to follow in making movements	recognizing a correct description of what to do

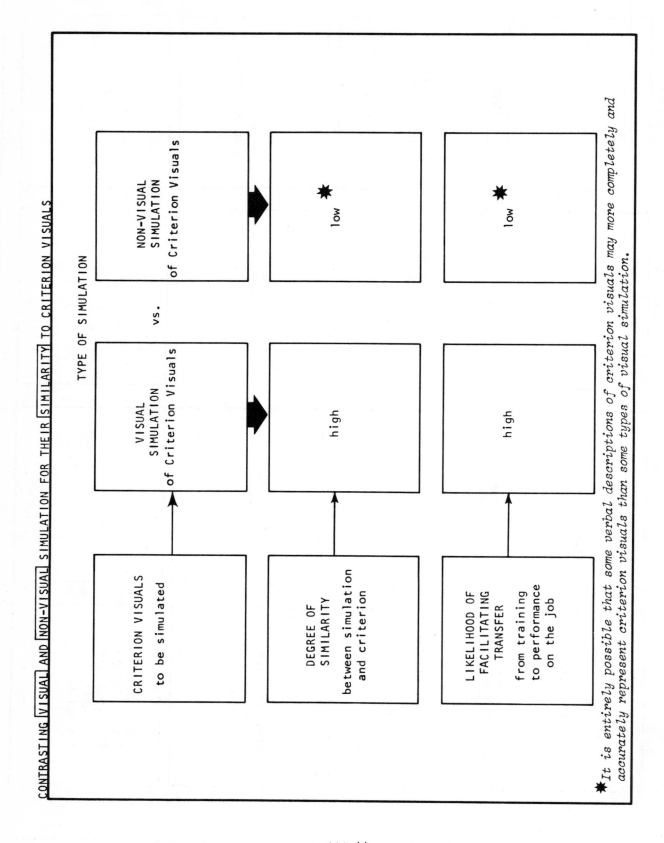

CONTRASTING [VISUAL] AND [NON-VISUAL] SIMULATION FOR THEIR [SIMILARITY] TO CRITERION VISUALS

TYPE OF SIMULATION

VISUAL SIMULATION of Criterion Visuals

vs.

NON-VISUAL SIMULATION of Criterion Visuals

CRITERION VISUALS to be simulated

DEGREE OF SIMILARITY between simulation and criterion

high

low

LIKELIHOOD OF FACILITATING TRANSFER from training to performance on the job

high

low

★ *It is entirely possible that some verbal descriptions of criterion visuals may more completely and accurately represent criterion visuals than some types of visual simulation.*

	EXAMPLE #1	EXAMPLE #2	EXAMPLE #3
Criterion Visuals that need to be simulated	Trajectory of a missile	Locations of parts in complex circuitry	Speed of automobiles in front of driver
VISUAL SIMULATION: *greater similarity to criterion visual*	Film of missile in flight	Diagram of circuitry with location of parts marked	Film of driving scene
vs.			
NON-VISUAL SIMULATION: *lesser similarity to criterion visual*	Verbal description of missile trajectory	Verbal description of where particular parts are in relation to other parts	Descriptions of distances and speeds

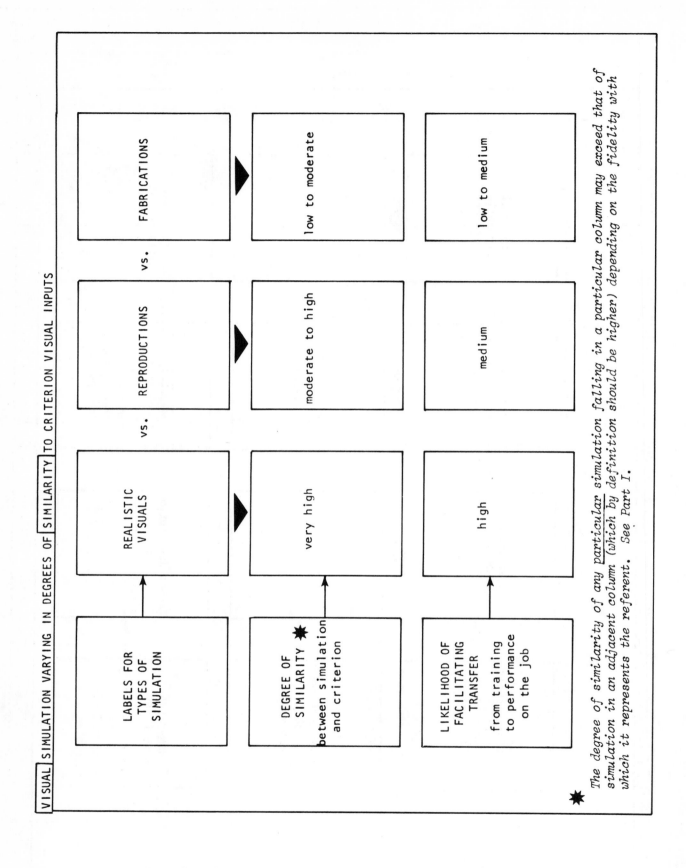

VISUAL SIMULATION VARYING IN DEGREES OF SIMILARITY TO CRITERION VISUAL INPUTS

LABELS FOR TYPES OF SIMULATION

REALISTIC VISUALS vs. REPRODUCTIONS vs. FABRICATIONS

DEGREE OF SIMILARITY ✳
between simulation and criterion

very high   moderate to high   low to moderate

LIKELIHOOD OF FACILITATING TRANSFER

from training to performance on the job

high   medium   low to medium

✳ *The degree of similarity of any particular simulation falling in a particular column may exceed that of simulation in an adjacent column (which by definition should be higher) depending on the fidelity with which it represents the referent. See Part I.*

EXAMPLES OF [VISUAL] SIMULATION VARYING IN DEGREES OF [SIMILARITY] TO CRITERION VISUAL [INPUTS]

	EXAMPLE #1	EXAMPLE #2	EXAMPLE #3
Criterion Visual INPUTS that need to be simulated	Levels of chemical foam (inputs) needed to extinguish fires	Ground approaching (inputs) as man in parachute nears ground	Customers requesting service from sales clerk
SIMULATION Simulated by REALISTIC VISUALS	Soap suds at comparable level *Very high similarity*	Ground approaching in jump from parachute tower *Very high similarity*	Live actors role playing customers *Very high similarity*
vs. Simulated by REPRODUCTIONS	Photographs of foam levels *Moderate similarity*	Film (from point of view of jumper) of ground approaching *Moderate to high similarity*	Photographs of customers' facial expressions *Moderate similarity*
vs. Simulated by FABRICATIONS	Cutaway drawing of foam levels *Low similarity*	Animation (from point of view of jumper) of ground approaching *Low similarity*	Sketches of customers' facial expressions *Very low similarity*

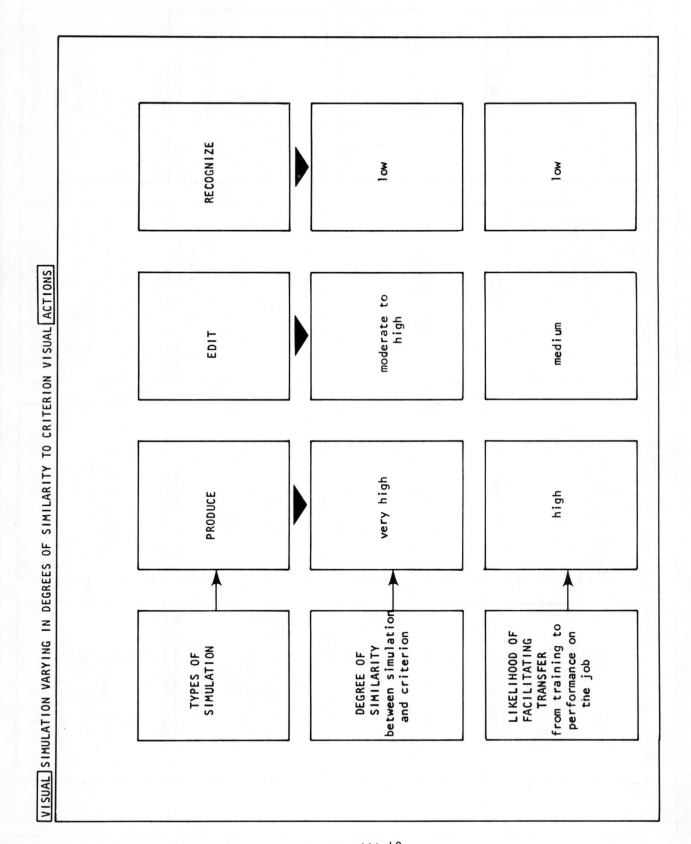

VISUAL SIMULATION VARYING IN DEGREES OF SIMILARITY TO CRITERION VISUAL ACTIONS

TYPES OF SIMULATION	PRODUCE	EDIT	RECOGNIZE
DEGREE OF SIMILARITY between simulation and criterion	very high	moderate to high	low
LIKELIHOOD OF FACILITATING TRANSFER from training to performance on the job	high	medium	low

EXAMPLES OF VISUAL SIMULATION VARYING IN DEGREES OF SIMILARITY TO CRITERION VISUAL ACTIONS

	EXAMPLE #1	EXAMPLE #2	EXAMPLE #3
Criterion Visual ACTIONS that need to be simulated	locating a malfunctioning component in complex equipment	soldering connections	orienting or positioning parts in motor assembly
SIMULATION Simulated by PRODUCTION practice	locating a malfunctioning component (on mockup) *high similarity*	soldering substitute materials *high similarity*	positioning parts on mockup *high similarity*
vs. Simulated by EDITING practice	editing (i.e., changing the identification of) the incorrectly identified component (on mockup) *medium similarity*	correcting an imperfect soldering job *medium similarity*	editing (changing) incorrectly positioned parts on mockup *medium similarity*
vs. Simulated by RECOGNITION practice	recognizing which of several components is the malfunctioning one (on mockup) *low similarity*	selecting the best of several soldering jobs *low similarity*	selecting which of the two or more positioned parts is correct; or indicating whether an example is correct or incorrect *low similarity*

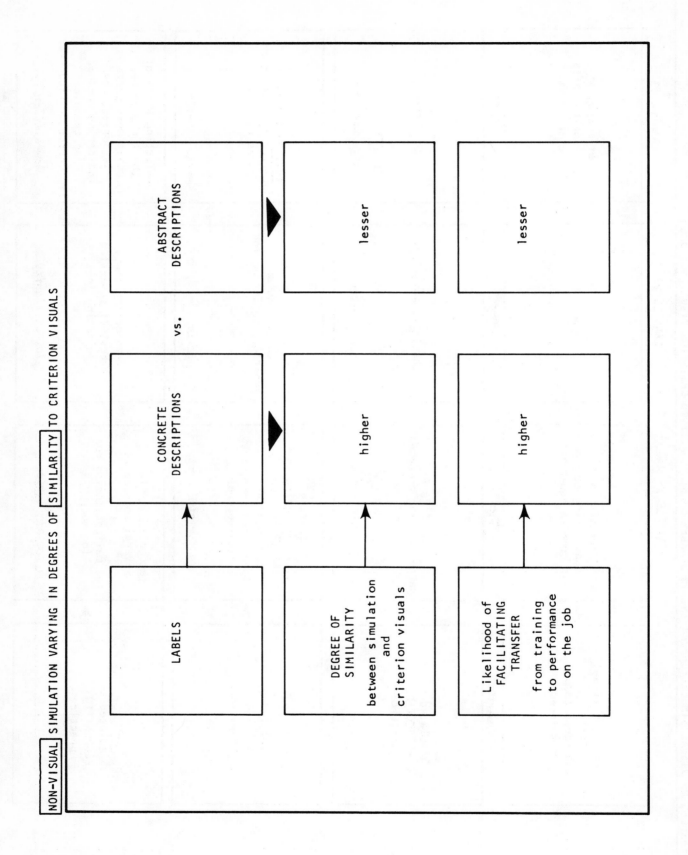

NON-VISUAL SIMULATION VARYING IN DEGREES OF SIMILARITY TO CRITERION VISUALS

CONCRETE DESCRIPTIONS vs. ABSTRACT DESCRIPTIONS

LABELS

DEGREE OF SIMILARITY between simulation and criterion visuals → higher / lesser

Likelihood of FACILITATING TRANSFER from training to performance on the job → higher / lesser

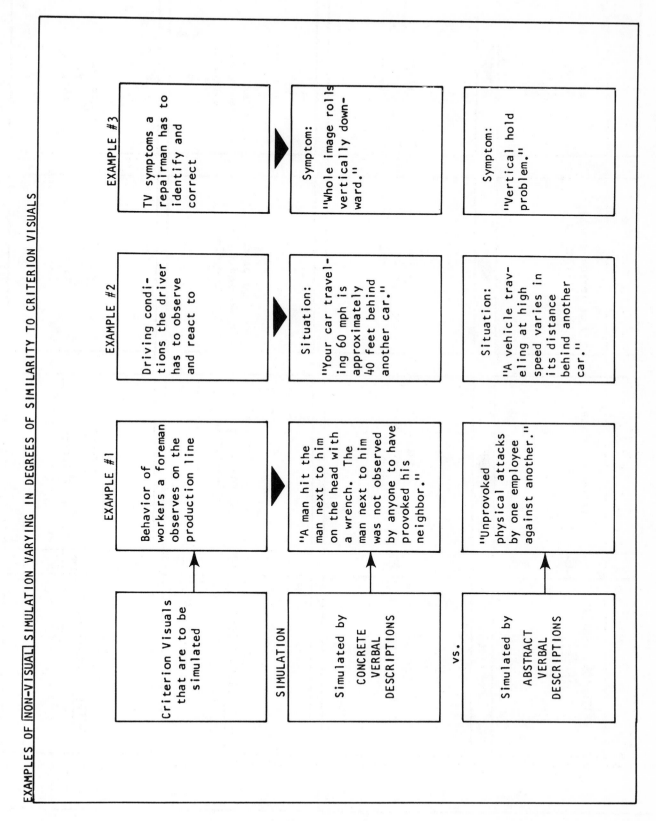

EXAMPLE #1

Behavior of workers a foreman observes on the production line

EXAMPLE #2

Driving conditions the driver has to observe and react to

EXAMPLE #3

TV symptoms a repairman has to identify and correct

SIMULATION

Simulated by
CONCRETE
VERBAL
DESCRIPTIONS

Criterion Visuals that are to be simulated

"A man hit the man next to him on the head with a wrench. The man next to him was not observed by anyone to have provoked his neighbor."

Situation:

"Your car traveling 60 mph is approximately 40 feet behind another car."

Symptom:

"Whole image rolls vertically downward."

vs.

Simulated by
ABSTRACT
VERBAL
DESCRIPTIONS

"Unprovoked physical attacks by one employee against another."

Situation:

"A vehicle traveling at high speed varies in its distance behind another car."

Symptom:

"Vertical hold problem."

III.51

SUMMARY OF PROPERTIES OF SIMULATION THAT AFFECT POSSIBILITIES OF TRANSFER

SUMMARY OF DESIRABLE CHARACTERISTICS OF SIMULATION

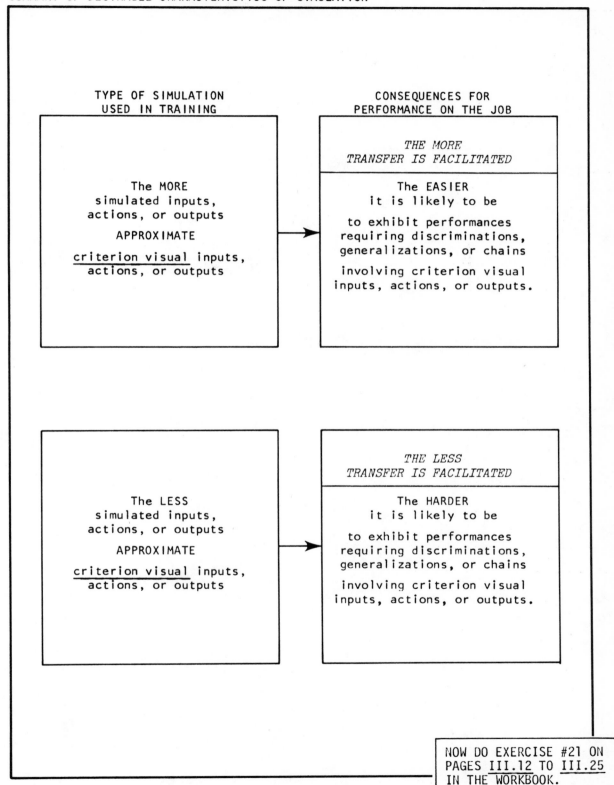

TYPE OF SIMULATION
USED IN TRAINING

CONSEQUENCES FOR
PERFORMANCE ON THE JOB

The MORE
simulated inputs,
actions, or outputs

APPROXIMATE

criterion visual inputs,
actions, or outputs

*THE MORE
TRANSFER IS FACILITATED*

The EASIER
it is likely to be

to exhibit performances
requiring discriminations,
generalizations, or chains

involving criterion visual
inputs, actions, or outputs.

The LESS
simulated inputs,
actions, or outputs

APPROXIMATE

criterion visual inputs,
actions, or outputs

*THE LESS
TRANSFER IS FACILITATED*

The HARDER
it is likely to be

to exhibit performances
requiring discriminations,
generalizations, or chains

involving criterion visual
inputs, actions, or outputs.

NOW DO EXERCISE #21 ON
PAGES III.12 TO III.25
IN THE WORKBOOK.

III.53

III.4   OBJECTIVES OF THIS UNIT

At the end of this unit, you will be able to determine PRIORITIES in deciding between practice with Criterion Visuals and practice with simulations of Criterion Visuals and among various types of simulation.

DIAGRAM OF YOUR JOB

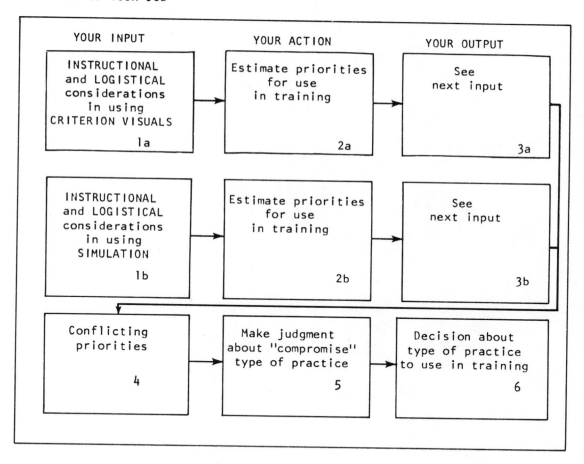

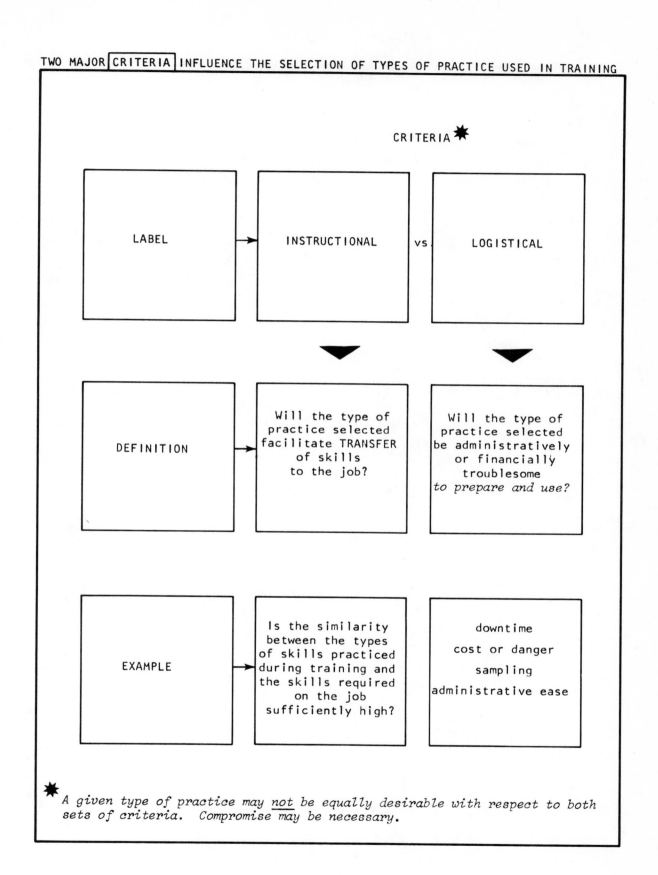

CRITERIA ✷

| LABEL | INSTRUCTIONAL | vs | LOGISTICAL |

| DEFINITION | Will the type of practice selected facilitate TRANSFER of skills to the job? | Will the type of practice selected be administratively or financially troublesome *to prepare and use?* |

| EXAMPLE | Is the similarity between the types of skills practiced during training and the skills required on the job sufficiently high? | downtime cost or danger sampling administrative ease |

✷ *A given type of practice may* <u>*not*</u> *be equally desirable with respect to both sets of criteria. Compromise may be necessary.*

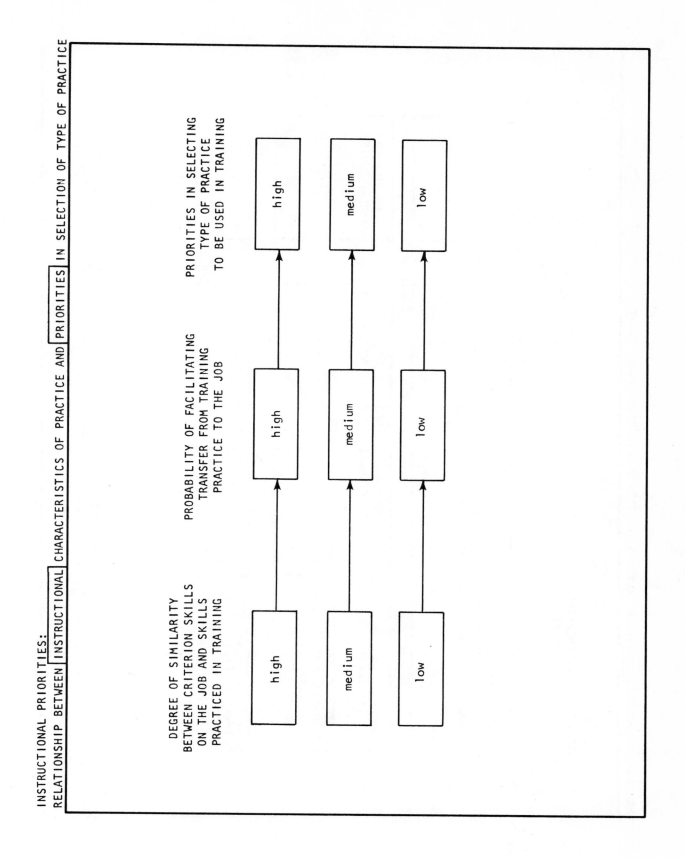

DEGREE OF SIMILARITY WITH
CRITERION VISUAL INPUTS
ON THE JOB

TYPES OF SIMULATED INPUTS

Identity

Therefore, highest probability of successful TRANSFER

→ CRITERION VISUAL INPUTS — I

Moderate to high similarity

Therefore, moderate to high probability of successful TRANSFER

→ REALISTIC SIMULATED VISUAL INPUTS — II

OR

REPRODUCED SIMULATED VISUAL INPUTS — III

OR

FABRICATED SIMULATED VISUAL INPUTS — IV

Least similarity

Therefore, lower probability of successful TRANSFER

→ CONCRETE NON-VISUAL SIMULATION OF INPUTS — V

OR

ABSTRACT NON-VISUAL SIMULATION OF INPUTS — VI

★ This is a general ordering of types of practice from I (most similar) to VI (least similar). In specific situations, one type of practice might achieve greater similarity than an adjacent, higher-ranked category.

★

TYPES OF INPUTS

		FABRICATED SIMULATED VISUAL INPUTS IV	

CRITERION VISUAL INPUTS I	REPRODUCED SIMULATED VISUAL INPUTS III	ABSTRACT NON-VISUAL SIMULATION OF INPUTS VI
REALISTIC SIMULATED VISUAL INPUTS II		
CONCRETE NON-VISUAL SIMULATION OF INPUTS V		

FIRST PRIORITY:

Highest probability of successful TRANSFER

SECOND PRIORITY:

High probability of successful TRANSFER

THIRD PRIORITY:

Lower probability of successful TRANSFER

★ *This is a general ordering of types of practice from I (most preferred) to VI (least preferred), based on assumed similarity between practice and criterion performance. In specific situations, one type of practice might be superior to one or two rated categories above it; e.g., concrete verbal descriptions (V) might be superior to fabricated visuals (IV).*

RANKING SIMULATED ACTIONS FOR THEIR SIMILARITY TO CRITERION VISUAL ACTIONS

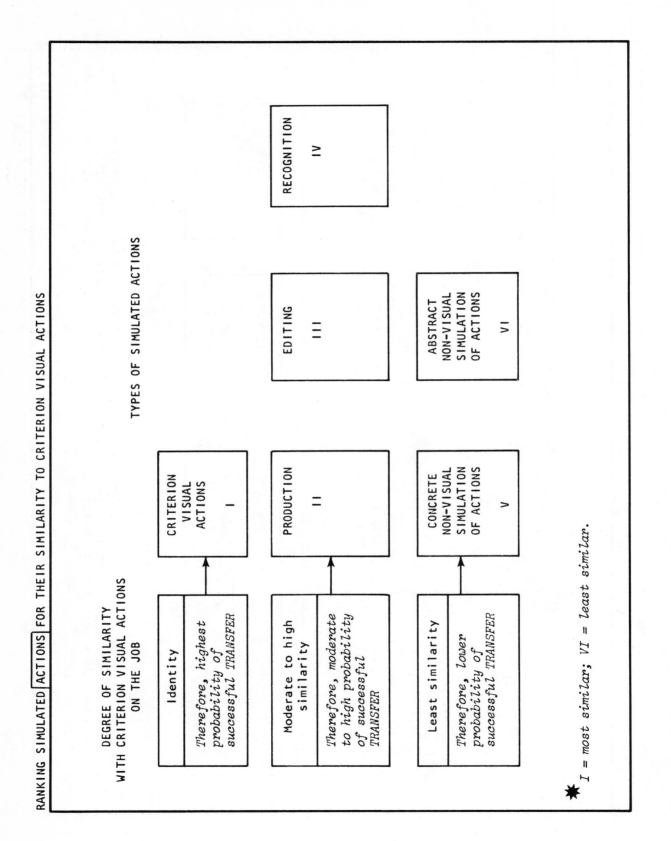

INSTRUCTIONAL PRIORITIES IN SELECTING TYPES OF SIMULATED [ACTIONS] TO INCLUDE IN TRAINING

TYPES OF ACTIONS

CRITERION VISUAL ACTIONS — I	EDITING — III	RECOGNITION — IV
PRODUCTION — II	ABSTRACT NON-VISUAL SIMULATION OF ACTIONS — VI	
CONCRETE NON-VISUAL SIMULATION OF ACTIONS — V		

FIRST PRIORITY: *Highest probability of successful TRANSFER* → CRITERION VISUAL ACTIONS

SECOND PRIORITY: *High probability of successful TRANSFER* → PRODUCTION

THIRD PRIORITY: *Lower probability of successful TRANSFER* → CONCRETE NON-VISUAL SIMULATION OF ACTIONS

✴ *I = most preferred; VI = least preferred.*

NOW DO EXERCISE #22 ON PAGES III.26 TO III.29 IN THE WORKBOOK.

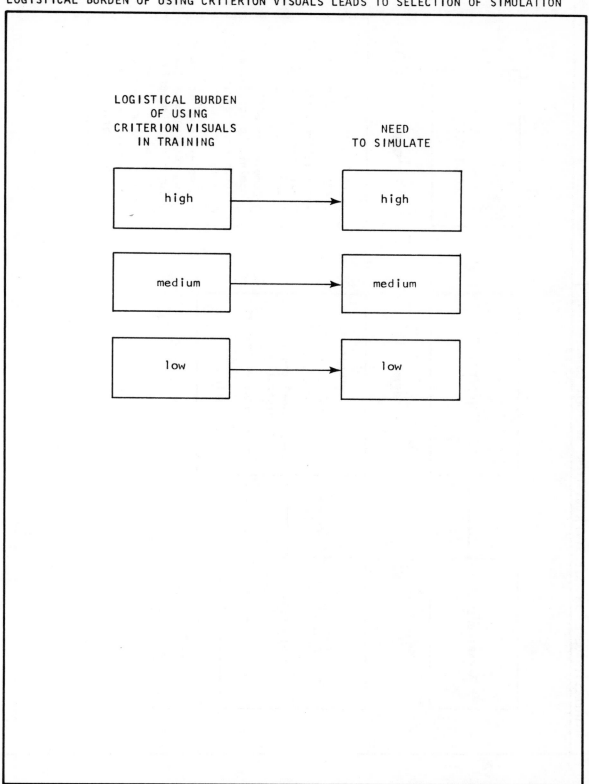

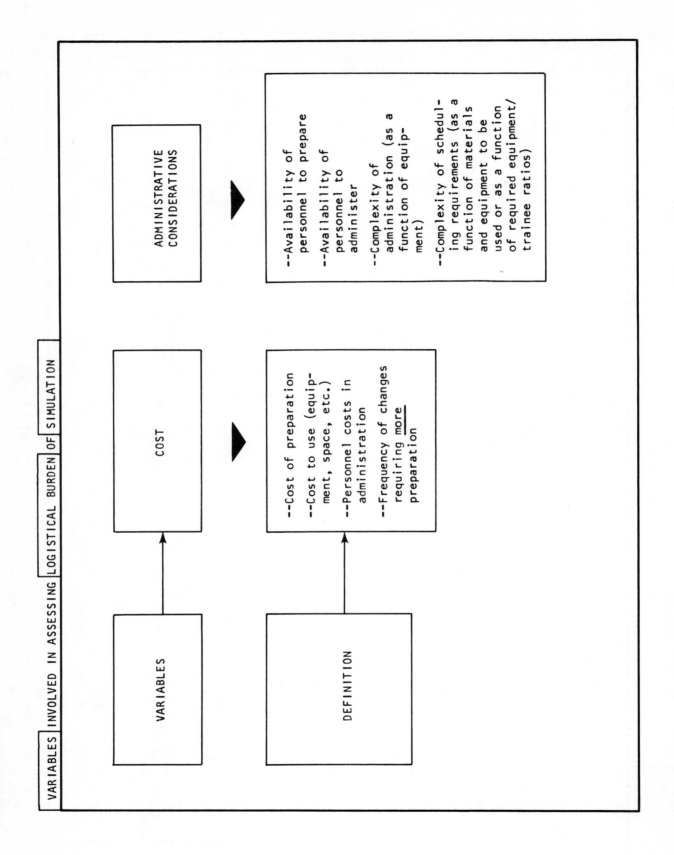

VARIABLES INVOLVED IN ASSESSING LOGISTICAL BURDEN OF SIMULATION

VARIABLES

COST

ADMINISTRATIVE
CONSIDERATIONS

DEFINITION

--Cost of preparation
--Cost to use (equip-
  ment, space, etc.)
--Personnel costs in
  administration
--Frequency of changes
  requiring more
  preparation

--Availability of
  personnel to prepare
--Availability of
  personnel to
  administer
--Complexity of
  administration (as a
  function of equip-
  ment)
--Complexity of schedul-
  ing requirements (as a
  function of materials
  and equipment to be
  used or as a function
  of required equipment/
  trainee ratios)

III.66

ILLUSTRATIVE COMPARATIVE RANKINGS OF VARIOUS TYPES OF SIMULATION AS TO THEIR LOGISTICAL BURDEN

GREATER LOGISTICAL BURDEN   vs.   LESSER LOGISTICAL BURDEN

	a		b		c
Comparison #1	Visual simulation	vs.		vs.	Paper-and-pencil non-visual simulation
Comparison #2	Film	vs.	Photographs	vs.	Sketches
Comparison #3	Animations	vs.	Slides	vs.	Photographs
Comparison #4	Three-dimensional functional mock-up	vs.	Photographs or films	vs.	

RELATIONSHIP BETWEEN LOGISTICAL CHARACTERISTICS OF PRACTICE
AND PRIORITIES IN SELECTION OF TYPE OF PRACTICE

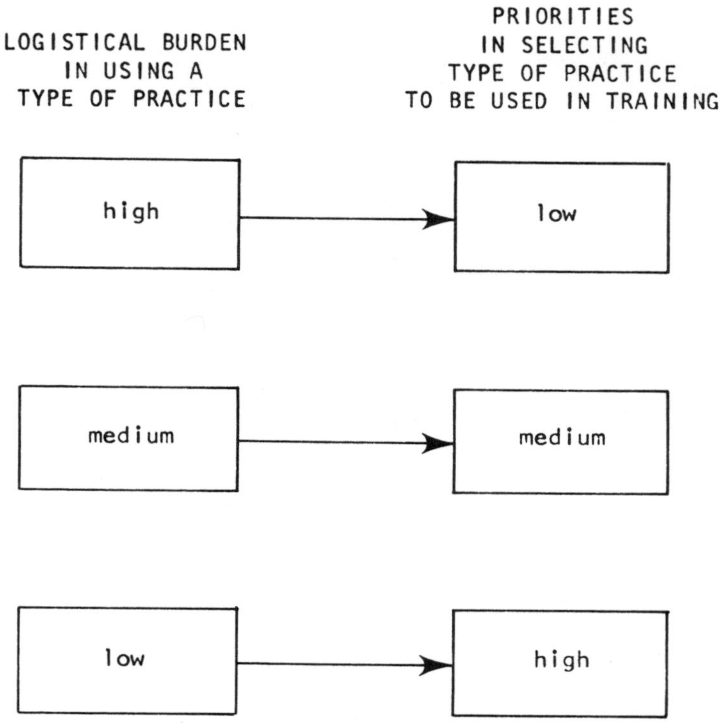

LOGISTICAL BURDEN
IN USING A
TYPE OF PRACTICE

PRIORITIES
IN SELECTING
TYPE OF PRACTICE
TO BE USED IN TRAINING

| high | → | low |

| medium | → | medium |

| low | → | high |

NOW DO EXERCISE #23 ON
PAGES III.30 TO III.31
IN THE WORKBOOK.

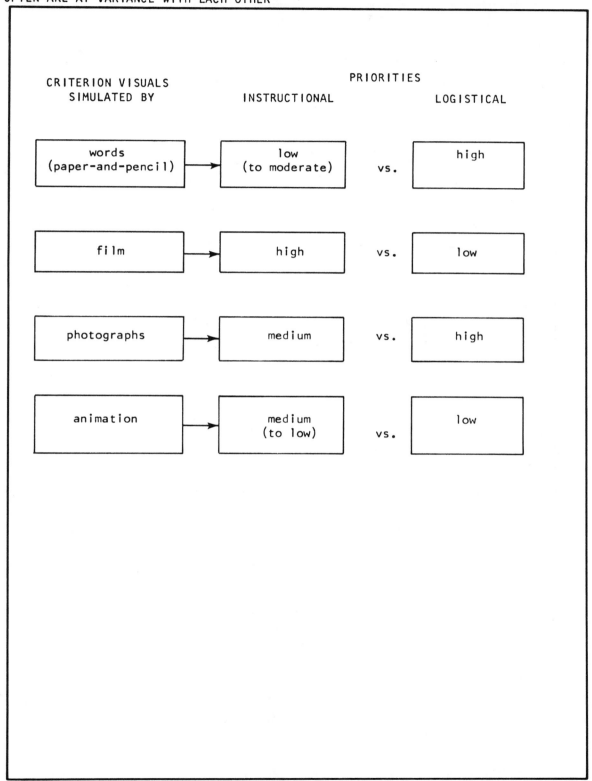

	CONDITIONS	RULES FOR SELECTING TYPE OF SIMULATION ✹
1.	There are <u>limitations</u> on the budget and resources that are available Logistical Burden <u>must</u> be considered	Select simulation with <u>highest instructional</u> priority (i.e., based on capacity to promote transfer) within the limitations of the budget *Biggest instructional bang for available bucks*
2.	There are <u>minimal</u> limitations on the budget and resources that are available Logistical Burden <u>may</u> be considered	Select simulation with <u>lowest</u> logistical burden (i.e., cheapest, easiest administratively) that leads to acceptable levels of transfer (instructional priority) *Smallest number of bucks for the same instructional bang*

✹*Decisions of this kind have to be <u>judgmental</u>.*

CRUCIAL INSTRUCTIONAL CONSIDERATIONS IN SETTLING ON COMPROMISE SIMULATION

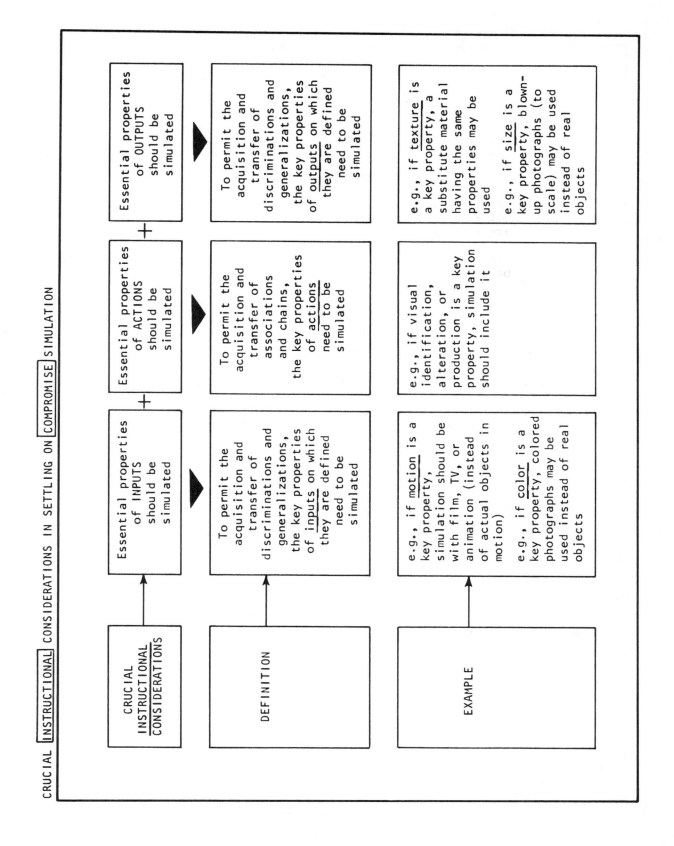

	Essential properties of INPUTS should be simulated	Essential properties of ACTIONS should be simulated	Essential properties of OUTPUTS should be simulated
CRUCIAL INSTRUCTIONAL CONSIDERATIONS			
DEFINITION	To permit the acquisition and transfer of discriminations and generalizations, the key properties of inputs on which they are defined need to be simulated	To permit the acquisition and transfer of associations and chains, the key properties of actions need to be simulated	To permit the acquisition and transfer of discriminations and generalizations, the key properties of outputs on which they are defined need to be simulated
EXAMPLE	e.g., if motion is a key property, simulation should be with film, TV, or animation (instead of actual objects in motion) e.g., if color is a key property, colored photographs may be used instead of real objects	e.g., if visual identification, alteration, or production is a key property, simulation should include it	e.g., if texture is a key property, a substitute material having the same properties may be used e.g., if size is a key property, blown-up photographs (to scale) may be used instead of real objects

EXAMPLES OF COMPROMISE SELECTION OF SIMULATION FOR CRITERION VISUALS

	EXAMPLE #1	EXAMPLE #2	EXAMPLE #3
Criterion visuals that have to be simulated (use in training criterion visuals themselves have been ruled out)	Job performance on production line (to be evaluated by foreman)	Molecular motion (in study of physics principles)	Complex electronic products a salesman has to describe and sell
HIGHEST INSTRUCTIONAL PRIORITY	Film of job performance	Animation of molecular motion	Functional working models
vs.			
HIGHEST LOGISTICAL PRIORITY	Written case study of job performance	Verbal description of molecular motion	Drawings or sketches of equipment
FINAL COMPROMISE DECISION	Photograph-assisted case study	Drawings of molecular motion	Photographs of equipment and equipment parts

NOW DO EXERCISE #24 ON PAGES III.32 TO III.33 IN THE WORKBOOK.

III.5   OBJECTIVES OF THIS UNIT

> At the end of this unit, you will be able to identify MEDIA REQUIREMENTS for SIMULATION OF CRITERION VISUALS.

DIAGRAM OF YOUR JOB

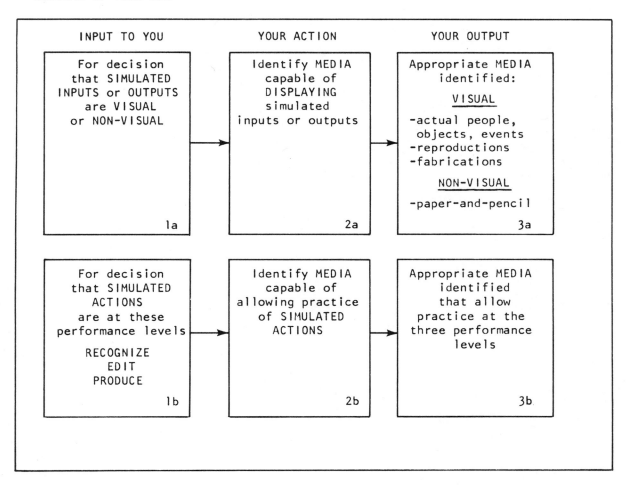

INPUT TO YOU	YOUR ACTION	YOUR OUTPUT
For decision that SIMULATED INPUTS or OUTPUTS are VISUAL or NON-VISUAL 1a	Identify MEDIA capable of DISPLAYING simulated inputs or outputs 2a	Appropriate MEDIA identified: VISUAL -actual people, objects, events -reproductions -fabrications NON-VISUAL -paper-and-pencil 3a
For decision that SIMULATED ACTIONS are at these performance levels RECOGNIZE EDIT PRODUCE 1b	Identify MEDIA capable of allowing practice of SIMULATED ACTIONS 2b	Appropriate MEDIA identified that allow practice at the three performance levels 3b

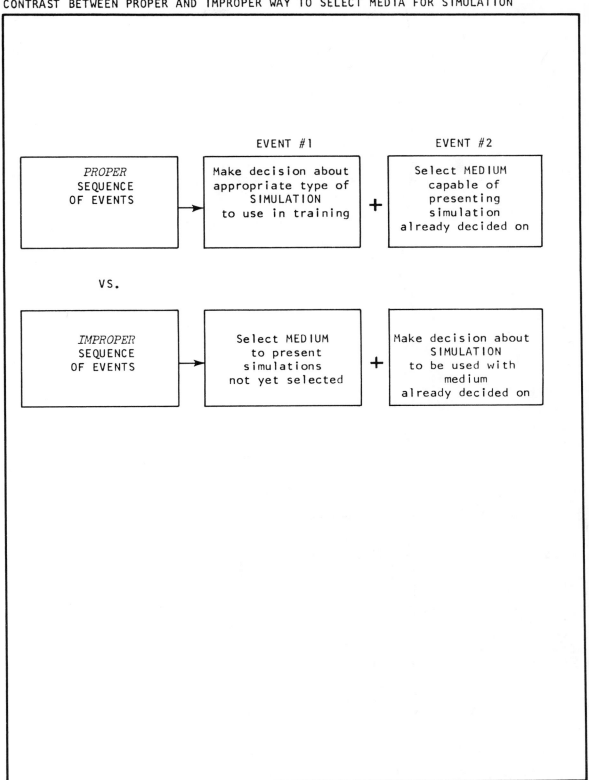

	REALISTIC VISUALS: Actual Objects Actual People Actual Events	REPRODUCTIONS	FABRICATIONS
TYPE OF MEDIA REQUIREMENT	►	►	►
CRITERION VISUALS used in practice	✕		
vs.			
SIMULATION used in practice	✕	✕	✕

* *Reproductions and fabrications are media candidates in CRITERION practice only for specialized jobs that typically include them, such as photographs for the photographer or paintings for the painter. All types of media are candidates for SIMULATED practice.*

SELECTION OF MEDIA IN SIMULATED PRACTICE IS LESS RESTRICTED THAN IN CRITERION PRACTICE

CRITERION PRACTICE

IN TRAINING

MEDIA REQUIREMENTS for Criterion Practice

JOB DIAGRAM

CRITERION VISUALS

Realistic Visuals

Realistic Visuals

Reproductions

Reproductions

Fabrications

Fabrications

SIMULATED PRACTICE

IN TRAINING

MEDIA POSSIBILITIES for Simulated Practice ✸

JOB DIAGRAM

CRITERION VISUALS

Realistic Visuals | Realistic Visuals | Reproductions | Fabrications

Reproductions | | Fabrications

Fabrications

✸ *The empty cells suggest that administratively and financially more costly media (or equally costly media) are less likely to be selected for simulation than less costly ones.*

III.81

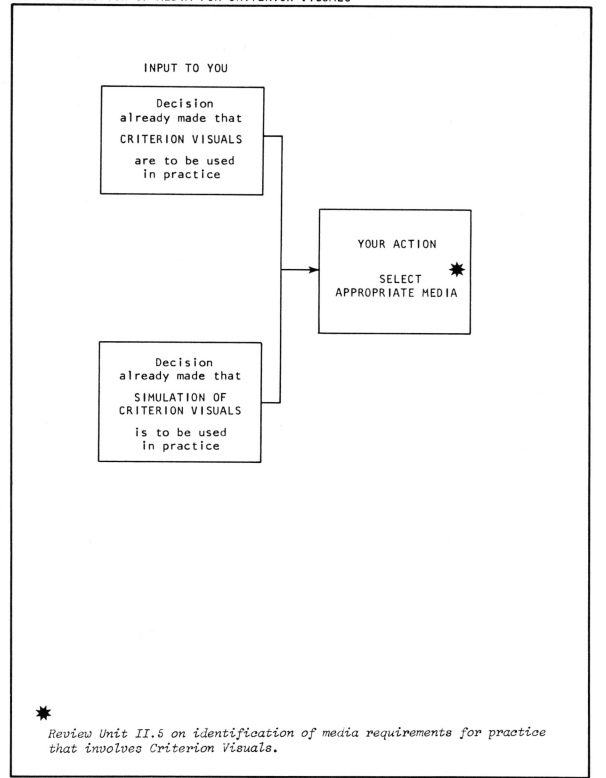

INPUT TO YOU

Decision
already made that
CRITERION VISUALS
are to be used
in practice

YOUR ACTION

SELECT
APPROPRIATE MEDIA

Decision
already made that
SIMULATION OF
CRITERION VISUALS
is to be used
in practice

*Review Unit II.5 on identification of media requirements for practice
that involves Criterion Visuals.*

NOW DO EXERCISE #25 ON
PAGES III.34 TO III.35
IN THE WORKBOOK.

PART I

Introduction to the Use of Visuals in Instruction

PART II

The Use of Criterion Visuals in Instruction

PART III

The Use of Simulated Criterion Visuals in Instruction

PART IV

√ The Use of Mediating Visuals in Instruction

PART V

Procedures to Follow in Selecting and Using Visuals
in Instruction

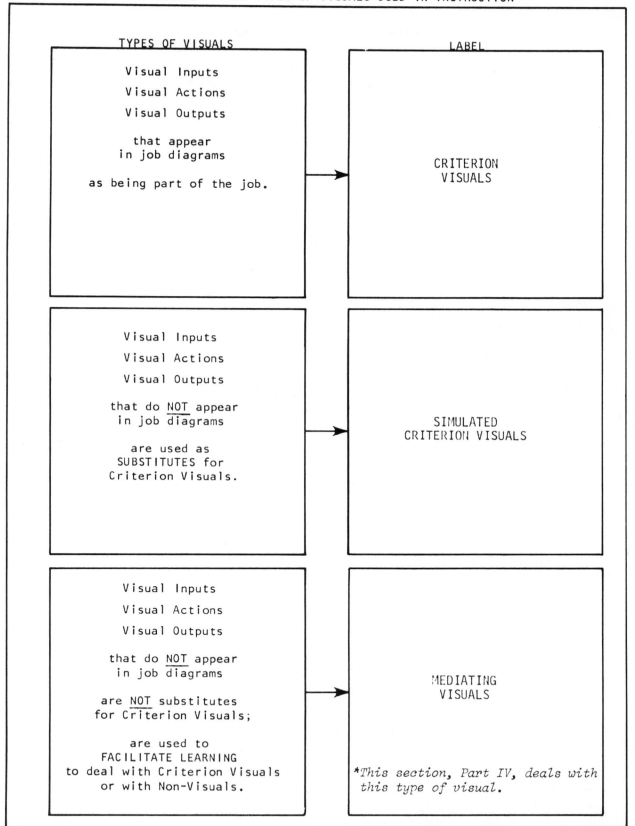

TYPES OF VISUALS

Visual Inputs

Visual Actions

Visual Outputs

that appear
in job diagrams

as being part of the job.

LABEL

CRITERION
VISUALS

Visual Inputs

Visual Actions

Visual Outputs

that do NOT appear
in job diagrams

are used as
SUBSTITUTES for
Criterion Visuals.

SIMULATED
CRITERION VISUALS

Visual Inputs

Visual Actions

Visual Outputs

that do NOT appear
in job diagrams

are NOT substitutes
for Criterion Visuals;

are used to
FACILITATE LEARNING
to deal with Criterion Visuals
or with Non-Visuals.

MEDIATING
VISUALS

*This section, Part IV, deals with
this type of visual.

PART IV

The Use of <u>Mediating</u> Visuals in Instruction

OBJECTIVES

IV.1   Distinguishing Between CRITERION PERFORMANCE and
        ASSISTED PERFORMANCE and Identifying Conditions
        Calling for Each

IV.2   Identifying Ways in Which MEDIATING VISUALS Can
        Provide ASSISTANCE in Lessening the Difficulties of
        Criterion Performance

IV.3   Identifying and Producing the Major Types of
        MEDIATING VISUALS

IV.4   Identifying MEDIA REQUIREMENTS When Using MEDIATING
        VISUALS in Instruction

IV.1   OBJECTIVES OF THIS UNIT

> At the end of this unit, you will be able to distinguish between CRITERION PERFORMANCE and ASSISTED PERFORMANCE and to identify CONDITIONS calling for each type.

DIAGRAM OF YOUR JOB

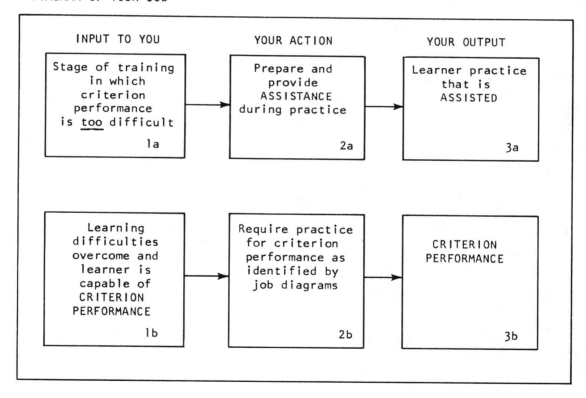

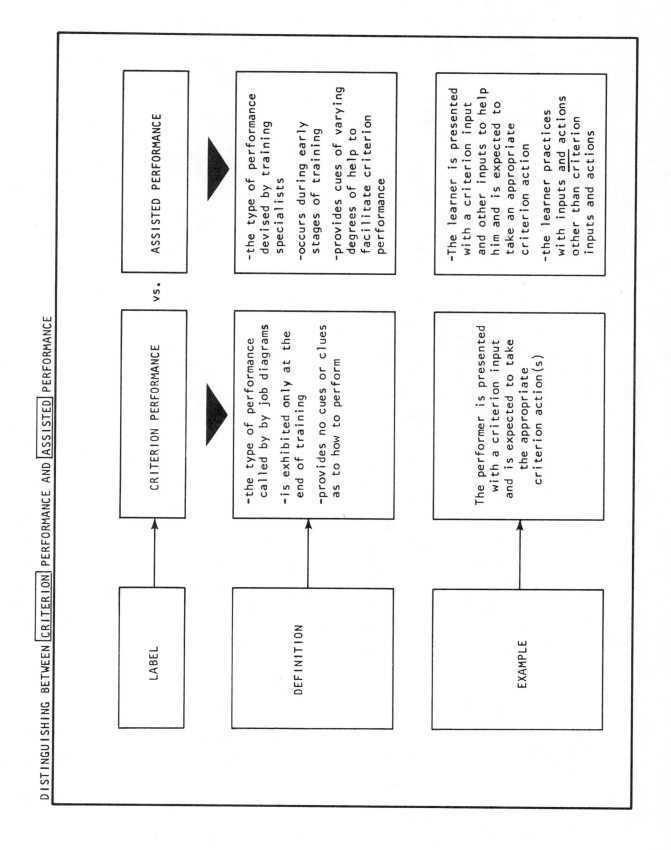

LABEL

CRITERION PERFORMANCE

vs.

ASSISTED PERFORMANCE

DEFINITION

-the type of performance called by job diagrams

-is exhibited only at the end of training

-provides no cues or clues as to how to perform

-the type of performance devised by training specialists

-occurs during early stages of training

-provides cues of varying degrees of help to facilitate criterion performance

EXAMPLE

The performer is presented with a criterion input and is expected to take the appropriate criterion action(s)

-The learner is presented with a criterion input and other inputs to help him and is expected to take an appropriate criterion action

-the learner practices with inputs and actions other than criterion inputs and actions

EXAMPLES OF NON-VISUAL CRITERION PERFORMANCE AND ASSISTED PERFORMANCE

	EXAMPLE #1	EXAMPLE #2	EXAMPLE #3
JOB TASK	Training specialist giving lecture on programmed instruction	Electronics maintenance man performs on qualifying test on basic electronics	Physics student
CRITERION PERFORMANCE on the job	Defines "programmed instruction" for class (without notes)	Given test question: "What is a semi-conductor," gives verbal definition	On test: describes the difference between perfectly and non-perfectly elastic objects
vs.			
ASSISTED PERFORMANCE during training	From notes defines "programmed instruction" (as he rehearses lecture)	With training aid in front of him, answers question, "What is a semiconductor?"	During training, with examples in front of him, describes the difference between perfectly and non-perfectly elastic objects

EXAMPLES OF [VISUAL] CRITERION PERFORMANCE AND ASSISTED PERFORMANCE

	EXAMPLE #1	EXAMPLE #2	EXAMPLE #3
JOB TASK	Television repairman repairs TV set	Airplane spotter	Draftsman
CRITERION PERFORMANCE on the job	When presented with a symptom (e.g., rolling image), diagnoses problem and makes appropriate adjustment	When he sees an enemy plane, reports type of plane spotted	From verbal request, draws blueprints
vs.			
ASSISTED PERFORMANCE during training	In addition to being presented with a symptom, may be given photographs of various types of symptoms for malfunction categories makes adjustments based on assisted diagnosis	In training, is allowed to consult guide to types of planes when he reports type of plane spotted	In training, may be allowed to keep model or sample drawing in front of him as he draws blueprints

CRITICAL DIFFERENCES BETWEEN CRITERION PERFORMANCE AND ASSISTED PERFORMANCE

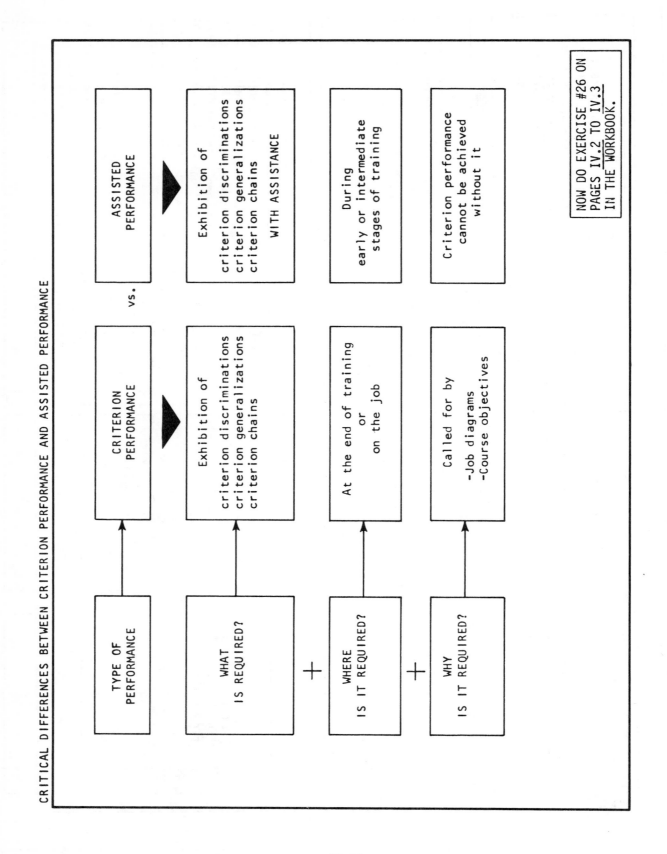

	CRITERION PERFORMANCE	vs.	ASSISTED PERFORMANCE
TYPE OF PERFORMANCE			
WHAT IS REQUIRED?	Exhibition of criterion discriminations criterion generalizations criterion chains		Exhibition of criterion discriminations criterion generalizations criterion chains WITH ASSISTANCE
+ WHERE IS IT REQUIRED?	At the end of training or on the job		During early or intermediate stages of training
+ WHY IS IT REQUIRED?	Called for by -Job diagrams -Course objectives		Criterion performance cannot be achieved without it

NOW DO EXERCISE #26 ON PAGES IV.2 TO IV.3 IN THE WORKBOOK.

IV.12

CONDITIONS THAT MAKE DISCRIMINATIONS AMONG INPUTS DIFFICULT AND MAKE ASSISTANCE NECESSARY

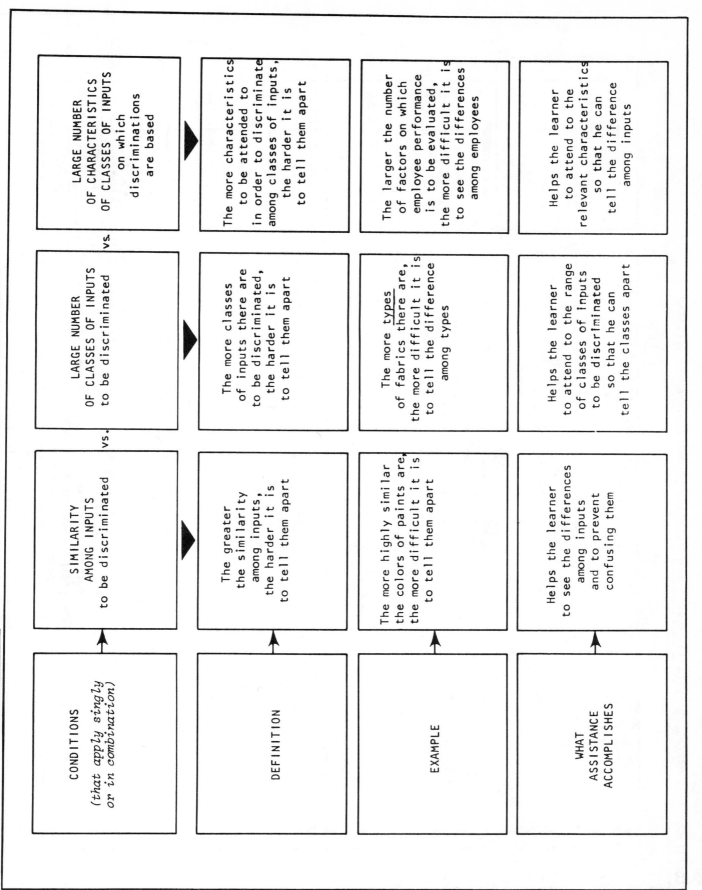

CONDITIONS (that apply singly or in combination)	SIMILARITY AMONG INPUTS to be discriminated	vs.	LARGE NUMBER OF CLASSES OF INPUTS to be discriminated	vs.	LARGE NUMBER OF CHARACTERISTICS OF CLASSES OF INPUTS on which discriminations are based
DEFINITION	The greater the similarity among inputs, the harder it is to tell them apart		The more classes of inputs there are to be discriminated, the harder it is to tell them apart		The more characteristics to be attended to in order to discriminate among classes of inputs, the harder it is to tell them apart
EXAMPLE	The more highly similar the colors of paints are, the more difficult it is to tell them apart		The more types of fabrics there are, the more difficult it is to tell the difference among types		The larger the number of factors on which employee performance is to be evaluated, the more difficult it is to see the differences among employees
WHAT ASSISTANCE ACCOMPLISHES	Helps the learner to see the differences among inputs and to prevent confusing them		Helps the learner to attend to the range of classes of inputs to be discriminated so that he can tell the classes apart		Helps the learner to attend to the relevant characteristics so that he can tell the difference among inputs

	CONDITIONS (that apply singly or in combination)		
CONDITIONS (that apply singly or in combination)	DISSIMILARITY AMONG INPUTS WITHIN A CLASS requiring generalization	vs. LARGE NUMBER OF INPUTS IN A CLASS OF INPUTS requiring generalization	vs. LARGE NUMBER OF CHARACTERISTICS OF INPUTS on which generalizations are based
DEFINITION	The greater the apparent dissimilarity among inputs belonging to the same class, the harder it is to see their essential similarity	The more inputs there are belonging to the same class, the harder it is to see them belonging to the same class	The more characteristics to be attended to in order to generalize across inputs, the harder it is to see them belonging to the same class
EXAMPLE	Symptoms of malfunctions in the horizontal circuit of a TV set can be as dissimilar as: jagged diagonal lines, shrinking picture, or vertical lines	The more types of man-made fibers there are, the harder it is to see them belonging to the same class (man-made)	The more characteristics to attend to in judging the quality of performance, the harder it is to see the similarity of the same level of performance
WHAT ASSISTANCE ACCOMPLISHES	Helps the learner to see the essential similarity among inputs belonging to the same class and prevents seeing them as being different	Helps the learner to treat all inputs that belong to the same class as members of that class	Helps the learner to attend to the relevant characteristics so that he can see the similarity among inputs

IV.14

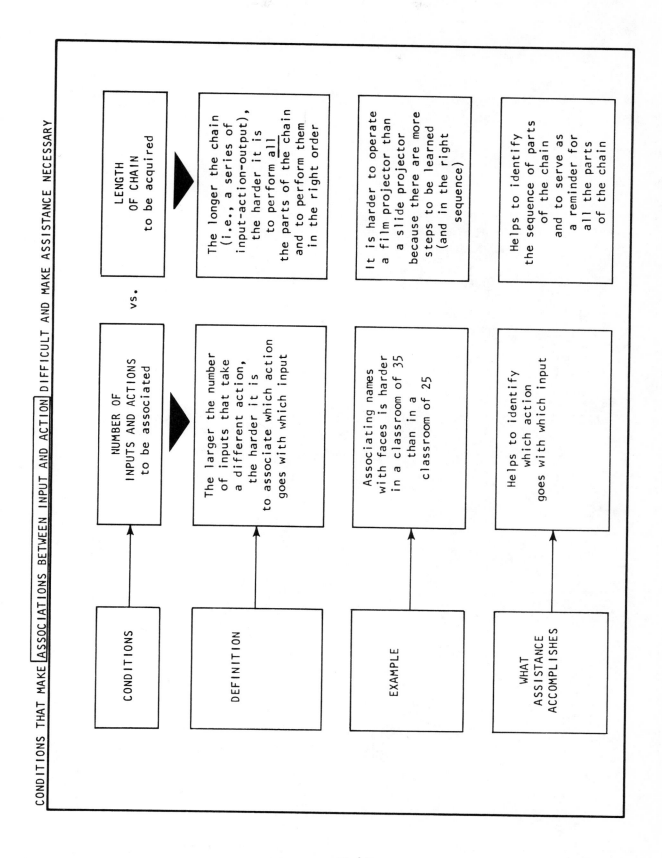

LENGTH
OF CHAIN
to be acquired

vs.

NUMBER OF
INPUTS AND ACTIONS
to be associated

CONDITIONS

The longer the chain
(i.e., a series of
input-action-output),
the harder it is
to perform all
the parts of the chain
and to perform them
in the right order

The larger the number
of inputs that take
a different action,
the harder it is
to associate which action
goes with which input

DEFINITION

It is harder to operate
a film projector than
a slide projector
because there are more
steps to be learned
(and in the right
sequence)

Associating names
with faces
in a classroom of 35
than in a
classroom of 25

EXAMPLE

Helps to identify
the sequence of parts
of the chain
and to serve as
a reminder for
all the parts
of the chain

Helps to identify
which action
goes with which input

WHAT
ASSISTANCE
ACCOMPLISHES

SUMMARY OF PROBLEMS IN THE WAY OF CRITERION PERFORMANCE THAT MAKE ASSISTANCE NECESSARY

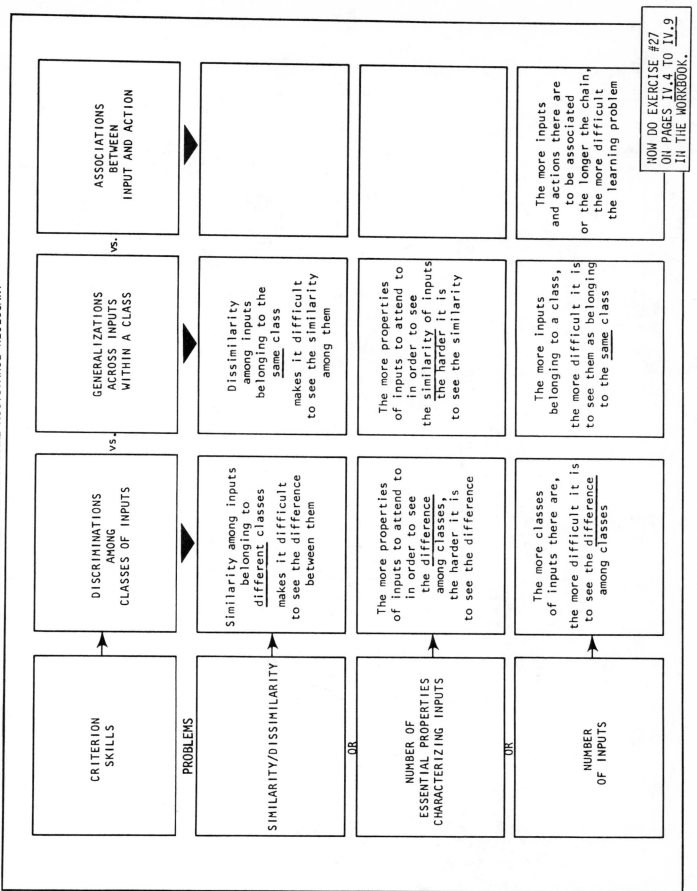

CRITERION
SKILLS

DISCRIMINATIONS
AMONG
CLASSES OF INPUTS

vs.

GENERALIZATIONS
ACROSS INPUTS
WITHIN A CLASS

vs.

ASSOCIATIONS
BETWEEN
INPUT AND ACTION

PROBLEMS

SIMILARITY/DISSIMILARITY

Similarity among inputs
belonging to
different classes
makes it difficult
to see the difference
between them

Dissimilarity
among inputs
belonging to the
same class
makes it difficult
to see the similarity
among them

OR

NUMBER OF
ESSENTIAL PROPERTIES
CHARACTERIZING INPUTS

The more properties
of inputs to attend to
in order to see
the difference
among classes,
the harder it is
to see the difference

The more properties
of inputs to attend to
in order to see
the similarity of inputs
the harder it is
to see the similarity

OR

NUMBER
OF INPUTS

The more classes
of inputs there are,
the more difficult it is
to see the difference
among classes

The more inputs
belonging to a class,
the more difficult it is
to see them as belonging
to the same class

The more inputs
and actions there are
to be associated
or the longer the chain,
the more difficult
the learning problem

NOW DO EXERCISE #27
ON PAGES IV.4 TO IV.9
IN THE WORKBOOK.

IV.2 OBJECTIVES OF THIS UNIT

> At the end of this unit, you will be able to identify ways in which MEDIATING VISUALS can provide ASSISTANCE to lessen the difficulties of criterion performance.

DIAGRAM OF YOUR JOB

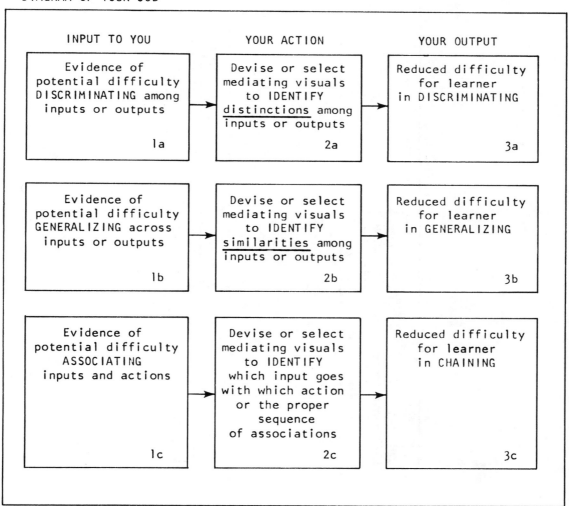

INPUT TO YOU	YOUR ACTION	YOUR OUTPUT
Evidence of potential difficulty DISCRIMINATING among inputs or outputs 1a	Devise or select mediating visuals to IDENTIFY distinctions among inputs or outputs 2a	Reduced difficulty for learner in DISCRIMINATING 3a
Evidence of potential difficulty GENERALIZING across inputs or outputs 1b	Devise or select mediating visuals to IDENTIFY similarities among inputs or outputs 2b	Reduced difficulty for learner in GENERALIZING 3b
Evidence of potential difficulty ASSOCIATING inputs and actions 1c	Devise or select mediating visuals to IDENTIFY which input goes with which action or the proper sequence of associations 2c	Reduced difficulty for learner in CHAINING 3c

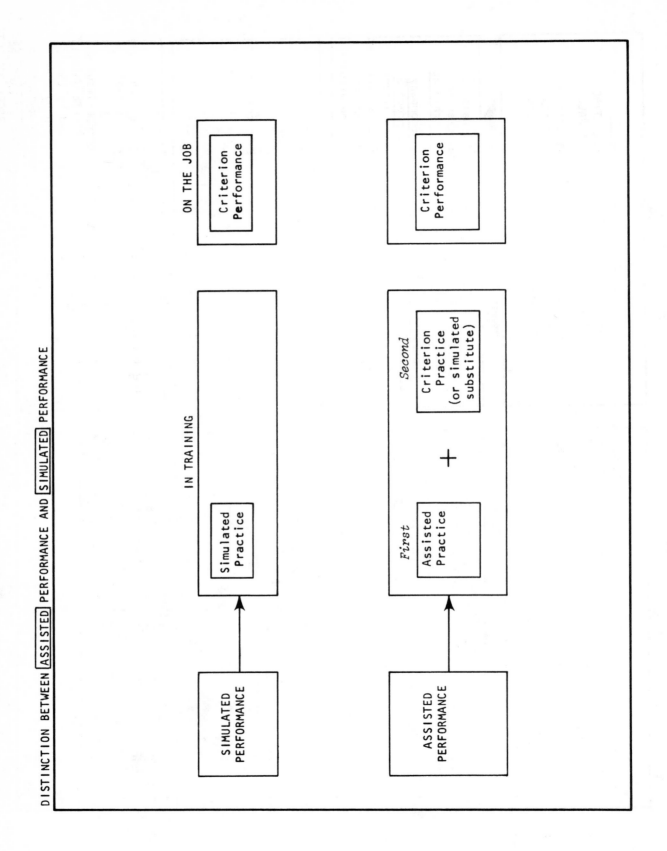

DISTINCTION BETWEEN ASSISTED PERFORMANCE AND SIMULATED PERFORMANCE

IN TRAINING

ON THE JOB

SIMULATED PERFORMANCE

Simulated Practice

Criterion Performance

ASSISTED PERFORMANCE

First

Assisted Practice

+

Second

Criterion Practice (or simulated substitute)

Criterion Performance

DESCRIPTION OF THE THREE TYPES OF VISUALS USED IN TRAINING

	CRITERION VISUALS	vs.	SIMULATED VISUALS	vs.	MEDIATING VISUALS
LABEL	inputs actions outputs		inputs actions outputs		inputs actions outputs
DEFINITION	Visuals identified by job diagrams to be part of job performance (or criterion performance)		Visuals selected for use in training as substitutes as criterion visuals		Visuals selected for use in training to accompany or to precede criterion visuals (or simulated substitutes for them) or criterion non-visuals
WHERE THEY APPEAR	on the job and (whenever possible) in training		only in training		only in training
WHY THEY ARE USED IN TRAINING	They make the best kind of practice; transfer to the job is easiest		The logistical burden of using criterion visuals is too high		Practice with criterion visuals or with criterion non-visuals is too difficult unless accompanied by them or preceded by them *they provide assistance*

NOW DO EXERCISE #28 ON PAGES IV.10 TO IV.11 IN THE WORKBOOK.

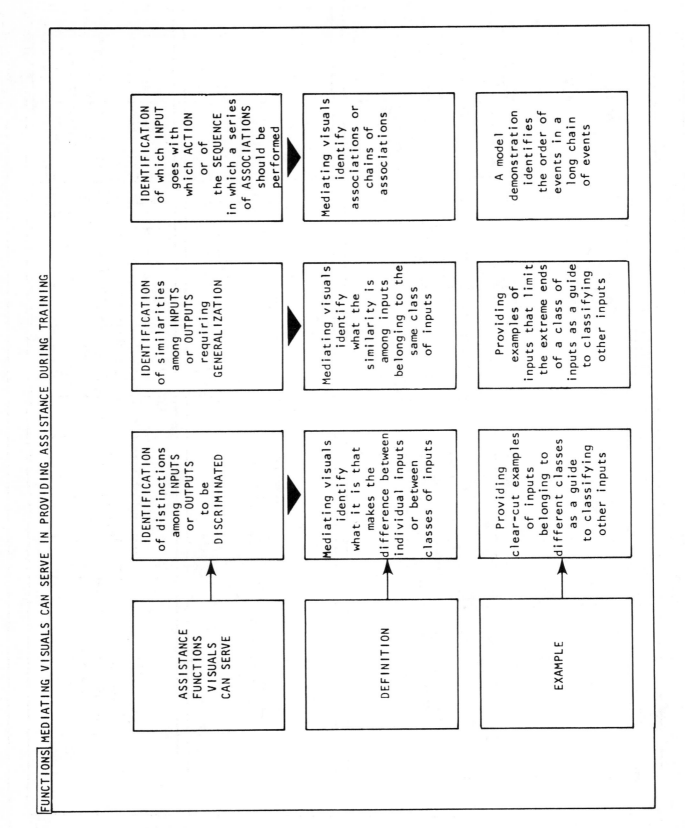

FUNCTIONS MEDIATING VISUALS CAN SERVE IN PROVIDING ASSISTANCE DURING TRAINING

ASSISTANCE FUNCTIONS VISUALS CAN SERVE

IDENTIFICATION of distinctions among INPUTS or OUTPUTS to be DISCRIMINATED

IDENTIFICATION of similarities among INPUTS or OUTPUTS requiring GENERALIZATION

IDENTIFICATION of which INPUT goes with which ACTION or of the SEQUENCE in which a series of ASSOCIATIONS should be performed

DEFINITION

Mediating visuals identify what it is that makes the difference between individual inputs or between classes of inputs

Mediating visuals identify what the similarity is among inputs belonging to the same class of inputs

Mediating visuals identify associations or chains of associations

EXAMPLE

Providing clear-cut examples of inputs belonging to different classes as a guide to classifying other inputs

Providing examples of inputs that limit the extreme ends of a class of inputs as a guide to classifying other inputs

A model demonstration identifies the order of events in a long chain of events

IV.22

EXAMPLES OF HOW MEDIATING VISUALS PROVIDE ASSISTANCE FOR | DISCRIMINATIONS |

	EXAMPLE #1	EXAMPLE #2	EXAMPLE #3
JOB TASKS	TV repairman diagnosing problems and correcting them	Seaman identifying classes of ships	Movie projectionist threading film through projector (e.g., making loops)
Assisting DISCRIMINATIONS among INPUTS	Photographs of the different spacing between horizontal lines running through picture indicating good and poor vertical linearity adjustment	Overlay used over photographs of ships calls attention to key property in the distinction among classes of ships: e.g., overlay outlines number of stacks	
or			
Assisting DISCRIMINATIONS among OUTPUTS	Some photographs can be used after adjustments are made to discriminate between properly adjusted and improperly adjusted vertical linearity		Markers indicating when a loop is O.K. and when it is either too high or too low

IV.23

EXAMPLES OF HOW MEDIATING VISUALS PROVIDE ASSISTANCE FOR GENERALIZATIONS

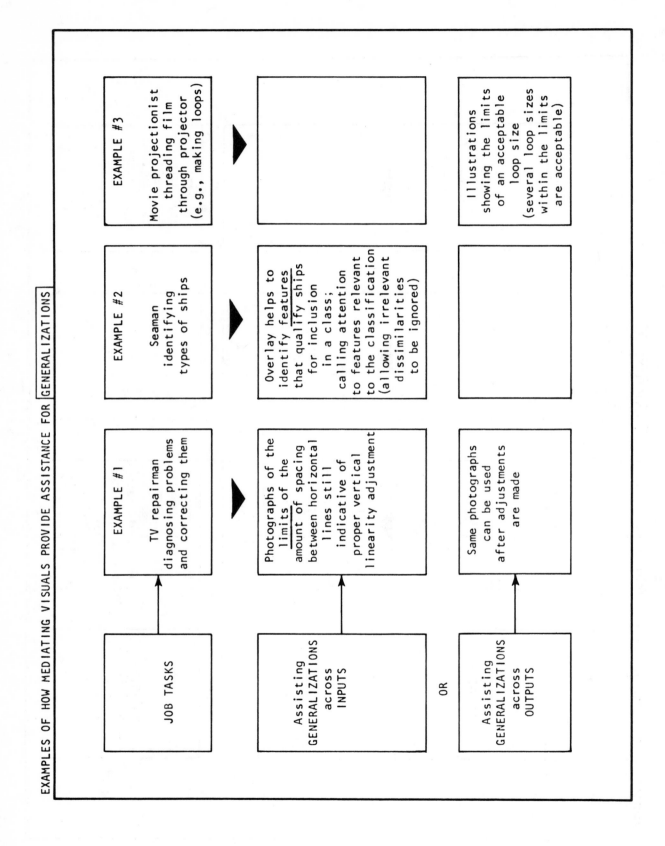

EXAMPLE #1

TV repairman
diagnosing problems
and correcting them

EXAMPLE #2

Seaman
identifying
types of ships

EXAMPLE #3

Movie projectionist
threading film
through projector
(e.g., making loops)

JOB TASKS

Assisting
GENERALIZATIONS
across
INPUTS

Photographs of the
limits of the
amount of spacing
between horizontal
lines still
indicative of
proper vertical
linearity adjustment

Overlay helps to
identify features
that qualify ships
for inclusion
in a class;
calling attention
to features relevant
to the classification
(allowing irrelevant
dissimilarities
to be ignored)

Illustrations
showing the limits
of an acceptable
loop size
(several loop sizes
within the limits
are acceptable)

OR

Assisting
GENERALIZATIONS
across
OUTPUTS

Same photographs
can be used
after adjustments
are made

EXAMPLE #1

TV repairman diagnosing problems and correcting them

JOB TASKS

A catalogue of photographs of symptoms and the corrective actions to be taken for each problem helps the learner to associate input and action

Assisting ASSOCIATIONS between INPUTS and ACTIONS

or

A diagram may be used to identify a preferred sequence of troubleshooting operations

Assisting CHAINING of a series of ASSOCIATIONS

EXAMPLE #2

Soldier has to disassemble and assemble a rifle

Demonstration of the procedures facilitates learning the sequence of events

EXAMPLE #3

Movie projectionist has to perform all the operations in threading a projector

Illustrative diagram identifies the action to be taken when a new input is reached (i.e., the output of a previous step)

Live or filmed demonstrations of the entire threading operations assists the learner to follow all procedures in correct sequence

IV.25

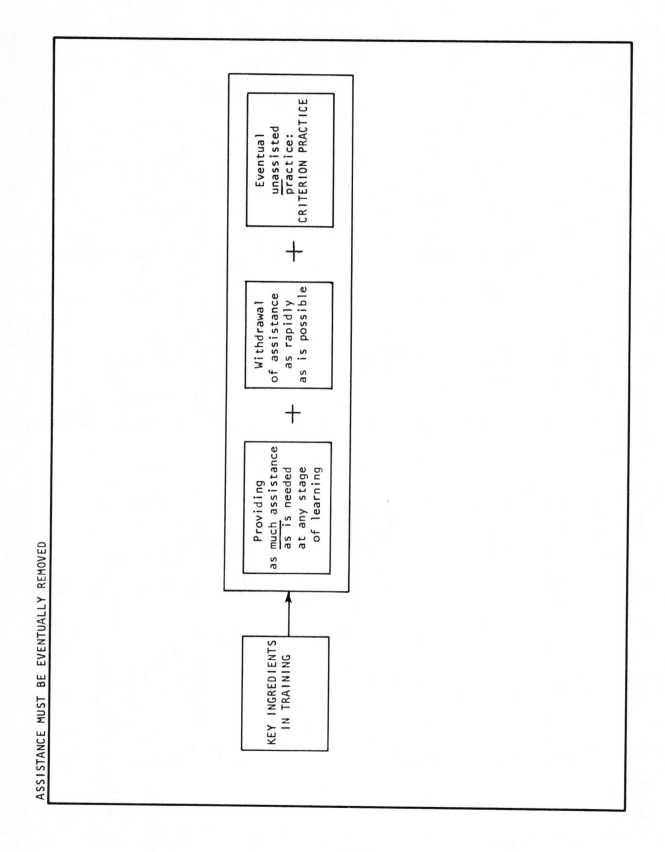

ASSISTANCE MUST BE EVENTUALLY REMOVED

KEY INGREDIENTS
IN TRAINING

Providing
as much assistance
as is needed
at any stage
of learning

+

Withdrawal
of assistance
as rapidly
as is possible

+

Eventual
unassisted
practice:
CRITERION PRACTICE

IV.26

RELATIONSHIP BETWEEN THE DIFFICULTY OF CRITERION PERFORMANCE AND AMOUNT OF ASSISTANCE PROVIDED

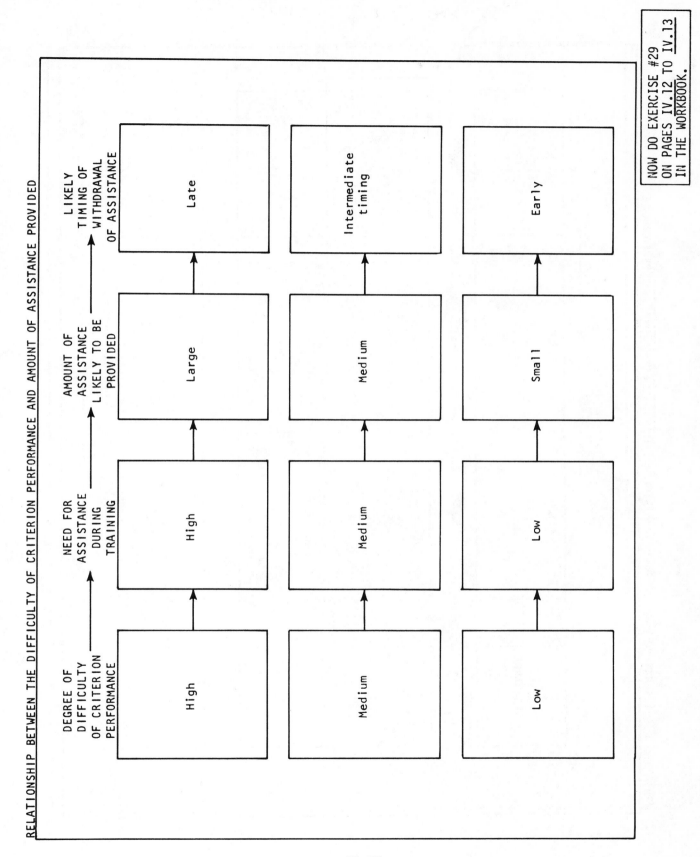

NOW DO EXERCISE #29 ON PAGES IV.12 TO IV.13 IN THE WORKBOOK.

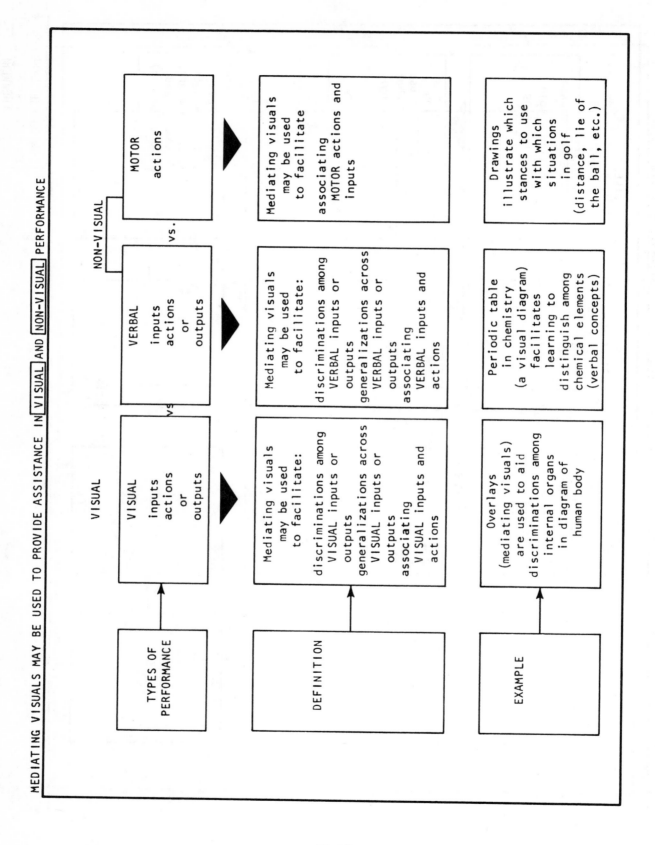

EXAMPLES OF THE USE OF MEDIATING ASSISTANCE PROVIDING ASSISTANCE IN THE [THREE] TYPES OF PERFORMANCE

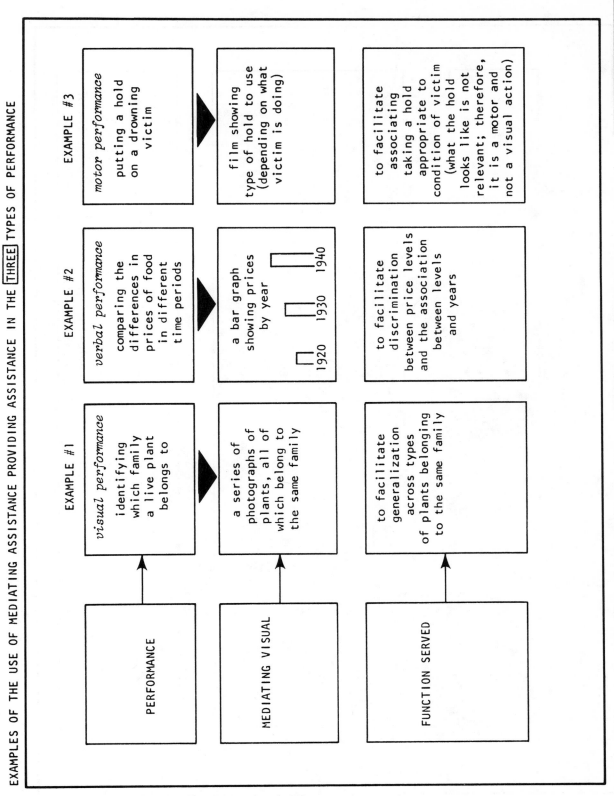

	EXAMPLE #1	EXAMPLE #2	EXAMPLE #3
PERFORMANCE	*visual performance* identifying which family a live plant belongs to	*verbal performance* comparing the differences in prices of food in different time periods	*motor performance* putting a hold on a drowning victim
MEDIATING VISUAL	a series of photographs of plants, all of which belong to the same family	a bar graph showing prices by year 1920 1930 1940	film showing type of hold to use (depending on what victim is doing)
FUNCTION SERVED	to facilitate generalization across types of plants belonging to the same family	to facilitate discrimination between price levels and the association between levels and years	to facilitate associating taking a hold appropriate to condition of victim (what the hold looks like is not relevant; therefore, it is a motor and not a visual action)

NOW DO EXERCISE #30
ON PAGES IV.14 TO IV.15
IN THE WORKBOOK.

IV.3   OBJECTIVES OF THIS UNIT

At the end of this unit, you will be able to IDENTIFY and PRODUCE the major types of MEDIATING VISUALS.

DIAGRAM OF YOUR JOB

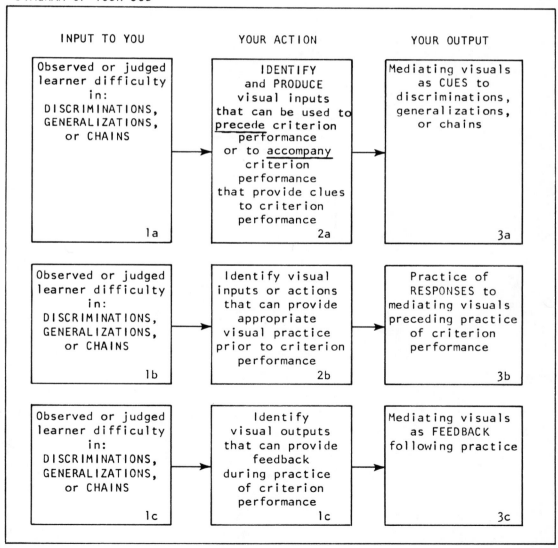

INPUT TO YOU	YOUR ACTION	YOUR OUTPUT
Observed or judged learner difficulty in: DISCRIMINATIONS, GENERALIZATIONS, or CHAINS 1a	IDENTIFY and PRODUCE visual inputs that can be used to precede criterion performance or to accompany criterion performance that provide clues to criterion performance 2a	Mediating visuals as CUES to discriminations, generalizations, or chains 3a
Observed or judged learner difficulty in: DISCRIMINATIONS, GENERALIZATIONS, or CHAINS 1b	Identify visual inputs or actions that can provide appropriate visual practice prior to criterion performance 2b	Practice of RESPONSES to mediating visuals preceding practice of criterion performance 3b
Observed or judged learner difficulty in: DISCRIMINATIONS, GENERALIZATIONS, or CHAINS 1c	Identify visual outputs that can provide feedback during practice of criterion performance 1c	Mediating visuals as FEEDBACK following practice 3c

OVERVIEW: THREE USES OF MEDIATING VISUALS TO FACILITATE CRITERION PERFORMANCE

	TYPE I	TYPE II	TYPE III
TYPES OF MEDIATING VISUALS	Mediating visuals as CUES	RESPONSES to mediating visuals	Mediating visuals as FEEDBACK
DEFINITION	Visuals used during practice to provide a clue about correct criterion performance	Practice involving inputs and/or actions other than those found in criterion performance	Use of feedback about correctness of performance other than the type found in criterion performance
EXAMPLE	Visuals assist: -discriminations about or generalizations across criterion inputs -associations between criterion inputs and actions	Practice involving visuals when criterion performance involves non-visuals	During practice, feedback is visual when in criterion performance it is non-visual
SEE FURTHER DISCUSSION	Pages IV.35 to IV.51	Pages IV.53 to IV.81	Pages IV.83 to IV.87

IV.3.a   OBJECTIVES OF THIS SUBUNIT

> At the end of this subunit, you will be able to IDENTIFY and PRODUCE mediating visuals that can serve as $\boxed{\text{CUES}}$ to aid in the learning of discriminations, generalizations, or chains.

DIAGRAM OF YOUR JOB

INPUT TO YOU	YOUR ACTION	YOUR OUTPUT
Long chain to be learned: all operations must be performed and they must be performed in the correct sequence. 1a	Develop a model performance (actual or on film) demonstrating the entire operations. 2a	Model demonstration that can be shown to the learner before he begins practicing the chain. 3a
Potential difficulties for the learner in learning discriminations, generalizations, or chains in visual, verbal, or motor performances. 1b	Develop visual cues that facilitate the practice of the discriminations, generalizations, or chains. 2b	Visual cues that can accompany and make the practice of discriminations, generalizations, or chains easier. 3b

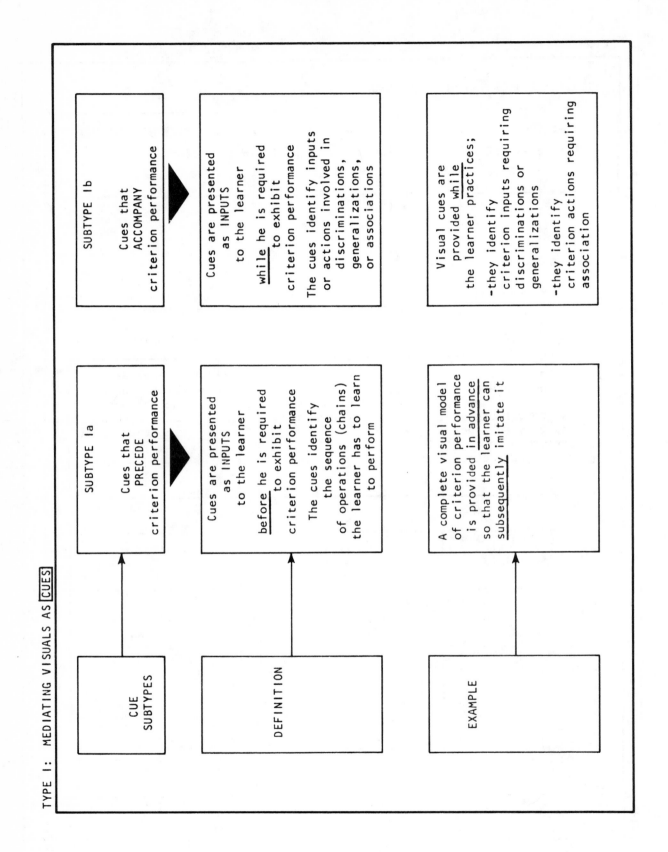

TYPE I: MEDIATING VISUALS AS [CUES]

CUE SUBTYPES

SUBTYPE Ia

Cues that
PRECEDE
criterion performance

SUBTYPE Ib

Cues that
ACCOMPANY
criterion performance

DEFINITION

Cues are presented
as INPUTS
to the learner

before he is required
to exhibit
criterion performance

The cues identify
the sequence
of operations (chains)
the learner has to learn
to perform

Cues are presented
as INPUTS
to the learner

while he is required
to exhibit
criterion performance

The cues identify inputs
or actions involved in
discriminations,
generalizations,
or associations

EXAMPLE

A complete visual model
of criterion performance
is provided in advance
so that the learner can
subsequently imitate it

Visual cues are
provided while
the learner practices;

-they identify
criterion inputs requiring
discriminations or
generalizations

-they identify
criterion actions requiring
association

EXAMPLES OF TWO [SUBTYPES] OF [VISUAL CUES]

	EXAMPLE #1	EXAMPLE #2	EXAMPLE #3
JOB TASK	Mechanic performs maintenance functions on carburetor	A dancer performing a new dance	Operator of movie projector threads film through projector
SUBTYPES *Ia* CUES THAT PRECEDE PRACTICE OF CRITERION SKILLS	The learner first sees a film demonstrating the disassembly of part of the carburetor; the learner then disassembles the <u>same part</u>.	Choreographer demonstrates steps to take. Dancer then imitates the same steps.	A demonstration provides a model for the operator of how to thread the projector. After seeing the demonstration, he threads the projector.
vs. *Ib* CUES THAT <u>ACCOMPANY</u> PRACTICE OF CRITERION SKILLS	The learner sees a series of photographs involving the disassembly of a carburetor; with each photograph in front of him, he takes the appropriate action on an actual carburetor.	Steps are marked out on the floor; dancer follows and practices the marked out steps.	<u>Diagram aids the operator</u> as he threads the whole film.

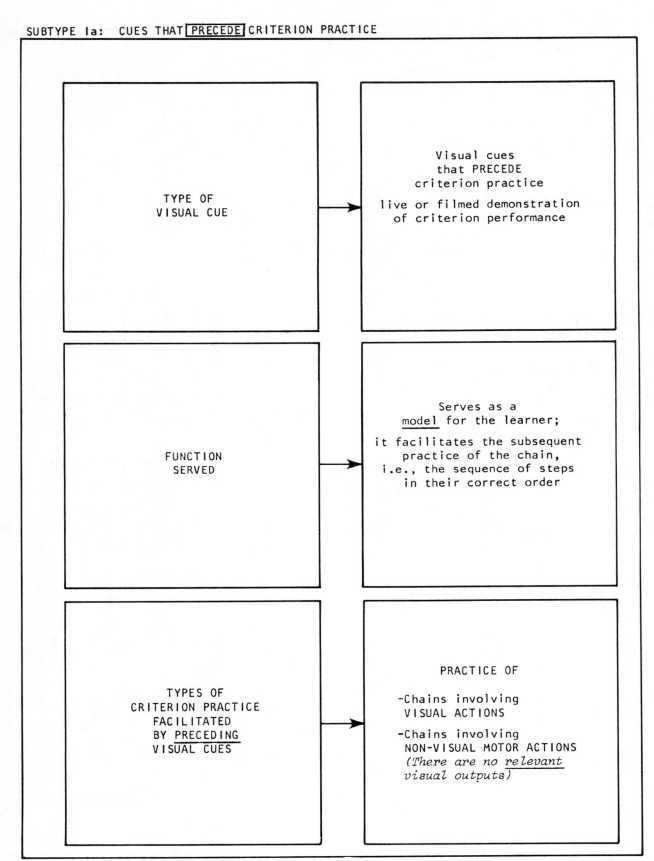

TYPE OF
VISUAL CUE

→

Visual cues
that PRECEDE
criterion practice

live or filmed demonstration
of criterion performance

FUNCTION
SERVED

→

Serves as a
model for the learner;

it facilitates the subsequent
practice of the chain,
i.e., the sequence of steps
in their correct order

TYPES OF
CRITERION PRACTICE
FACILITATED
BY PRECEDING
VISUAL CUES

→

PRACTICE OF

-Chains involving
VISUAL ACTIONS

-Chains involving
NON-VISUAL MOTOR ACTIONS
(There are no relevant
visual outputs)

EXAMPLES OF SUBTYPE 1a: VISUAL [CUES] THAT [PRECEDE] CRITERION PRACTICE

	EXAMPLE #1	EXAMPLE #2	EXAMPLE #3
JOB TASK	Assembly and disassembly of rifle	Operating a desk calculator	Actor performing a scene
CRITERION PERFORMANCE	All the assembly and disassembly operations are performed in the correct sequence	All the steps involved in a specific operation (e.g., finding square roots), are performed	Making all the movements, gestures, etc. in the scene
PRIOR USE OF MEDIATING VISUAL AS A CUE	An expert on film demonstrates the assembly of a partly or wholly disassembled rifle	An expert demonstrates the complete operation	The director demonstrates what should be done
SUBSEQUENT CRITERION PRACTICE	Following the demonstration, the learner practices assembling the rifle exactly as the expert did	Following the demonstration, the learner practices taking a square root exactly as the expert did	Following the demonstration, the actor performs all the movements, gestures, etc., just the way the director did and in the same order

NOW DO EXERCISE #31 ON PAGES IV.16 TO IV.17 IN THE WORKBOOK.

SUBTYPE 1b: CUES THAT [ACCOMPANY] CRITERION PRACTICE

TYPE OF VISUAL CUE	Visual cues that ACCOMPANY criterion inputs, actions, or outputs DURING criterion practice
FUNCTION SERVED	Visual cues facilitate the identification of -inputs or outputs to be discriminated or generalized -actions to be associated with inputs -sequence of associations in long chains

TWO TYPES OF CUES SERVING THE IDENTIFICATION FUNCTION	-content cues:
	  e.g., visual examples of inputs in photographs or on film
	
	-attentional cues:
	  e.g., cues that call attention to distinctions--as the boxed diagrams in this handbook
	(See discussion on page IV.42.)

TYPES OF CRITERION PRACTICE FACILITATED BY ACCOMPANYING VISUAL CUES	PRACTICE OF Discriminations, Generalizations, Associations or Chains involving -VISUAL INPUTS OR ACTIONS -NON-VISUAL VERBAL INPUTS OR ACTIONS -NON-VISUAL MOTOR ACTIONS *(See discussion on next page.)*

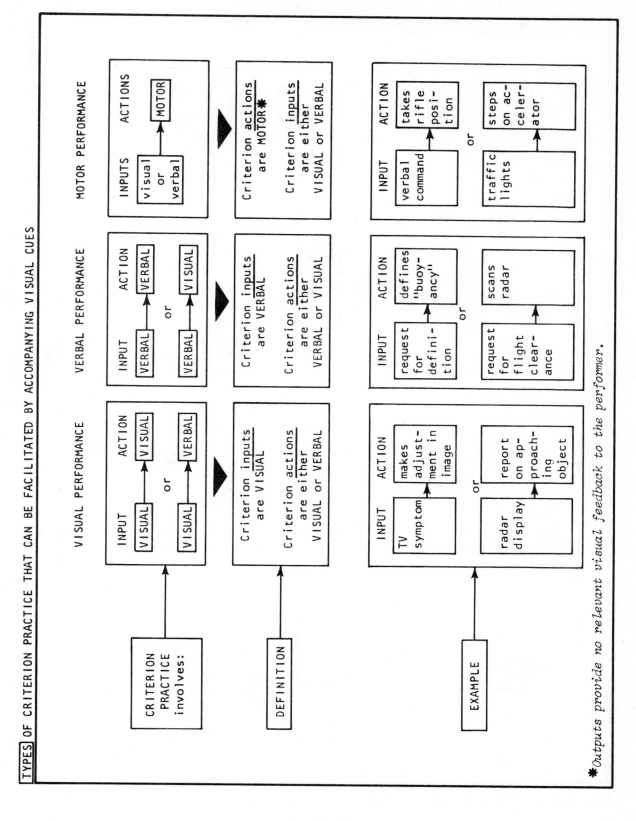

TYPES OF CRITERION PRACTICE THAT CAN BE FACILITATED BY ACCOMPANYING VISUAL CUES

VISUAL PERFORMANCE

INPUT   ACTION

VISUAL → VISUAL

or

VISUAL → VERBAL

Criterion inputs
are VISUAL

Criterion actions
are either
VISUAL or VERBAL

VERBAL PERFORMANCE

INPUT   ACTION

VERBAL → VERBAL

or

VERBAL → VISUAL

Criterion inputs
are VERBAL

Criterion actions
are either
VERBAL or VISUAL

MOTOR PERFORMANCE

INPUTS   ACTIONS

visual
or   → MOTOR
verbal

Criterion actions
are MOTOR*

Criterion inputs
are either
VISUAL or VERBAL

CRITERION
PRACTICE
involves:

DEFINITION

EXAMPLE

INPUT   ACTION

TV
symptom → makes adjust-
ment in
image

or

radar
display → report
on ap-
proach-
ing
object

INPUT   ACTION

request
for
defini-
tion → defines
"buoy-
ancy"

or

request
for
flight
clear-
ance → scans
radar

INPUT   ACTION

verbal
command → takes
rifle
posi-
tion

or

traffic
lights → steps
on ac-
celer-
ator

*Outputs provide no relevant visual feedback to the performer.

IV.41

DEFINITION OF CONTENT AND ATTENTIONAL CUES

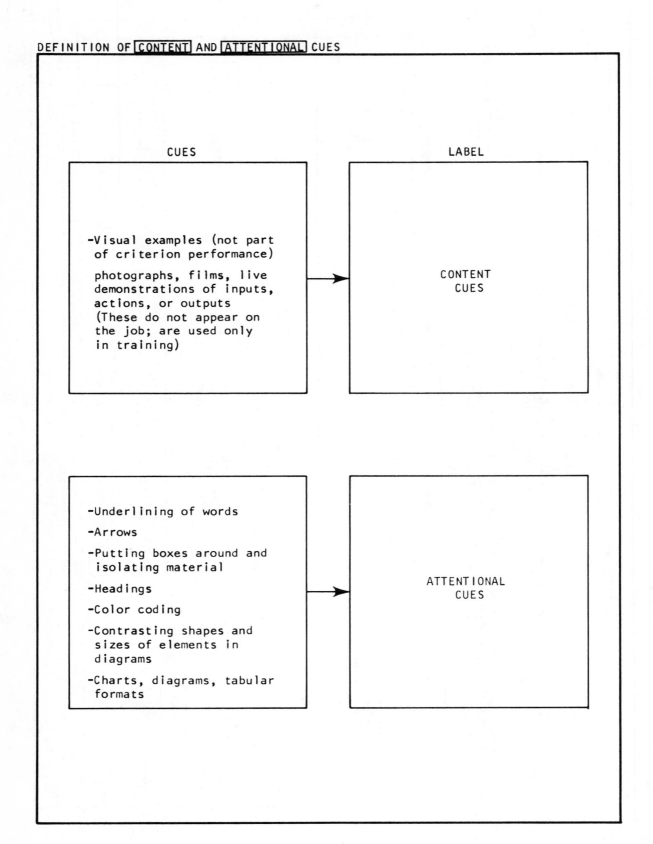

CUES

-Visual examples (not part of criterion performance)

photographs, films, live demonstrations of inputs, actions, or outputs (These do not appear on the job; are used only in training)

LABEL

CONTENT CUES

-Underlining of words

-Arrows

-Putting boxes around and isolating material

-Headings

-Color coding

-Contrasting shapes and sizes of elements in diagrams

-Charts, diagrams, tabular formats

ATTENTIONAL CUES

CONTRASTING EXAMPLES OF CONTENT AND ATTENTIONAL CUES

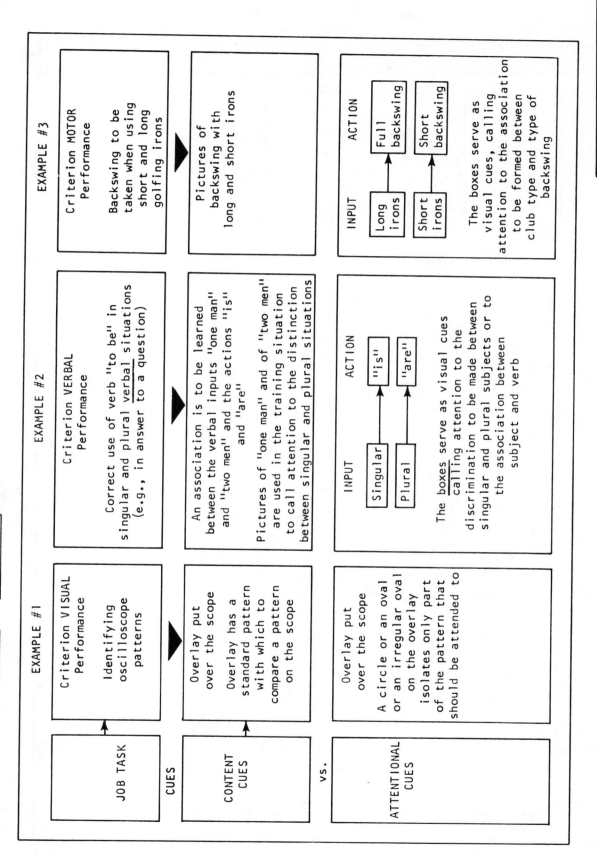

	EXAMPLE #1	EXAMPLE #2	EXAMPLE #3
	Criterion VISUAL Performance	Criterion VERBAL Performance	Criterion MOTOR Performance

JOB TASK

EXAMPLE #1 — Identifying oscilloscope patterns

EXAMPLE #2 — Correct use of verb "to be" in singular and plural verbal situations (e.g., in answer to a question)

EXAMPLE #3 — Backswing to be taken when using short and long golfing irons

CUES

CONTENT CUES

Overlay put over the scope

Overlay has a standard pattern with which to compare a pattern on the scope

An association is to be learned between the verbal inputs "one man" and "two men" and the actions "is" and "are"

Pictures of "one man" and of "two men" are used in the training situation to call attention to the distinction between singular and plural situations

Pictures of backswing with long and short irons

vs.

ATTENTIONAL CUES

Overlay put over the scope

A circle or an oval or an irregular oval on the overlay isolates only part of the pattern that should be attended to

INPUT   ACTION

Singular → "is"

Plural → "are"

The boxes serve as visual cues calling attention to the discrimination to be made between singular and plural subjects or to the association between subject and verb

INPUT   ACTION

Long irons → Full backswing

Short irons → Short backswing

The boxes serve as visual cues, calling attention to the association to be formed between club type and type of backswing

NOW DO EXERCISE #32 ON PAGES IV.18 TO IV.19 IN THE WORKBOOK.

EXAMPLES OF MANNER IN WHICH VISUAL CUES ACCOMPANY THE VARIOUS TYPES OF CRITERION PRACTICE

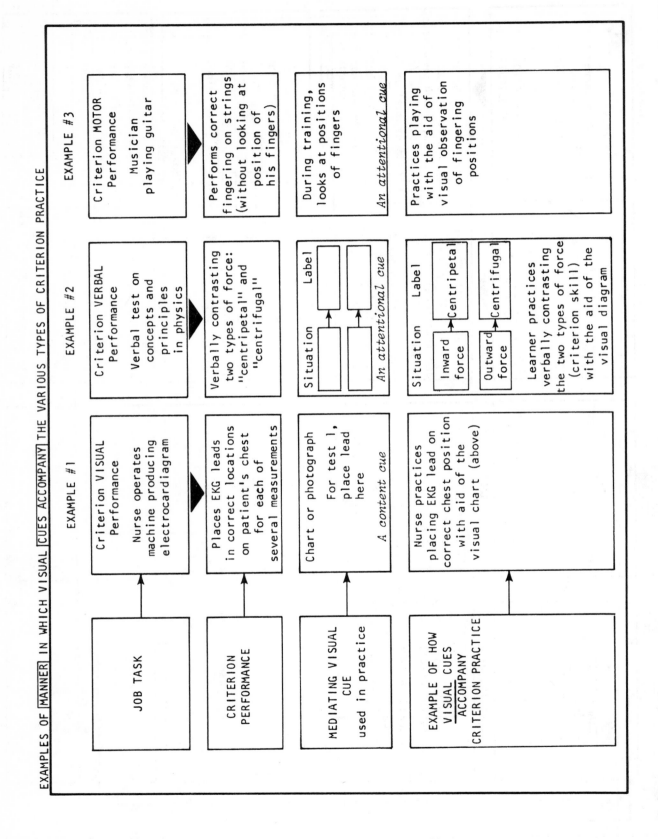

	EXAMPLE #1	EXAMPLE #2	EXAMPLE #3
EXAMPLES OF CRITERION VISUAL JOB PERFORMANCE	Airplane pilot inspects plane exterior for evidence of damage IDENTIFICATION OF INPUTS	Soldier has to assemble rifle parts ALTERATION OF INPUTS	Wood carver carves furniture legs PRODUCTION OF OUTPUTS
DURING TRAINING Visual cues facilitating practice of DISCRIMINATIONS AMONG VISUAL INPUTS OR VISUAL OUTPUTS	Pilot has to locate a defect and decide on the seriousness *The general area of the damaged part may be identified by arrows painted on the plane (attentional cue)*	Soldier has to discriminate between correctly and incorrectly positioned parts *Series of photographs showing orientation of individual parts helps the learner to determine if he has oriented parts correctly*	*Learner may be given pictures of what a curved French provincial leg looks like (a content cue) or he may have lines drawn to guide him and help him determine whether his output is correct or not (attentional cues)*
or Visual cues facilitating practice of GENERALIZATIONS ACROSS VISUAL INPUTS OR VISUAL OUTPUTS	*The pilot may be given photographs showing examples of the limits of "tolerable" changes in appearance of plane parts*	*(Since parts are either correctly positioned or not, generalization across degrees of proper orientation is not a learning problem)*	*Photographs of the limits of an acceptable leg may be used to facilitate generalization across outputs*
or Visual cues facilitating practice of ASSOCIATIONS (OR CHAINS) BETWEEN VISUAL ACTIONS AND INPUTS	*The pilot may be given photographs of visual check-out operations to verify the existence or seriousness of a defect*	The soldier has to assemble all the parts in the correct order (a long chain) *Each in a numbered series of photographs can help him to select parts in the correct order*	*A series of photographs may guide the learner through a series of steps (the chain)*

EXAMPLE #1

Audio-visual specialist has to verbally identify and define types of visuals used in instruction

Blocks below serve as visual cues

EXAMPLE #2

Public opinion analyst presents results in tabular format to facilitate public's understanding of results

Tabular formats below serve as visual cues

EXAMPLE #3

Manager gets indoctrination on horizontal and vertical relationships he will be involved in

Table of organization serves as visual cue

EXAMPLES OF CRITERION VERBAL JOB PERFORMANCE

Visual cues facilitating DISCRIMINATIONS AMONG VERBAL INPUTS OR VERBAL OUTPUTS

EXAMPLE #1:

Blocks as visual cues

Types	Label
ACTUAL OBJECTS	REALISTIC
FILM	REPRODUCED
SKETCHES	FABRICATED

EXAMPLE #2:

	June	July	August
N.E.	25%	30%	40%
Midwest	17%	18%	18%
South	50%	40%	30%
West	20%	25%	30%

Columns facilitate the discriminations between months; rows, between geographic regions

EXAMPLE #3:

Table facilitates discriminating between those with whom he will have relations and those with whom he will not

---

Visual cues facilitating GENERALIZATIONS ACROSS VERBAL INPUTS OR VERBAL OUTPUTS

EXAMPLE #1:

Types	Label
ACTUAL OBJECTS	
ACTUAL PEOPLE	REALISTIC
ACTUAL EVENTS	

EXAMPLE #2:

MIDWEST	June	July	Aug.
Elementary	17%	18%	18%
H. School	17%	18%	18%
College	16%	17%	18%

Tabular format (and results) shows the generalization across types of education (results stay the same).

EXAMPLE #3:

Same diagram illustrates all those he will be dealing with

Visual cues facilitating ASSOCIATIONS (or CHAINS) BETWEEN VERBAL INPUTS AND ACTIONS

EXAMPLE #1:

See diagram above for "discriminations"; "associations" are also shown there

EXAMPLE #2:

Tabular format for "discriminations" above facilitates association between months or regions and numerical values

EXAMPLES OF VISUAL [CUES] THAT FACILITATE CRITERION [NON-VISUAL, MOTOR] PRACTICE *

EXAMPLE #1

swimming strokes

pictures of
arm movements
in breast stroke,
crawl, backstroke,
etc.

EXAMPLE #2

braking car

film or pictures
of tires' short
braking motions
on brake pedal

EXAMPLE #3

climbing
telephone pole

film or pictures
of foot/hand
coordination in
climbing pole

EXAMPLES OF
CRITERION MOTOR
JOB PERFORMANCE

Visual cues
facilitating
ASSOCIATIONS
or CHAINS
involving
MOTOR ACTIONS
and
VISUAL or VERBAL
INPUTS

* *Motor actions are those actions which produce outputs whose visual properties are irrelevant when they (the outputs) become inputs for the next action to be taken. Thus, the actions neither identify visual inputs, nor alter visual inputs, nor produce visual outputs (relevant to continuing performance).*

IV.47

SUMMARY CONSIDERATIONS IN THE USE OF VISUAL CUES IN MEDIATING PRACTICE

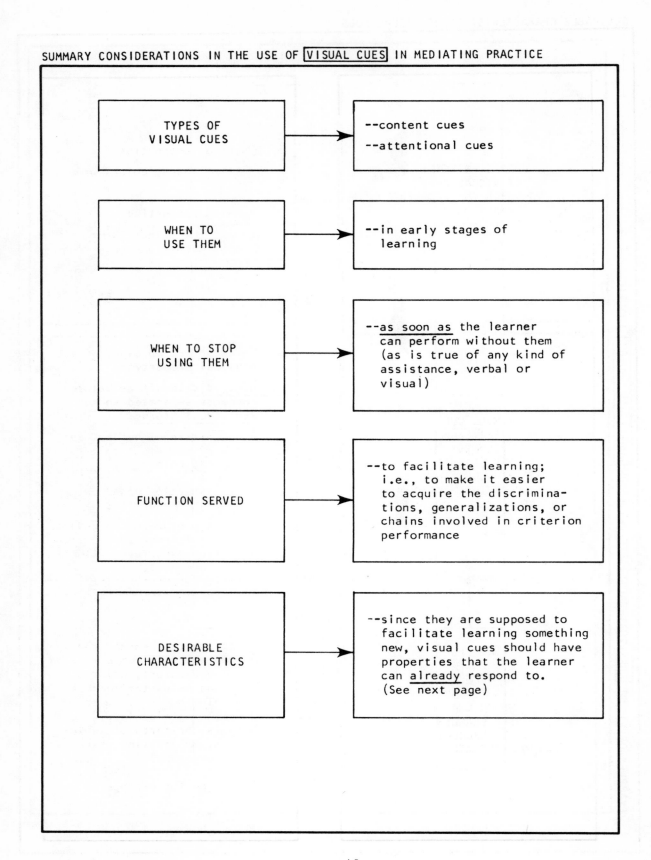

| TYPES OF VISUAL CUES | → | --content cues
--attentional cues |

| WHEN TO USE THEM | → | --in early stages of learning |

| WHEN TO STOP USING THEM | → | --as soon as the learner can perform without them (as is true of any kind of assistance, verbal or visual) |

| FUNCTION SERVED | → | --to facilitate learning; i.e., to make it easier to acquire the discriminations, generalizations, or chains involved in criterion performance |

| DESIRABLE CHARACTERISTICS | → | --since they are supposed to facilitate learning something new, visual cues should have properties that the learner can already respond to. (See next page) |

CHARACTERISTICS
OF VISUAL CUES
TO WHICH THE LEARNER
RESPONDS

1. Physical properties

   --size, shape, color, order, etc.

2. Meaning properties

   --what the object is or what events are occurring

VISUAL CUES
SERVE AS
INPUTS;
THE LEARNER
PRODUCES AN
APPROPRIATE ACTION

1. Takes an action based on a physical property:

   e.g., distinguishes between concepts separated in individual blocks;

   e.g., distinguishes between parts of equipment colored different colors

2. Takes an action based on "meaning" properties:

   e.g., a picture of an object gets the learner to practice an action associated with it (i.e., naming it)

SELECT
VISUAL CUES
WHICH ENABLE
THE LEARNER
TO PRODUCE
AN APPROPRIATE ACTION

e.g., because the learner can tell the difference between colors, color coding helps the learner to distinguish between something else (e.g., tools, or parts of equipment, or location of parts in equipment)

See next page for examples.

WHAT NEEDS TO BE LEARNED	VISUAL CUE SELECTED	EXPLANATION
E.G. In biology, the learner has to distinguish between the vascular system and the digestive system.	On a cutaway drawing of inner organs, the vascular system is colored <u>blue</u>, the digestive system <u>red</u>.	Since the learner can already distinguish between the colors red and blue, this capability is used to help the learner distinguish between the two systems in the body.
E.G. A teacher has to learn to manage problems in the classroom; she must follow certain routines in the proper order (a long chain).	The sequence of events is presented in a series of boxes connected with arrows; these are presented in correct sequence from left to right. ▢→▢→▢→▢	Since the learner can already follow a left-to-right sequence and interpret it to mean the order of events, procedures written up in the boxes can be learned in the left-to-right order.
E.G. A TV repairman has to identify TV malfunctions from symptoms on the screen (discriminations and associations).	Pictures of various problems presented to him as he learns enables him to distinguish between symptoms.	Since the learner can compare what he sees on the screen and in a book of photographs, he is enabled to make the appropriate diagnosis during training.

SITUATION	RULE
1. -A long chain must be learned: --The chain must be performed in its entirety --All parts of the chain must be performed in the correct sequence	-Provide a model demonstration (live or on film) of the chain: --The length of the demonstration is determined by a judgment as to how much of the chain the learner can imitate after seeing it --The model demonstration serves as a cue to the subsequent practice of the chain
2. -Discriminations, generalizations, or chains must be learned in criterion tasks that are either <u>visual</u>, <u>verbal</u>, or <u>motor</u>: --Potential difficulties exist in learning these skills	-Select or develop visual cues to which the learner can already respond (i.e., take an appropriate action) -Use this ability to respond to visual cues to facilitate practice of discriminations, generalizations, or chains which would be more difficult without them

NOW DO EXERCISE #33 ON PAGES IV.21 TO IV.27 IN THE WORKBOOK.

IV.3.b   OBJECTIVES OF THIS SUBUNIT

> At the end of this subunit, you will be able to IDENTIFY and PRODUCE practice that requires the learner to RESPOND to mediating visuals.

DIAGRAM OF YOUR JOB

INPUT TO YOU	YOUR ACTION	YOUR OUTPUT
Potential learner difficulty in learning the discriminations, generalizations, or chains involved in VERBAL OR QUANTITATIVE CONCEPTS. 1a	Prepare VISUAL EXAMPLES that illustrate the discriminations, generalizations, or chains in VERBAL CONCEPTS. 2a	VISUAL PRACTICE that can make the learning of concepts or principles EASIER. 3a
Potential learner difficulty in learning the associations or chains in a long procedural chain. 1b	Prepare a visual presentation performance of the chain that allows the learner to respond at a level lower than that required in criterion performance. 2b	RECOGNITION or EDITING practice based on the visual presentation; facilitates the subsequent, actual performance of the learner. 3b

TYPE II: RESPONSES TO MEDIATING VISUALS

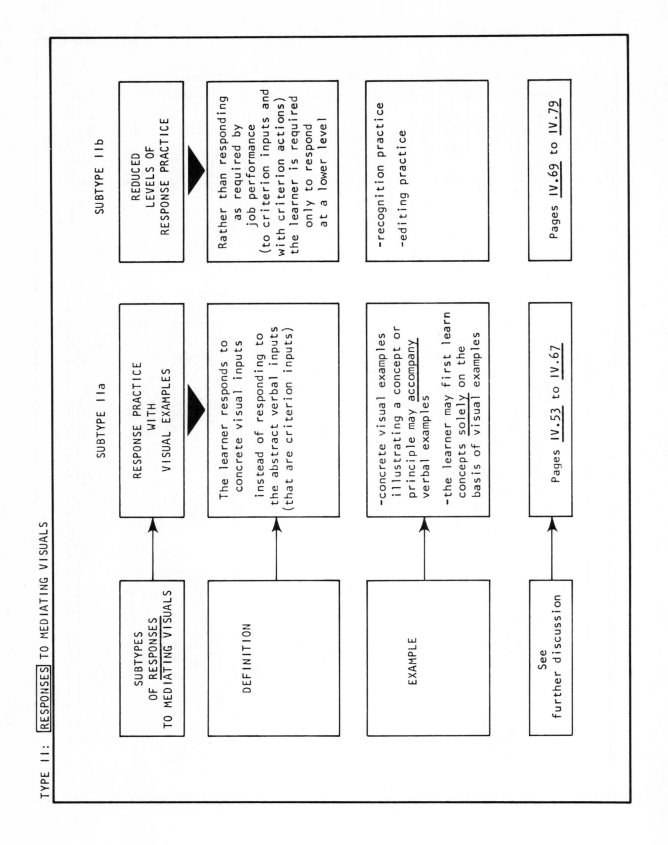

	SUBTYPE IIa	SUBTYPE IIb
SUBTYPES OF RESPONSES TO MEDIATING VISUALS	RESPONSE PRACTICE WITH VISUAL EXAMPLES	REDUCED LEVELS OF RESPONSE PRACTICE
DEFINITION	The learner responds to concrete visual inputs instead of responding to the abstract verbal inputs (that are criterion inputs)	Rather than responding as required by job performance (to criterion inputs and with criterion actions) the learner is required only to respond at a lower level
EXAMPLE	-concrete visual examples illustrating a concept or principle may accompany verbal examples -the learner may first learn concepts solely on the basis of visual examples	-recognition practice -editing practice
See further discussion	Pages IV.53 to IV.67	Pages IV.69 to IV.79

SUBTYPE IIa: RESPONSES TO VISUAL EXAMPLES

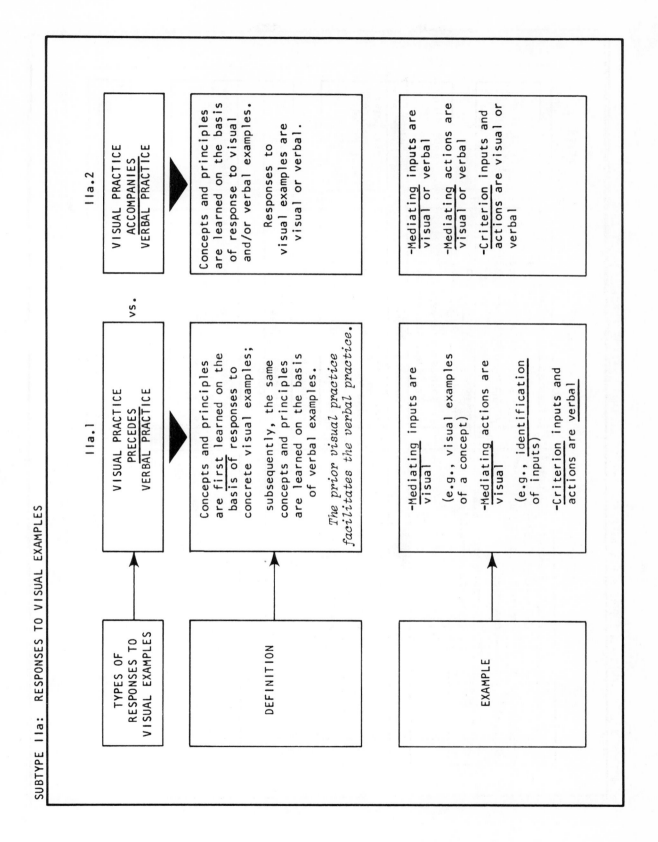

IIa.1   vs.   IIa.2

TYPES OF RESPONSES TO VISUAL EXAMPLES

VISUAL PRACTICE PRECEDES VERBAL PRACTICE

VISUAL PRACTICE ACCOMPANIES VERBAL PRACTICE

DEFINITION

Concepts and principles are first learned on the basis of responses to concrete visual examples;

subsequently, the same concepts and principles are learned on the basis of verbal examples.

The prior visual practice facilitates the verbal practice.

Concepts and principles are learned on the basis of response to visual and/or verbal examples.

Responses to visual examples are visual or verbal.

EXAMPLE

-Mediating inputs are visual

(e.g., visual examples of a concept)

-Mediating actions are visual

(e.g., identification of inputs)

-Criterion inputs and actions are verbal

-Mediating inputs are visual or verbal

-Mediating actions are visual or verbal

-Criterion inputs and actions are visual or verbal

SUBTYPE IIa.1   SEQUENCE OF EVENTS IN VISUAL PRACTICE THAT PRECEDES VERBAL PRACTICE

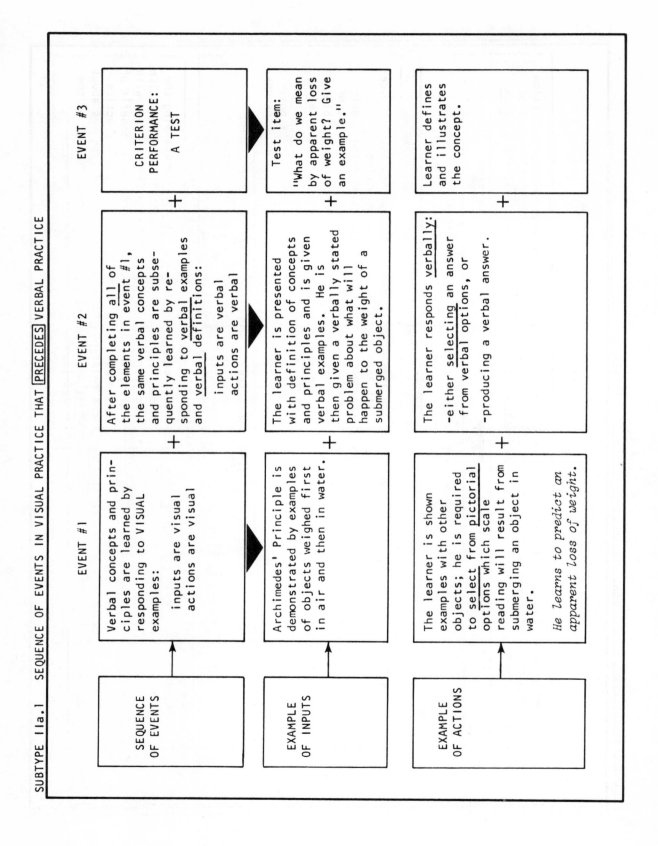

EVENT #1

EVENT #2

EVENT #3

SEQUENCE OF EVENTS

Verbal concepts and principles are learned by responding to VISUAL examples:

inputs are visual
actions are visual

+

After completing all of the elements in event #1, the same verbal concepts and principles are subsequently learned by responding to verbal examples and verbal definitions:

inputs are verbal
actions are verbal

+

CRITERION PERFORMANCE:

A TEST

EXAMPLE OF INPUTS

Archimedes' Principle is demonstrated by examples of objects weighed first in air and then in water.

+

The learner is presented with definition of concepts and principles and is given verbal examples. He is then given a verbally stated problem about what will happen to the weight of a submerged object.

+

Test item:
"What do we mean by apparent loss of weight? Give an example."

EXAMPLE OF ACTIONS

The learner is shown other examples with other objects; he is required to select from pictorial options which scale reading will result from submerging an object in water.

He learns to predict an apparent loss of weight.

+

The learner responds verbally:
-either selecting an answer from verbal options, or
-producing a verbal answer.

+

Learner defines and illustrates the concept.

EXAMPLES OF MEDIATING VISUAL PRACTICE THAT PRECEDES VERBAL PRACTICE

	EXAMPLE #1	EXAMPLE #2	EXAMPLE #3
REQUIRED CRITERION PERFORMANCE	A verbal differentiation between the type of link-up of poles of a power source and poles of a semiconductor device that occurs in "forward" and "reverse" bias	A verbal explanation of how heat affects the action of molecules	A verbal description of the link-ups of atoms in a complex molecule
PRIOR MEDIATING VISUAL PRACTICE	A filmed or live demonstration is shown in which connections are made between positive and negative poles of a power source and positive and negative poles of a semiconductor. The learner either selects different types of link-ups or produces them himself for forward and reverse bias.	The learner practices with an animated sequence showing the speed of molecular movement as a function of the application and removal of heat. Problems may consist of recognizing (selecting from pictorial options) what will happen, e.g., when heat is applied.	The learner practices with a three-dimensional model; different types of atoms may be color coded. Practice may consist of discriminations about positioning and link-ups of atoms.
SUBSEQUENT VERBAL PRACTICE	Following completion of above practice, the learner practices verbally stating the difference between link-ups in forward and reverse bias.	After completing the above type of practice, the learner is given solely verbal problems (as practice) concerning the relationship between heat and movement of molecules.	After completing the above visual practice, the learner may, with or without benefit of the model, practice verbal problems about the structure of the molecule.

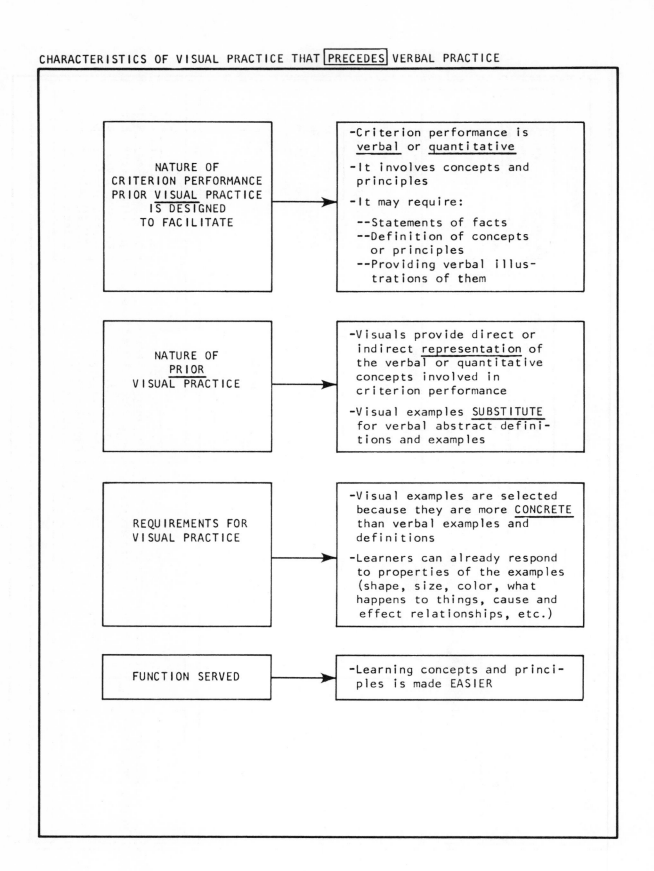

NATURE OF
CRITERION PERFORMANCE
PRIOR VISUAL PRACTICE
IS DESIGNED
TO FACILITATE

-Criterion performance is
verbal or quantitative

-It involves concepts and
principles

-It may require:

--Statements of facts
--Definition of concepts
or principles
--Providing verbal illus-
trations of them

NATURE OF
PRIOR
VISUAL PRACTICE

-Visuals provide direct or
indirect representation of
the verbal or quantitative
concepts involved in
criterion performance

-Visual examples SUBSTITUTE
for verbal abstract definitions and examples

REQUIREMENTS FOR
VISUAL PRACTICE

-Visual examples are selected
because they are more CONCRETE
than verbal examples and
definitions

-Learners can already respond
to properties of the examples
(shape, size, color, what
happens to things, cause and
effect relationships, etc.)

FUNCTION SERVED

-Learning concepts and principles is made EASIER

	Practice with SIMULATED VISUALS	Practice with MEDIATING VISUALS
TYPE OF VISUALS		
NATURE OF THE SUBSTITUTION	Simulated visual inputs or actions are selected which are intended to be as nearly like criterion inputs or actions as possible.	Mediating visual inputs or actions are selected which are intended to be different from criterion inputs or actions. *Mediating visuals are concrete, while verbal materials are abstract.*
PURPOSE OF THE SUBSTITUTION	To facilitate TRANSFER from practice situation to criterion situation. *For purposes of simulation, use of visuals to substitute for words may be undesirable.*	To facilitate ACQUISITION of concepts in the first place. They are easier to learn on the basis of the visual examples. *For purposes of mediating practice, use of visuals to substitute for words can be helpful.*
WHEN ARE THEY USED	When it is not logistically feasible to use criterion inputs or actions in training.	When verbal criterion performance is expected to be difficult for the learners.

IV.59

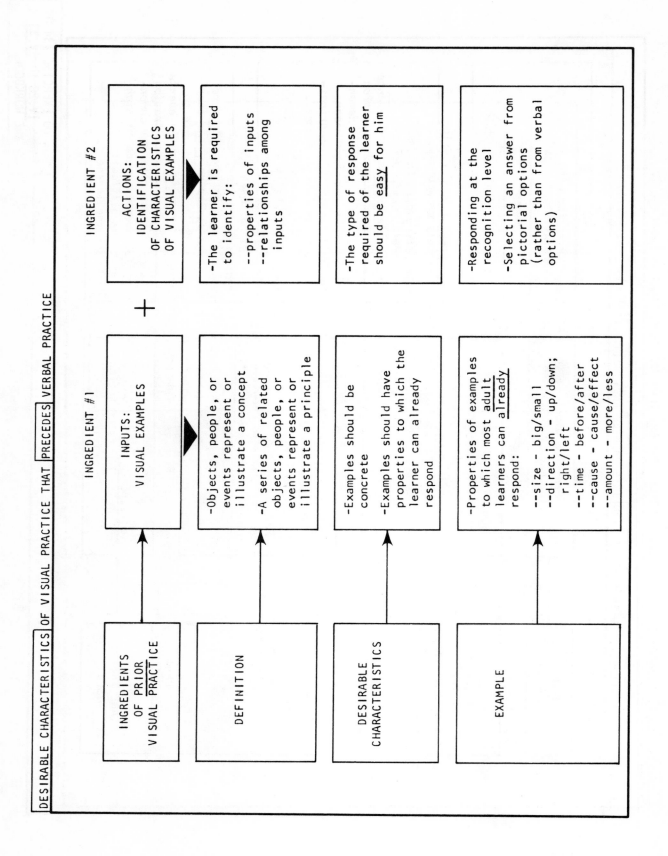

INGREDIENT #1

INPUTS:
VISUAL EXAMPLES

+

INGREDIENT #2

ACTIONS:
IDENTIFICATION
OF CHARACTERISTICS
OF VISUAL EXAMPLES

INGREDIENTS
OF PRIOR
VISUAL PRACTICE

-Objects, people, or
 events represent or
 illustrate a concept

-A series of related
 objects, people, or
 events represent or
 illustrate a principle

-The learner is required
 to identify:

--properties of inputs
--relationships among
  inputs

DEFINITION

DESIRABLE
CHARACTERISTICS

-Examples should be
 concrete

-Examples should have
 properties to which the
 learner can already
 respond

-The type of response
 required of the learner
 should be easy for him

EXAMPLE

-Properties of examples
 to which most adult
 learners can already
 respond:

--size - big/small
--direction - up/down;
  right/left
--time - before/after
--cause - cause/effect
--amount - more/less

-Responding at the
 recognition level

-Selecting an answer from
 pictorial options
 (rather than from verbal
 options)

CONCRETENESS OF VISUAL REPRESENTATION IS MORE IMPORTANT THAN ITS DIRECTNESS OR FIDELITY

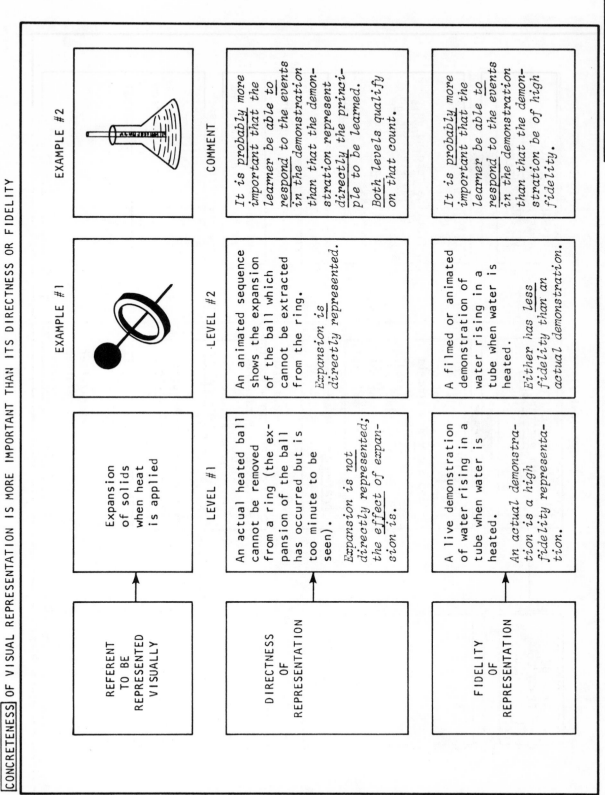

EXAMPLE #1   EXAMPLE #2

REFERENT TO BE REPRESENTED VISUALLY

Expansion of solids when heat is applied

DIRECTNESS OF REPRESENTATION

LEVEL #1

An actual heated ball cannot be removed from a ring (the expansion of the ball has occurred but is too minute to be seen).

Expansion is not directly represented; the effect of expansion is.

LEVEL #2

An animated sequence shows the expansion of the ball which cannot be extracted from the ring.

Expansion is directly represented.

COMMENT

It is probably more important that the learner be able to respond to the events in the demonstration than that the demonstration represent directly the principle to be learned.

Both levels qualify on that count.

FIDELITY OF REPRESENTATION

A live demonstration of water rising in a tube when water is heated.

An actual demonstration is a high fidelity representation.

A filmed or animated demonstration of water rising in a tube when water is heated.

Either has less fidelity than an actual demonstration.

It is probably more important that the learner be able to respond to the events in the demonstration than that the demonstration be of high fidelity.

NOW DO EXERCISE #34 ON PAGES IV.28 TO IV.33 IN THE WORKBOOK.

SUBTYPE IIa.2: VISUAL PRACTICE THAT ACCOMPANIES VERBAL PRACTICE
CONTRASTING DIFFERENCES BETWEEN VISUAL PRACTICE THAT PRECEDES AND ACCOMPANIES VERBAL PRACTICE

	VISUAL PRACTICE THAT PRECEDES VERBAL PRACTICE	vs.	VISUAL PRACTICE THAT ACCOMPANIES VERBAL PRACTICE
TYPE OF PRACTICE			
DEFINITION	-Criterion performance is VERBAL -Before any practice is had with verbal inputs or actions, visual practice (e.g., visual examples) is had *Practice with visuals precedes practice with words.*		-Criterion performance is VERBAL -Practice leading up to criterion practice consists of a mixture of visual and verbal examples *Practice with visuals and words is integrated.*
EXAMPLE	-Practice is first with visual examples -Actions are more apt to be visual than verbal -Only upon completing the visual practice does verbal practice begin		-Visual and verbal examples are intermixed -Actions practiced are more apt to be verbal to either visual or verbal inputs (examples)

IIa.2: SEQUENCE OF EVENTS IN VISUAL PRACTICE THAT [ACCOMPANIES] VERBAL PRACTICE

	EVENT #1	EVENT #2	OTHER EVENTS
SEQUENCE OF EVENTS	Verbal concepts and principles are learned by responding to a VISUAL example. Responses (i.e., actions taken) to examples may be either visual or verbal.	The same concepts or principles may immediately be followed by another visual or verbal example.	Visual and verbal examples are inter-mixed.
	+	+	+
EXAMPLE OF INPUTS	The expansion of solids when heated may be illustrated by a visual example.	The visual example may be followed by a verbally stated example.	Demonstration of visual examples and verbal statements and examples are intermixed.
	+	+	+
EXAMPLE OF ACTIONS	The learner can predict what will happen in the visual example -either by selecting from visual options, or -by a verbal action: --selecting a verbal answer --producing a statement (e.g., ball will or won't pass through a metal ring)	The learner predicts verbally what will happen in the verbal example: -selects from verbal options -produces a statement	Actions can be a mixture of visual and verbal actions.

IV.63

EXAMPLES OF MEDIATING VISUAL PRACTICE THAT [ACCOMPANIES] VERBAL PRACTICE

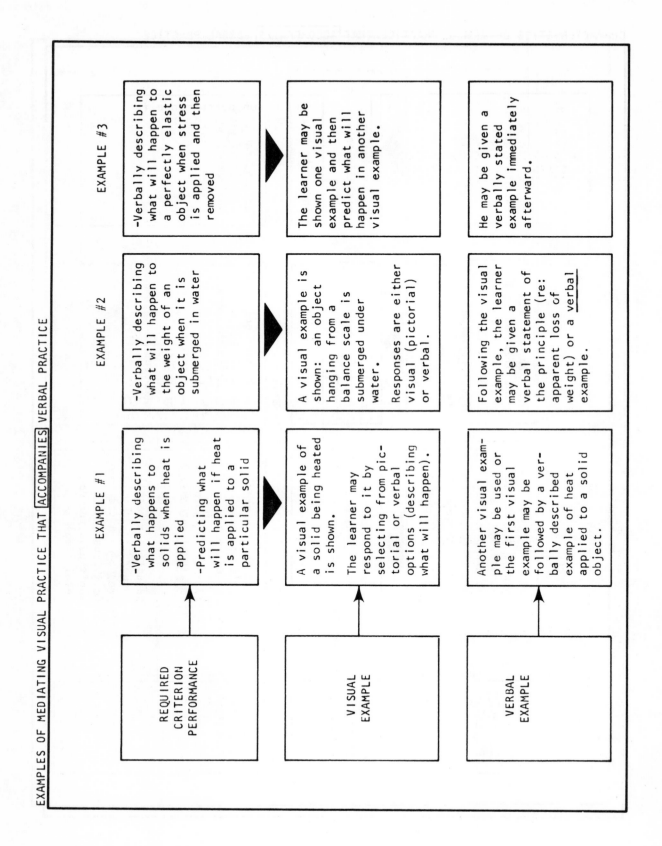

	EXAMPLE #1	EXAMPLE #2	EXAMPLE #3
REQUIRED CRITERION PERFORMANCE	-Verbally describing what happens to solids when heat is applied -Predicting what will happen if heat is applied to a particular solid	-Verbally describing what will happen to the weight of an object when it is submerged in water	-Verbally describing what will happen to a perfectly elastic object when stress is applied and then removed
VISUAL EXAMPLE	A visual example of a solid being heated is shown. The learner may respond to it by selecting from pictorial or verbal options (describing what will happen).	A visual example is shown: an object hanging from a balance scale is submerged under water. Responses are either visual (pictorial) or verbal.	The learner may be shown one visual example and then predict what will happen in another visual example.
VERBAL EXAMPLE	Another visual example may be used or the first visual example may be followed by a verbally described example of heat applied to a solid object.	Following the visual example, the learner may be given a verbal statement of the principle (re: apparent loss of weight) or a _verbal_ example.	He may be given a verbally stated example immediately afterward.

NATURE OF CRITERION PERFORMANCE ACCOMPANYING VISUAL PRACTICE IS DESIGNED TO FACILITATE	-Criterion performance is verbal or quantitative -It involves concepts and principles -It may require: --Statements of facts --Definition of concepts or principles --Providing verbal illustrations of them
NATURE OF ACCOMPANYING VISUAL PRACTICE	-Visuals provide direct or indirect representation of the verbal or quantitative concepts involved in criterion performance -Visual examples SUBSTITUTE for verbal abstract definitions and examples
REQUIREMENTS FOR VISUAL PRACTICE	-Visual examples are selected because they are more CONCRETE than verbal examples and definitions -Learners can already respond to properties of the examples (shape, size, color, what happens to things, cause and effect relationships, etc.)
FUNCTION SERVED	-Learning concepts and principles is made EASIER

COMPARISON OF MEDIATING VISUAL PRACTICE
THAT [ACCOMPANIES] AND [PRECEDES] VERBAL PRACTICE

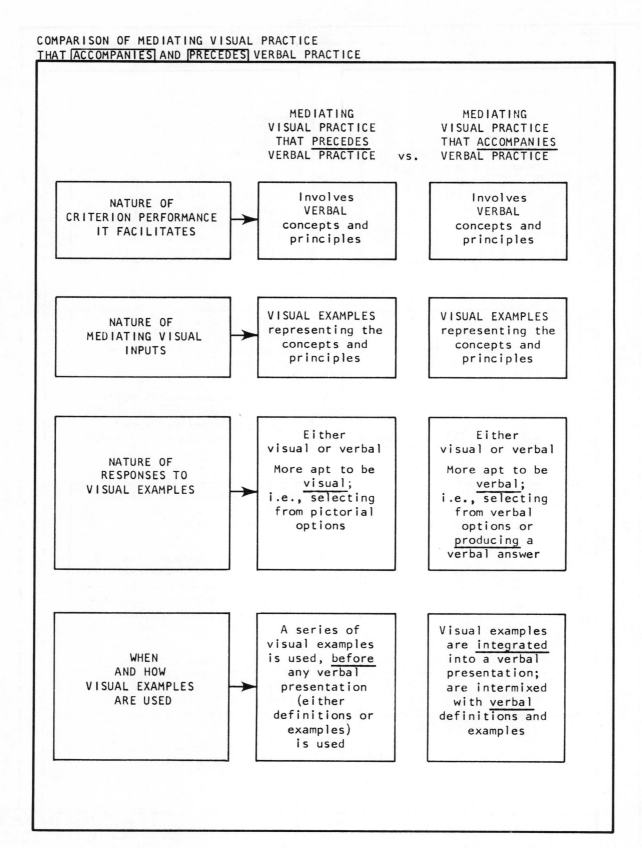

	MEDIATING VISUAL PRACTICE THAT PRECEDES VERBAL PRACTICE	vs.	MEDIATING VISUAL PRACTICE THAT ACCOMPANIES VERBAL PRACTICE
NATURE OF CRITERION PERFORMANCE IT FACILITATES	Involves VERBAL concepts and principles		Involves VERBAL concepts and principles
NATURE OF MEDIATING VISUAL INPUTS	VISUAL EXAMPLES representing the concepts and principles		VISUAL EXAMPLES representing the concepts and principles
NATURE OF RESPONSES TO VISUAL EXAMPLES	Either visual or verbal More apt to be visual; i.e., selecting from pictorial options		Either visual or verbal More apt to be verbal; i.e., selecting from verbal options or producing a verbal answer
WHEN AND HOW VISUAL EXAMPLES ARE USED	A series of visual examples is used, before any verbal presentation (either definitions or examples) is used		Visual examples are integrated into a verbal presentation; are intermixed with verbal definitions and examples

IV.66

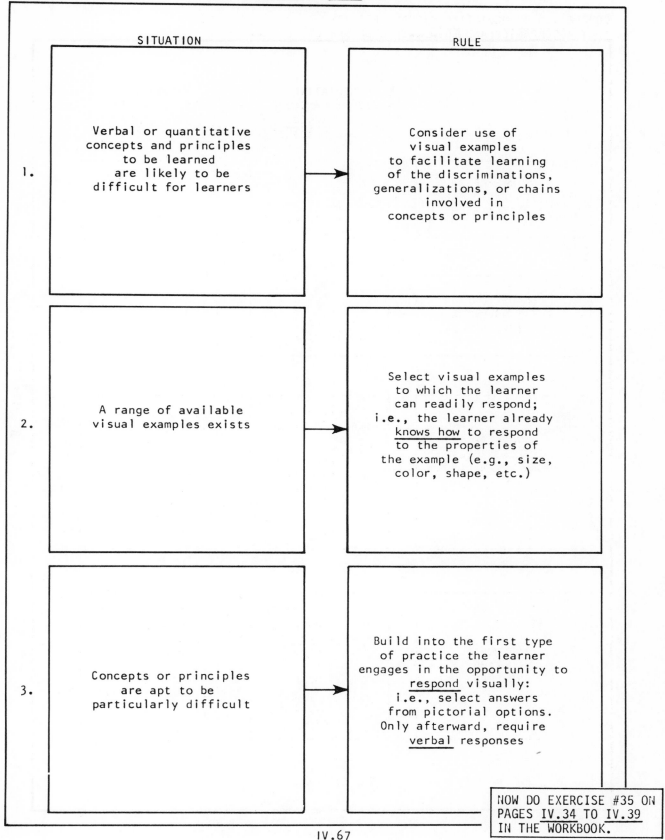

SITUATION | RULE

1. Verbal or quantitative concepts and principles to be learned are likely to be difficult for learners → Consider use of visual examples to facilitate learning of the discriminations, generalizations, or chains involved in concepts or principles

2. A range of available visual examples exists → Select visual examples to which the learner can readily respond; i.e., the learner already knows how to respond to the properties of the example (e.g., size, color, shape, etc.)

3. Concepts or principles are apt to be particularly difficult → Build into the first type of practice the learner engages in the opportunity to respond visually: i.e., select answers from pictorial options. Only afterward, require verbal responses

NOW DO EXERCISE #35 ON PAGES IV.34 TO IV.39 IN THE WORKBOOK.

SUBTYPE IIb: REDUCED LEVELS OF RESPONSE PRACTICE

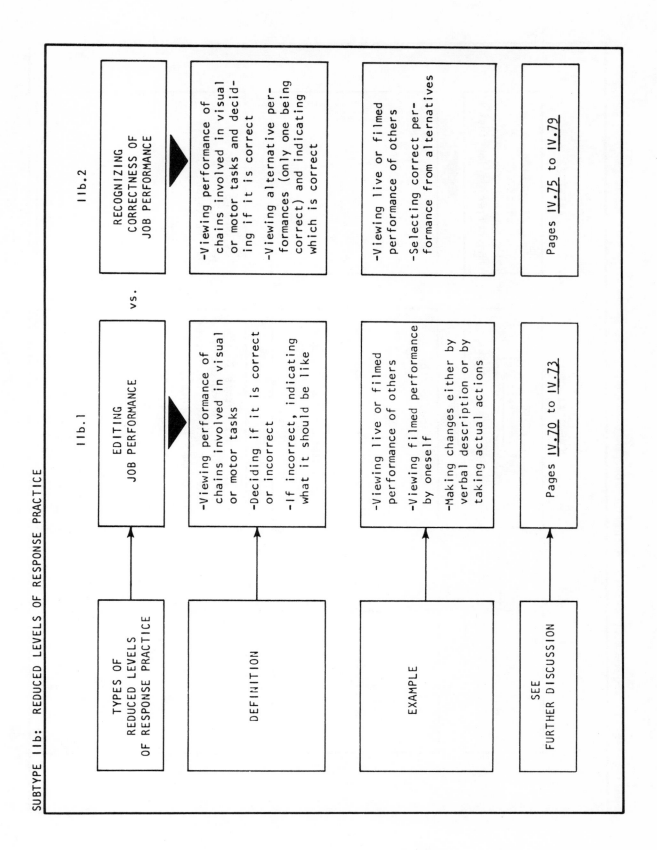

	IIb.1	vs.	IIb.2
TYPES OF REDUCED LEVELS OF RESPONSE PRACTICE	EDITING JOB PERFORMANCE		RECOGNIZING CORRECTNESS OF JOB PERFORMANCE
DEFINITION	-Viewing performance of chains involved in visual or motor tasks -Deciding if it is correct or incorrect -If incorrect, indicating what it should be like		-Viewing performance of chains involved in visual or motor tasks and decid-ing if it is correct -Viewing alternative per-formances (only one being correct) and indicating which is correct
EXAMPLE	-Viewing live or filmed performance of others -Viewing filmed performance by oneself -Making changes either by verbal description or by taking actual actions		-Viewing live or filmed performance of others -Selecting correct per-formance from alternatives
SEE FURTHER DISCUSSION	Pages IV.70 to IV.73		Pages IV.75 to IV.79

SUBTYPE IIb.1: SEQUENCE OF EVENTS IN EDITING JOB PERFORMANCE

EVENT #1

SEQUENCE OF EVENTS	EDITING of incorrect performance of chains in visual or motor tasks
EXAMPLE OF INPUTS	-Live or filmed performance by another person of the chain -Filmed performance by oneself of the steps in the chain *The mediating visual inputs consist of the performance to be edited.*
EXAMPLE OF ACTIONS	If there are errors in the chain (i.e., wrong action taken or actions taken out of proper sequence), the learner edits the performance: i.e., indicates verbally what should be done or actually does it correctly. *The mediating action is editing rather than producing.*

+

EVENT #2

PRODUCTION practice: The learner practices the criterion job task
Inputs found on the job *Criterion inputs are used.*
Actions found on the job: i.e., the chain of inputs/actions *Criterion chains*

IV.70

EXAMPLES OF EDITING PRACTICE

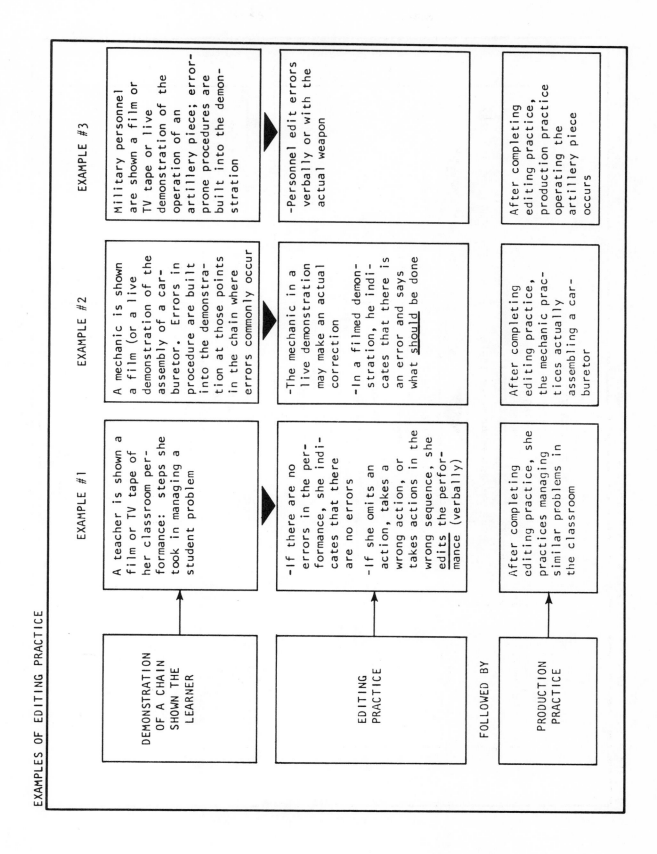

EXAMPLE #1

A teacher is shown a film or TV tape of her classroom performance: steps she took in managing a student problem

- If there are no errors in the performance, she indicates that there are no errors

- If she omits an action, takes a wrong action, or takes actions in the wrong sequence, she edits the performance (verbally)

DEMONSTRATION OF A CHAIN SHOWN THE LEARNER

EDITING PRACTICE

After completing editing practice, she practices managing similar problems in the classroom

EXAMPLE #2

A mechanic is shown a film (or a live demonstration of the assembly of a carburetor. Errors in procedure are built into the demonstration at those points in the chain where errors commonly occur

- The mechanic in a live demonstration may make an actual correction

- In a filmed demonstration, he indicates that there is an error and says what should be done

After completing editing practice, the mechanic practices actually assembling a carburetor

EXAMPLE #3

Military personnel are shown a film or TV tape or live demonstration of the operation of an artillery piece; error-prone procedures are built into the demonstration

- Personnel edit errors verbally or with the actual weapon

After completing editing practice, production practice operating the artillery piece occurs

FOLLOWED BY

PRODUCTION PRACTICE

IV.71

NATURE OF CRITERION PERFORMANCE EDITING PRACTICE IS DESIGNED TO FACILITATE	→	Criterion performance involves long chains:
		
		--Tasks may be VISUAL or MOTOR
		
		   e.g., operating or maintaining
		     equipment
		
		   e.g., producing products

NATURE OF EDITING PRACTICE	→	--Visual input consists of a demonstration of the chain (actual or filmed) --Demonstrations are of the learner's own production or of someone else's --The learner edits errors in the performance (omission of actions, wrong actions taken, or actions taken out of sequence
REQUIREMENTS FOR EDITING PRACTICE	→	--Editing practice is selected because error-prone situations can be built into it; it provides opportunities for the learner to recognize errors and then correct them
FUNCTION SERVED	→	--Editing practice is easier than production practice; by preceding it, it makes it more likely that production practice can proceed WITH MINIMAL ERRORS

NOW DO EXERCISE #36 ON PAGES IV.40 TO IV.41 IN THE WORKBOOK.

SUBTYPE IIb.2: SEQUENCE OF EVENTS IN PRACTICE [RECOGNIZING] THE CORRECTNESS OF A PERFORMANCE

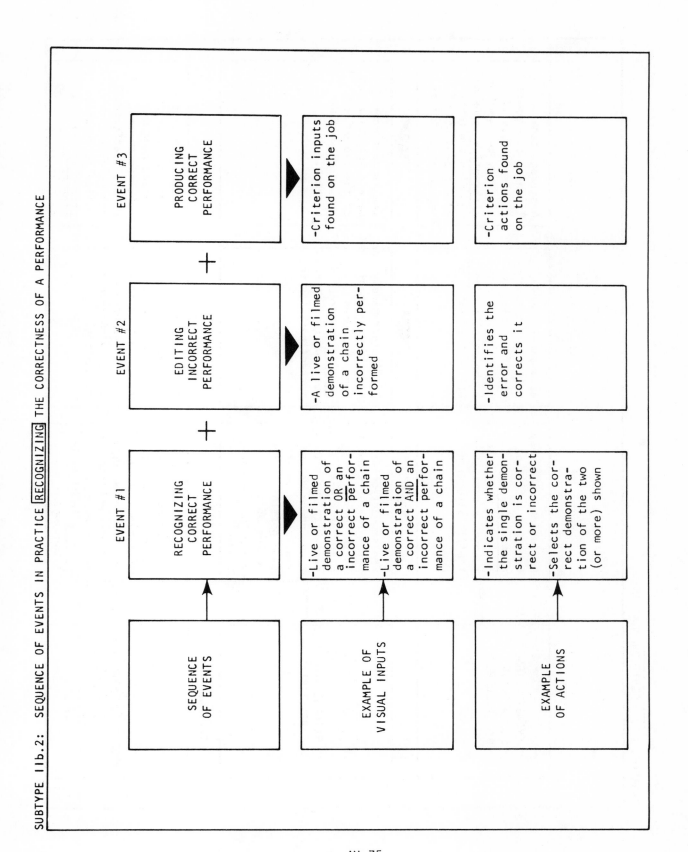

SEQUENCE OF EVENTS	EVENT #1 RECOGNIZING CORRECT PERFORMANCE	+	EVENT #2 EDITING INCORRECT PERFORMANCE	+	EVENT #3 PRODUCING CORRECT PERFORMANCE
EXAMPLE OF VISUAL INPUTS	-Live or filmed demonstration of a correct OR an incorrect performance of a chain -Live or filmed demonstration of a correct AND an incorrect performance of a chain		-A live or filmed demonstration of a chain incorrectly performed		-Criterion inputs found on the job
EXAMPLE OF ACTIONS	-Indicates whether the single demonstration is correct or incorrect -Selects the correct demonstration of the two (or more) shown		-Identifies the error and corrects it		-Criterion actions found on the job

IV.75

	EXAMPLE #1	EXAMPLE #2	EXAMPLE #3
DEMONSTRATION OF A CHAIN SHOWN THE LEARNER	A student driver may be shown a film of alternative ways (a series of steps) to take in a particular traffic situation	At a particular point in the assembly of a rifle, the learner may be given a choice of the next part to be assembled	A student cook learning to prepare a certain type of food may be shown an alternative sequence in which the order of addition of ingredients differs
RECOGNITION PRACTICE	The student driver merely selects which is the preferred order of steps to deal with the situation; or he may be required to select some portion of the series of steps as being an incorrect step.	The learner merely selects from remaining parts or a smaller number of parts which is the correct part for the next step.	The student cook merely selects which of the two or more presented ways is correct.
FOLLOWED BY			
EDITING AND PRODUCTION PRACTICE	Following recognition practice, the student driver may edit tapes of his own or others' performance. Ultimately, he practices driving in criterion situations.	Following recognition practice, editing and production practice follow (editing concentrating on error-prone situations).	Following recognition practice, the student cook may be required to edit others' performance and is always required to practice producing the type of food he is learning to prepare

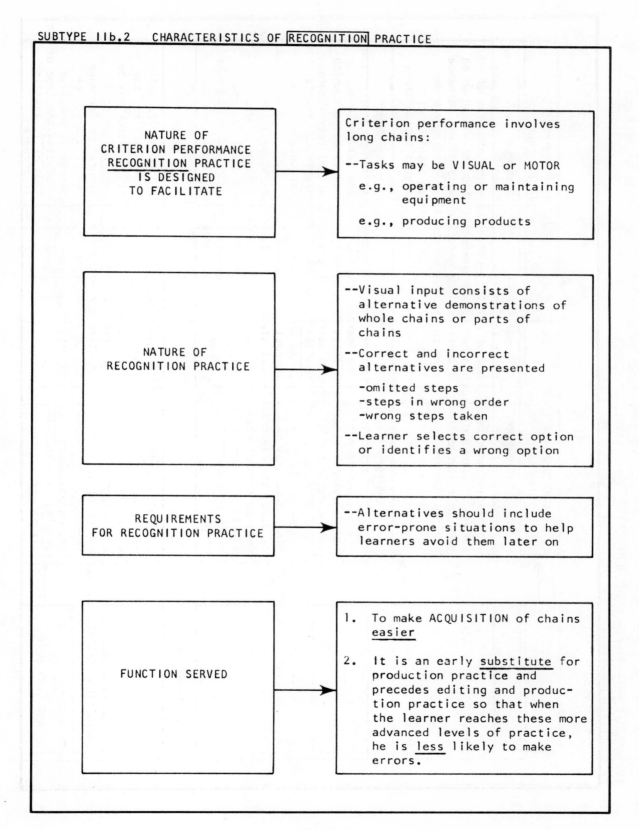

NATURE OF CRITERION PERFORMANCE RECOGNITION PRACTICE IS DESIGNED TO FACILITATE

Criterion performance involves long chains:

--Tasks may be VISUAL or MOTOR

    e.g., operating or maintaining equipment

    e.g., producing products

NATURE OF RECOGNITION PRACTICE

--Visual input consists of alternative demonstrations of whole chains or parts of chains

--Correct and incorrect alternatives are presented

    -omitted steps
    -steps in wrong order
    -wrong steps taken

--Learner selects correct option or identifies a wrong option

REQUIREMENTS FOR RECOGNITION PRACTICE

--Alternatives should include error-prone situations to help learners avoid them later on

FUNCTION SERVED

1. To make ACQUISITION of chains easier

2. It is an early substitute for production practice and precedes editing and production practice so that when the learner reaches these more advanced levels of practice, he is less likely to make errors.

CONTRASTING DIFFERENCES BETWEEN [SUBSTITUTION] OF LEVELS OF RESPONSE
IN [SIMULATED] AND [MEDIATING] RECOGNITION OR EDITING PRACTICE

	LOWER RESPONSE LEVELS AS SIMULATED PRACTICE	LOWER RESPONSE LEVELS AS MEDIATING PRACTICE
TYPE OF VISUALS		
NATURE OF THE SUBSTITUTION	-Criterion performance involves visual inputs and visual and/or motor actions. Instead of the learner being exposed to criterion inputs and being required to take criterion actions, the learner during training is presented with a record of criterion performance (e.g., demonstration or a film of it) and is expected to evaluate it and/or correct it.	-Criterion performance involves visual inputs and visual and/or motor actions. Instead of the learner being exposed to criterion inputs and being required to take criterion actions, the learner during training is presented with a record of criterion performance (e.g., demonstration or a film of it) and is expected to evaluate it and/or correct it.
PURPOSE OF THE SUBSTITUTION	To facilitate TRANSFER of a learned CHAIN to the criterion situation. *For purposes of TRANSFER, lower levels of responding (i.e., recognition or editing) as a replacement for and without subsequent production practice may not be effective.*	To facilitate ACQUISITION of a CHAIN in the first place. Recognition and editing are easier than production and make it more likely that when he reaches production practice, the learner will be successful. *For purposes of ACQUISITION, lower levels of responding early in training can be highly effective.*
WHEN ARE THEY USED	When it is not logistically feasible to use criterion inputs and actions (i.e., production practice).	When criterion performance is expected to be difficult.

IV.78

SUMMARY: TYPE IIb: LOWER RESPONSE LEVELS
PROCEDURES IN USING RECOGNITION AND EDITING PRACTICE

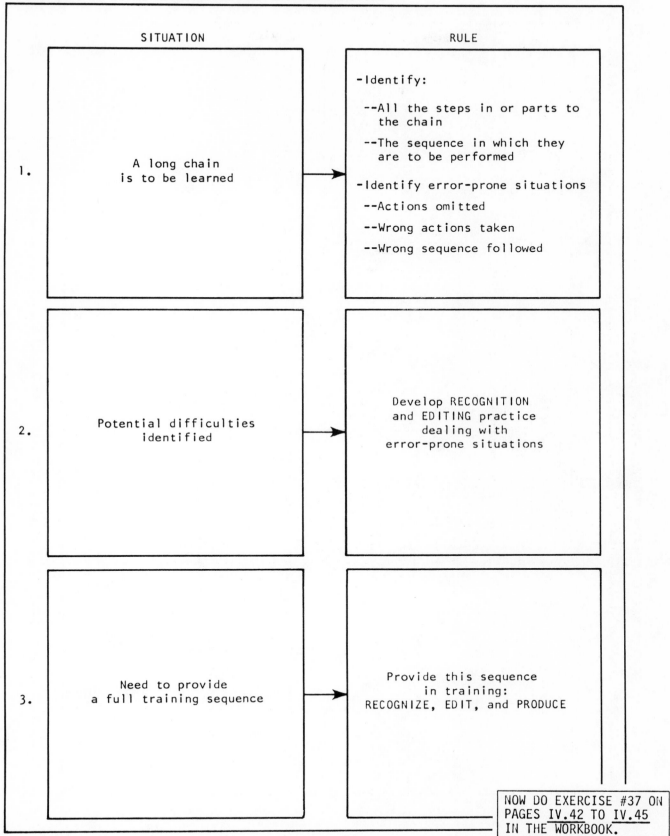

SITUATION

RULE

1.
A long chain
is to be learned

-Identify:

--All the steps in or parts to
the chain

--The sequence in which they
are to be performed

-Identify error-prone situations

--Actions omitted

--Wrong actions taken

--Wrong sequence followed

2.
Potential difficulties
identified

Develop RECOGNITION
and EDITING practice
dealing with
error-prone situations

3.
Need to provide
a full training sequence

Provide this sequence
in training:
RECOGNIZE, EDIT, and PRODUCE

NOW DO EXERCISE #37 ON
PAGES IV.42 TO IV.45
IN THE WORKBOOK.

SITUATION | RULE

1.

-A long chain must be learned:

--The chain must be performed in its entirety.

--All parts of the chain must be performed in the correct sequence.

-Provide a demonstration, live or filmed, showing alternative ways to perform the chain. Have the learner select correct ways or identify errors.

-Provide a demonstration, live or filmed, showing the chain performed with errors. Have the learner edit the performance.

2.

-Discriminations, generalizations, and chains must be learned in criterion tasks that involve verbal concepts and principles.

--Potential difficulties exist in learning these tasks.

-Use visual examples either before or during verbal practice exercises.

--Select concrete examples to which the learner can readily respond (thus making it easier for the learner to learn from the more abstract verbal materials).

IV.3.c. OBJECTIVES OF THIS UNIT

> At the end of this subunit, you will be able to IDENTIFY and PRODUCE
> practice that uses mediating visuals as FEEDBACK.

DIAGRAM OF YOUR JOB

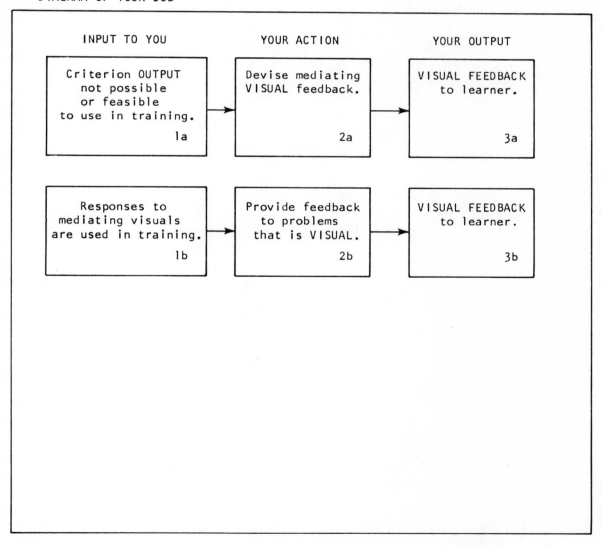

INPUT TO YOU | YOUR ACTION | YOUR OUTPUT

Criterion OUTPUT
not possible
or feasible
to use in training.
                    1a

Devise mediating
VISUAL feedback.

                    2a

VISUAL FEEDBACK
to learner.

                    3a

Responses to
mediating visuals
are used in training.
                    1b

Provide feedback
to problems
that is VISUAL.

                    2b

VISUAL FEEDBACK
to learner.

                    3b

	CONDITIONS	DEFINITION	EXAMPLE
	CRITERION OUTPUTS that provide FEEDBACK are not POSSIBLE OR FEASIBLE in training.	OUTPUTS that follow actions indicate the correctness of performance. When criterion outputs whether visual or non-visual are not feasible, mediating visual feedback may be used.	When the learner takes an action, he is given visual feedback to replace the feedback he otherwise would not get from criterion outputs that are unavailable.

vs.

VISUAL FEEDBACK is more EFFECTIVE for learning than NON-VISUAL FEEDBACK.	Whenever visual examples are used to teach concepts and principles, outputs of actions taken (problem solutions) should also be visual.	If the learner predicts the outcome of events, the answer or outcome should be presented visually.

IV.85

EXAMPLES OF MEDIATING VISUALS USED AS [FEEDBACK] WHEN CRITERION FEEDBACK IS [NOT POSSIBLE]

	EXAMPLE #1	EXAMPLE #2	EXAMPLE #3
CRITERION OUTPUTS	In rifle target practice, criterion OUTPUTS are visual (holes in the target) but the learner cannot see them from a distance.	Sound is a non-visual criterion output that a deaf person learning to speak cannot use for feedback.	Animated examples of non-observable sub-atomic events may be used to teach verbal concepts and principle. Outputs in practice may be verbal.
MEDIATING VISUAL USED AS FEEDBACK	"MAGGIES DRAWERS" indicates bullets missed target.	An oscilloscope pattern resulting from his speech can be used as visual feedback by a deaf person. He can match it up with the pattern produced by a teacher making the same sounds.	Visual outputs are used when visual examples are used (outputs being answer to problems posed visually).
FUNCTION SERVED BY VISUAL FEEDBACK	Feedback is provided by mediating visuals in a situation in which the criterion feedback is not possible to obtain visually.	Visual feedback is used in a situation in which the criterion output (sound) is not possible.	Feedback is visual (to go along with the visual example which is used to make learning easier).

EXAMPLES OF MEDIATING VISUALS AS | FEEDBACK | WHEN | RESPONSES TO MEDIATING VISUALS | ARE USED IN PRACTICE

NOW DO EXERCISE #38 ON
PAGES IV.46 TO IV.47
IN THE WORKBOOK.

	EXAMPLE #1	EXAMPLE #2	EXAMPLE #3
CRITERION PERFORMANCE	Predicting consequences of applying and removing stress to perfectly and imperfectly elastic bodies (learning concepts and principles).	Predicting consequences of lowering an object hanging from a balance scale (learning concepts and principles).	Correct assembly of a carburetor (learning procedures).
PRACTICE IN TRAINING	Visual examples illustrate the application and removal of stress. On practice problems, the learner predicts what will happen.	The learner predicts what will happen to the pointer on the scale face (i.e., go down, stay the same, or go up) for a problem about a visual example.	The learner edits an incorrect performance.
VISUAL FEEDBACK	What does happen is provided by finishing the visual demonstration; feedback is visual.	After the learner answers the problem question, the object is lowered into water and the change in the scale reading provides visual feedback.	Visual feedback consists of showing the learner how the performance should have been edited. He is thus able to assess his own editing.

IV.4   OBJECTIVES OF THIS UNIT

> At the end of this unit, you will be able to identify MEDIA requirements for MEDIATING VISUALS.

DIAGRAM OF YOUR JOB

INPUT TO YOU	YOUR ACTION	YOUR OUTPUT
Your decision to use MEDIATING VISUAL INPUTS. 1a	Identify MEDIA capable of DISPLAYING mediating visual _inputs_ or _outputs_ -visual cues -visual examples -visual feedback 2a	Appropriate MEDIA identified. 3a
Your decision to use MEDIATING VISUAL ACTIONS. 1b	Identify MEDIA capable of allowing PRACTICE of mediating visual actions -recognition -editing 2b	Appropriate MEDIA identified. 3b

SUMMARY OF PART IV: TYPES OF MEDIATING VISUALS FOR WHICH MEDIA ARE REQUIRED

TYPE OF LEARNING

| Learning CHAINS involved in VISUAL or MOTOR PROCEDURES | vs. | Learning DISCRIMINATIONS, GENERALIZATIONS, or CHAINS involved in VERBAL CONCEPTS and PRINCIPLES |

TYPES OF MEDIATING VISUALS

Mediating visuals as CUES

A model performance the learner can imitate

vs.

Use of visual cues: attentional or content to facilitate verbal practice

RESPONSES to mediating visuals

-Recognizing the correctness of perfor-mance by oneself or by others

-Editing incorrect per-formance by self or by others

vs.

-Responding to concrete, visual examples as a way to make concept and principle learning easier

Mediating visuals as FEEDBACK

When solving recognition or editing problems on the basis of live or filmed demonstrations, feedback is visual.

vs.

Visual feedback is pro-vided to problems solved on the basis of visual examples.

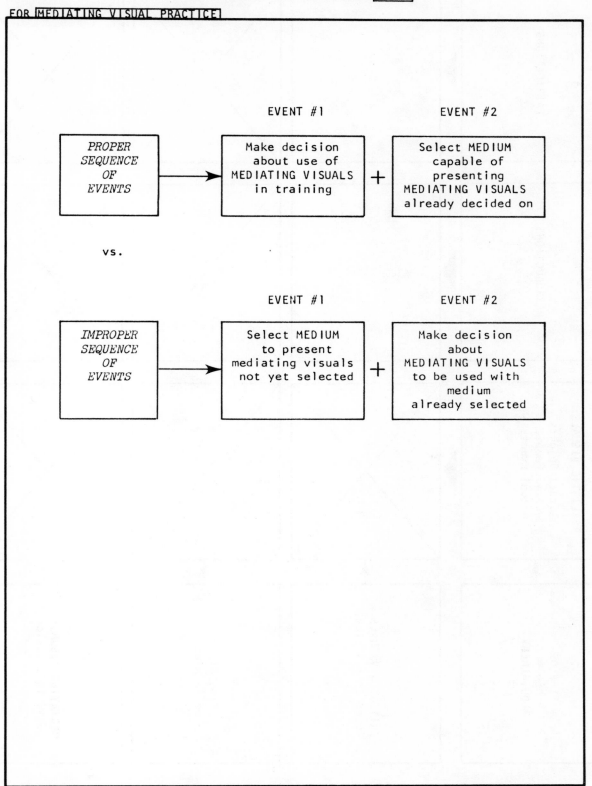

CONTRASTING MEDIA REQUIREMENTS IN CRITERION, SIMULATED, AND MEDIATING PRACTICE*

TYPE OF MEDIA REQUIREMENT	REALISTIC VISUALS: Actual Objects, Actual People, Actual Events	REPRODUCTIONS	FABRICATIONS
CRITERION VISUALS used in practice	✕		
vs.			
SIMULATION used in practice	✕	✕	✕
vs.			
MEDIATING VISUALS used in practice	✕	✕	✕

* X indicates media likely to be required.

CONTRASTING REFERENTS TO BE PRESENTED OR REPRESENTED BY MEDIA IN CRITERION, SIMULATED, AND MEDIATING PRACTICE

TYPE OF PRACTICE → CRITERION VISUAL PRACTICE vs. SIMULATED VISUAL PRACTICE vs. MEDIATING VISUAL PRACTICE

REFERENTS → CRITERION VISUAL inputs actions outputs ► VISUAL SIMULATION of criterion visual inputs actions outputs ► MEDIATING VISUALS: visual cues visual examples visual perfor- mances visual feedback ►

MEDIA LIKELY TO BE USED → REALISTIC VISUALS actual objects actual persons actual events | VISUALS: Realistic Reproduced Fabricated | VISUALS: Realistic Reproduced Fabricated

IV.95

	EXAMPLE #1	EXAMPLE #2	EXAMPLE #3
CRITERION PERFORMANCE	Performing assembly operations in putting a radio chassis together	Performing a series of sequential test operations in electronic equipment	Soldering
TYPE OF MEDIATING VISUAL FOR WHICH A MEDIUM IS NECESSARY	CUE The sequence of operations is demonstrated live serving as a model for the learner	RESPONSE An incorrect sequence is shown on film which the learner can edit	FEEDBACK The learner is shown alternative (correct and incorrect) soldering jobs and is asked to select the correct one. Photographs are used.
MEDIA REQUIREMENTS	Realistic Visuals Actual objects: radio parts Actual people: technicians Actual events: assembly operation	Reproductions Film showing objects, people, and events. Film presents all the motions and their sequence in time	Reproductions Photograph of the correct soldering job is used to provide feedback to the learner

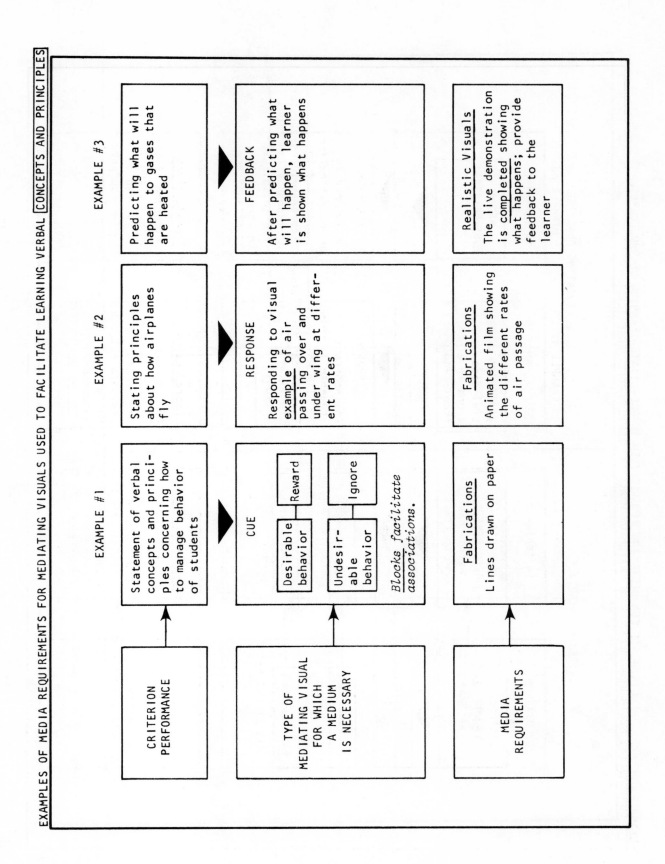

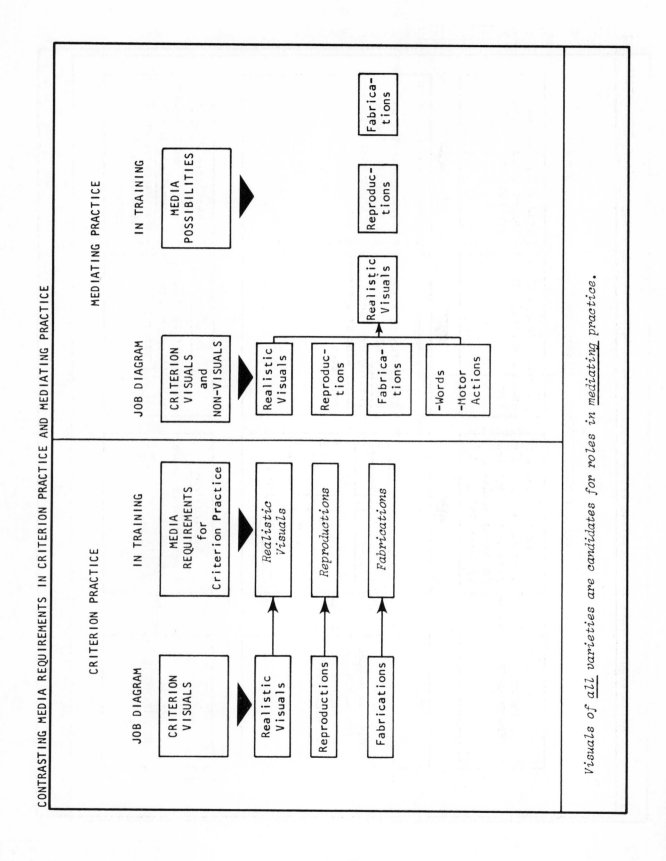

CONTRASTING MEDIA REQUIREMENTS IN CRITERION PRACTICE AND MEDIATING PRACTICE

CRITERION PRACTICE

JOB DIAGRAM — IN TRAINING

CRITERION VISUALS → MEDIA REQUIREMENTS for Criterion Practice

Realistic Visuals → *Realistic Visuals*

Reproductions → *Reproductions*

Fabrications → *Fabrications*

MEDIATING PRACTICE

JOB DIAGRAM — IN TRAINING

CRITERION VISUALS and NON-VISUALS → MEDIA POSSIBILITIES

Realistic Visuals
Reproductions
Fabrications
-Words
-Motor Actions
→ Realistic Visuals
Reproductions
Fabrications

Visuals of all varieties are candidates for roles in mediating practice.

SELECTION OF MEDIA FOR [MEDIATING] PRACTICE PROCEEDS
IN THE SAME WAY IT DOES FOR CRITERION AND SIMULATED PRACTICE

INPUT TO YOU

```
+-------------------+
|     Decision      |
| already made that |
| CRITERION VISUALS |
|   are to be used  |
|     in practice   |
+-------------------+
```

YOUR ACTION

```
+-------------------+
|      Select       |
| appropriate MEDIA |
| to present visuals|
|  already selected |
+-------------------+
```

```
+-------------------+
|     Decision      |
| already made that |
|   SIMULATION OF   |
|  CRITERION VISUALS|
|    is to be used  |
|     in practice   |
+-------------------+
```

```
+-------------------+
|     Decision      |
| already made that |
| MEDIATING VISUALS |
|   are to be used  |
|     in practice   |
+-------------------+
```

Review Unit II.5 for methods of identifying media requirements.

NOW DO EXERCISE #39 ON
PAGES IV.48 TO IV.49
IN THE WORKBOOK.

PART I

Introduction to the Use of Visuals in Instruction

PART II

The Use of Criterion Visuals in Instruction

PART III

The Use of Simulated Criterion Visuals in Instruction

PART IV

The Use of Mediating Visuals in Instruction

PART V

 Procedures to Follow in Selecting and Using Visuals
in Instruction

PART V

Procedures to Follow in Selecting and Using Visuals in Instruction

OBJECTIVES

V.1   Following Procedures in Selecting or Developing Visuals
        for Use in Instruction

V.1   OBJECTIVES OF THIS UNIT

> At the end of this unit, you will be able to follow appropriate procedures in selecting or developing visuals for use in instruction.

DIAGRAM OF YOUR JOB

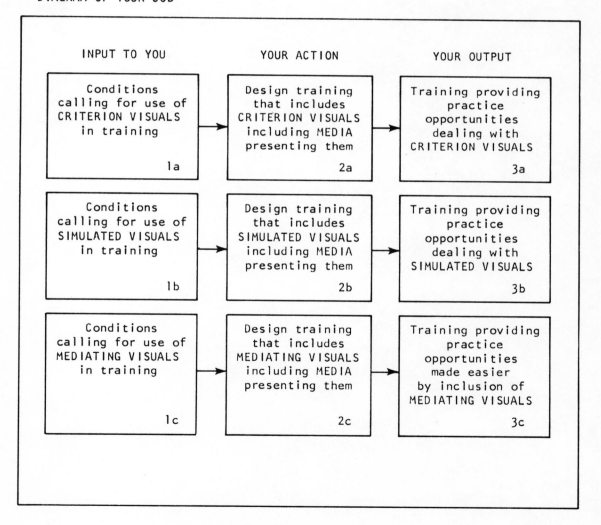

INPUT TO YOU	YOUR ACTION	YOUR OUTPUT
Conditions calling for use of CRITERION VISUALS in training 1a	Design training that includes CRITERION VISUALS including MEDIA presenting them 2a	Training providing practice opportunities dealing with CRITERION VISUALS 3a
Conditions calling for use of SIMULATED VISUALS in training 1b	Design training that includes SIMULATED VISUALS including MEDIA presenting them 2b	Training providing practice opportunities dealing with SIMULATED VISUALS 3b
Conditions calling for use of MEDIATING VISUALS in training 1c	Design training that includes MEDIATING VISUALS including MEDIA presenting them 2c	Training providing practice opportunities made easier by inclusion of MEDIATING VISUALS 3c

THREE CONDITIONS CALLING FOR THE DEVELOPMENT OR SELECTION OF VISUAL INSTRUCTION

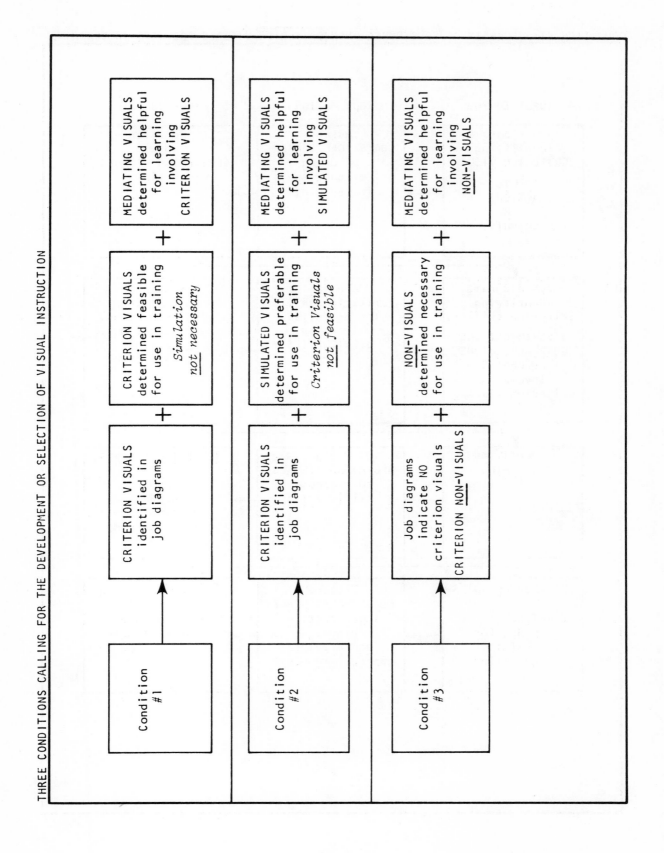

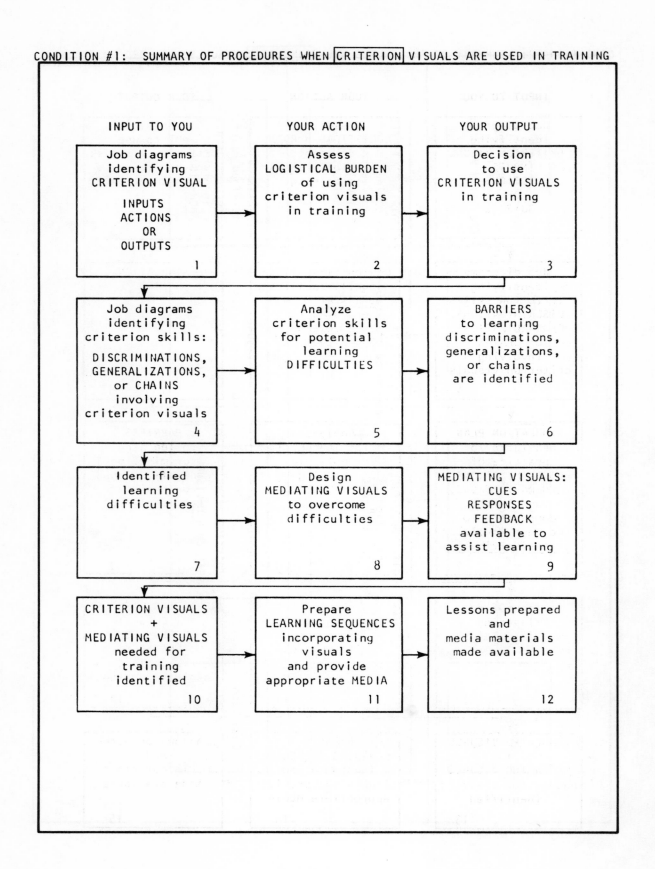

INPUT TO YOU

YOUR ACTION

YOUR OUTPUT

Job diagrams
identifying
CRITERION VISUAL

INPUTS
ACTIONS
OR
OUTPUTS

1

Assess
LOGISTICAL BURDEN
of using
criterion visuals
in training

2

Decision
to use
CRITERION VISUALS
in training

3

Job diagrams
identifying
criterion skills:

DISCRIMINATIONS,
GENERALIZATIONS,
or CHAINS
involving
criterion visuals

4

Analyze
criterion skills
for potential
learning
DIFFICULTIES

5

BARRIERS
to learning
discriminations,
generalizations,
or chains
are identified

6

Identified
learning
difficulties

7

Design
MEDIATING VISUALS
to overcome
difficulties

8

MEDIATING VISUALS:
CUES
RESPONSES
FEEDBACK
available to
assist learning

9

CRITERION VISUALS
+
MEDIATING VISUALS
needed for
training
identified

10

Prepare
LEARNING SEQUENCES
incorporating
visuals
and provide
appropriate MEDIA

11

Lessons prepared
and
media materials
made available

12

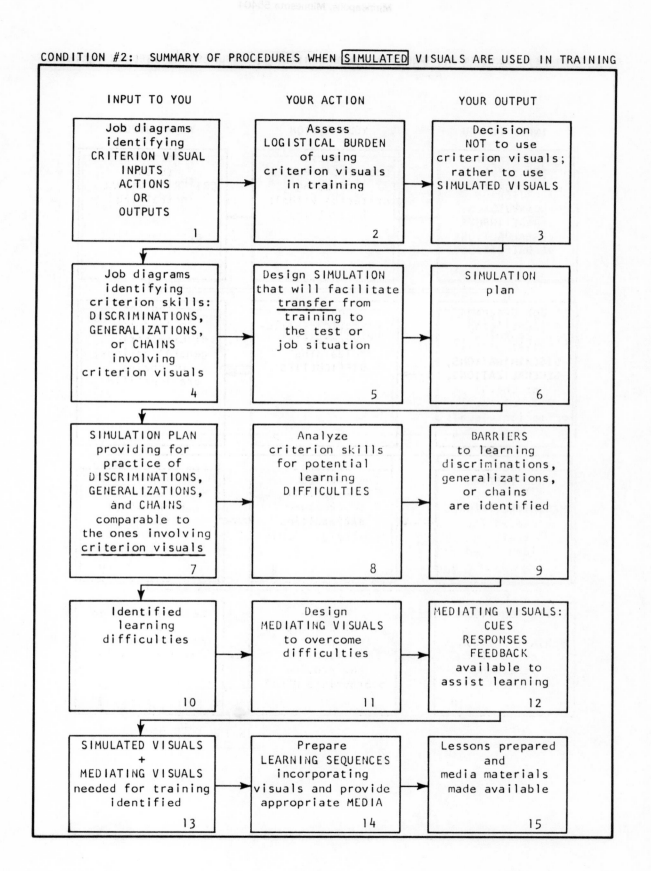

INPUT TO YOU	YOUR ACTION	YOUR OUTPUT
Job diagrams identifying CRITERION VISUAL INPUTS ACTIONS OR OUTPUTS **1**	Assess LOGISTICAL BURDEN of using criterion visuals in training **2**	Decision NOT to use criterion visuals; rather to use SIMULATED VISUALS **3**
Job diagrams identifying criterion skills: DISCRIMINATIONS, GENERALIZATIONS, or CHAINS involving criterion visuals **4**	Design SIMULATION that will facilitate transfer from training to the test or job situation **5**	SIMULATION plan **6**
SIMULATION PLAN providing for practice of DISCRIMINATIONS, GENERALIZATIONS, and CHAINS comparable to the ones involving criterion visuals **7**	Analyze criterion skills for potential learning DIFFICULTIES **8**	BARRIERS to learning discriminations, generalizations, or chains are identified **9**
Identified learning difficulties **10**	Design MEDIATING VISUALS to overcome difficulties **11**	MEDIATING VISUALS: CUES RESPONSES FEEDBACK available to assist learning **12**
SIMULATED VISUALS + MEDIATING VISUALS needed for training identified **13**	Prepare LEARNING SEQUENCES incorporating visuals and provide appropriate MEDIA **14**	Lessons prepared and media materials made available **15**

CONDITION #3: SUMMARY OF PROCEDURES WHEN NON-VISUALS ARE USED IN TRAINING

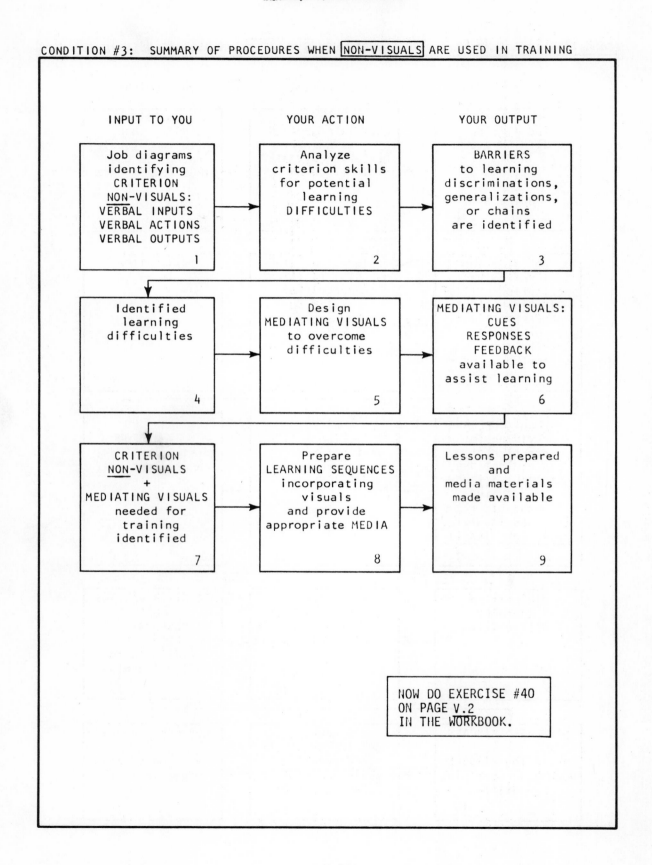

INPUT TO YOU

YOUR ACTION

YOUR OUTPUT

Job diagrams
identifying
CRITERION
NON-VISUALS:
VERBAL INPUTS
VERBAL ACTIONS
VERBAL OUTPUTS

1

Analyze
criterion skills
for potential
learning
DIFFICULTIES

2

BARRIERS
to learning
discriminations,
generalizations,
or chains
are identified

3

Identified
learning
difficulties

4

Design
MEDIATING VISUALS
to overcome
difficulties

5

MEDIATING VISUALS:
CUES
RESPONSES
FEEDBACK
available to
assist learning

6

CRITERION
NON-VISUALS
+
MEDIATING VISUALS
needed for
training
identified

7

Prepare
LEARNING SEQUENCES
incorporating
visuals
and provide
appropriate MEDIA

8

Lessons prepared
and
media materials
made available

9

NOW DO EXERCISE #40
ON PAGE V.2
IN THE WORKBOOK.